Human Learning

An holistic approach

Edited by
Peter Jarvis and Stella Parker

Routledge
Taylor & Francis Group

LONDON AND NEW YORK

First published 2005
by Routledge
2 Park Square, Milton Park, Abingdon, Oxon OX14 4RN

Simultaneously published in the USA and Canada
by Routledge
270 Madison Ave., New York, NY 10016

This edition published in paperback 2007

Routledge is an imprint of the Taylor & Francis Group, an informa business

Typeset in Gill Sans and Times New Roman by
Taylor & Francis Book
Printed and bound in Great Britain by
Antony Rowe Ltd, Chippenham, Wiltshire

British Library Cataloguing in Publication Data
A catalogue record for this book is available from the British Library

Library of Congress Cataloging in Publication Data
A catalog record for this book has been requested

ISBN10: 0-415-34098-5 (hbk)
ISBN10: 0-415-43218-9 (pbk)
ISBN10: 0-203-46332-3 (ebk)

ISBN13: 978-0-415-34098-4 (hbk)
ISBN13: 978-0-415-43218-4 (pbk)
ISBN13: 978-0-203-46332-1 (ebk)

Contents

Illustrations   vii
Contributors   viii
Preface   xiii

1 **Towards a philosophy of human learning: an existentialist
   perspective**   1
   PETER JARVIS

2 **The biology of learning**   16
   STELLA PARKER

3 **The brain and learning**   32
   JOHN STEIN

4 **Multiple intelligences theory in adult literacy education**   50
   JULIE VIENS AND SILJA KALLENBACH

5 **The role of individual differences in approaches to learning**   66
   LI-FANG ZHANG AND ROBERT J. STERNBERG

6 **A comprehensive understanding of human learning**   87
   KNUD ILLERIS

7 **Cognition**   101
   MARK TENNANT

8 **Human learning: the interrelationship of the individual
   and the social structures**   116
   PETER JARVIS

 9 **Morality and human learning** 128
 MAL LEICESTER AND ROGER TWELVETREES

10 **Emotional intelligence and experiential learning** 139
 CAROL HALL

11 **The spiritual and human learning** 157
 R. E. Y. WICKETT

12 **Fabricating new directions for women's learning: case studies
 in fabric crafts and fashion** 168
 JOYCE STALKER

13 **Life cycle development and human learning** 183
 MARY ALICE WOLF

14 **Learning trajectories: reconsidering the barriers to participation** 195
 STEPHEN GORARD

15 **Human learning: the themes** 209
 STELLA PARKER

 Index 220

Illustrations

Figures

1.1	Kolb's learning cycle	6
1.2	A revised model of the processes of human learning	8
3.1	A typical brain cell – a 'neurone'	34
3.2	Horizontal section through the cerebral hemispheres showing anticlockwise twist favouring back of left hemisphere, front of right hemisphere	40
6.1	The fundamental processes of learning	90
6.2	The processes and dimensions of learning	92
6.3	Positions in the learning triangle	98

Tables

5.1	Pearson Correlation Matrix for the scales in the Study Process Questionnaire and Thinking Styles Inventory	74
5.2	Predicting learning approaches from career personality types	77
5.3	Predicting learning approaches from personality traits	78
7.1	Contrasting internalisation and participation models	109
14.1	Frequency of four patterns of participation	197
14.2	Patterns of participation by age range	198
14.3	Patterns of participation by area of birth	200
14.4	Patterns of participation by parents' education	201
14.5	Patterns of participation by father's social class	201
14.6	Patterns of participation by mother's place of birth	202
14.7	Patterns of participation by attendance at school	202
14.8	Patterns of participation by school attended at age 16	203
14.9	Patterns of participation by family setup	204
14.10	Predictive power at each life stage	205
14.11	ICT use by trajectory	206

Contributors

Stephen Gorard is Anniversary Professor of Educational Studies at the University of York. His research is focused on issues of equity, especially in educational opportunities and outcomes, and on the effectiveness of educational systems. Recent project topics include widening participation in learning, the role of technology in lifelong learning, informal learning, the impact of targets, market forces and school compositions, under-achievement, teacher supply and retention, and developing international indicators of inequality. His interest stems from fourteen years as a school teacher and adult educator. He is the author of over three hundred publications, and an advocate of what has been termed the 'third methodological movement' involving the judicious mix of research methods, especially those traditionally referred to as 'qualitative' and 'quantitative'.

Carol Hall is Dean and Head of the School of Education and Director of the Centre for the Study of Human Relations at the University of Nottingham. She has worked as a teacher, lecturer and consultant on aspects of human relations in education and business in the UK and abroad. Her books include *Human Relations in Education* (Routledge, 1988), *Scripted Fantasy in the Classroom* (Routledge, 1990), *Developing Leadership in the Primary School* (Paul Chapman, 1998) and *Counselling Pupils in Schools* (Falmer, 2001).

Knud Illeris holds a PhD in Psychology and is Professor of Educational Research at Roskilde University, Denmark. He is also Research Leader of The Learning Lab Denmark Consortium for Research in Workplace Learning and Honorary Adjunct Professor of Adult Learning and Leadership at Teachers College, Columbia University, New York. In Scandinavia he is well known for his work on Project Education and his recent works on general learning theory and adult learning, including his books *The Three Dimensions of Learning* (NIACE, 2002) and *Adult Education and Adult Learning* (Krieger, 2004). He is the author, co-author or editor of more than seventy books and three hundred articles on subjects such as learning and motivation, educational planning and practice, theory of qualification and vocational training, and adult and youth education from the perspective of the learners. His new book, *Learning in Working Life*, is expected to be published in English in 2005.

Peter Jarvis is Professor of Continuing Education at the University of Surrey, where he was Head of Department of Educational Studies for a number of years. He is the author and editor of about thirty books, among his most recent being *Adult and Continuing Education: Major Themes* (5 vols; RoutledgeFalmer, 2003) which he edited with assistance from Colin Griffin; *The Theory and Practice of Learning* (with John Holford and Colin Griffin; Kogan Page, 2003); *Learning in Later Life* (Kogan Page, 2001) and *Adult Education and Lifelong Learning: Theory and Practice* (third edition; RoutledgeFalmer, 2004). He is founding editor of *The International Journal of Lifelong Education,* which he edits with Stella Parker. His work has been widely translated. He has received numerous awards including the C. O. Houle World Award for Adult Education Literature from the American Association of Adult and Continuing Education. He has been visiting professor in a number of universities and is a frequent lecturer at conferences and universities in many parts of the world.

Silja Kallenbach has over twenty years of experience in adult basic education as a teacher, administrator, researcher, professional development provider and programme developer. From 1996 to 2001 Silja co-directed with Julie Viens the Adult Multiple Intelligences (AMI) Study for the National Center for the Study of Adult Learning and Literacy with staff from Project Zero at Harvard, USA. Silja is co-author of *Multiple Intelligences in Adult Education, A Sourcebook for Practitioners* (Teachers College Press, 2004) and co-editor of *Multiple Intelligences in Practice* (NCSALL, 2001). Silja is the Director of the New England Literacy Resource Center at World Education, a six-state collaborative focused on staff development for adult educators. In that capacity, she has provided professional development through workshops, courses and publications on diverse topics. Silja is a former director of the City of Boston Adult Literacy Initiative, co-founder of the Boston Adult Literacy Fund and was an incorporator and coordinator of a Latina women's learning centre in Boston, Mujeres Unidas en Accion, 1981–5.

Mal Leicester's career in education has encompassed teaching in schools, teacher education, being adviser for multicultural education for the Avon Education Authority and most recently Professor of Adult Learning and Teaching at Nottingham University. She is a long serving member of the editorial board of the *Journal of Moral Education.* She is Emeritus Professor at Nottingham University and visiting professor at the universities of Derby and Nottingham Trent.

Stella Parker has worked in both further and higher education for almost thirty years, having started her academic career as a lecturer in biological sciences and later switching her interests to the study of adult and continuing education. She held appointments both in colleges and in higher education institutions, and before taking up her post at the University of Nottingham she was a Pro Vice Chancellor at City University. She worked at the University of Nottingham between 1997 and 2003, first as Head of the School of Continuing Education and then as Dean of the Faculty of Education. Stella's professional interests have been concerned with the boundary between further and higher education and the quality assurance and institutional issues associated with this. Her initial publications were in the area of science education, then later in the areas of policy and practice in continuing education. She is now Emeritus Professor at the University of Nottingham and an independent consultant. Her regular activities include being the Independent Academic Advisor to the Police Promotions Examinations Board and a lay Chair for the National Clinical Assessment Authority. Stella is the co-editor of the *International Journal of Lifelong Education* with Professor Peter Jarvis. She lives in and works from France.

Joyce Stalker left Canada thirteen years ago to become a Senior Lecturer at the University of Waikato, Hamilton, New Zealand/Aotearoa. Her research interest focuses on adult education as an advocacy activity for social justice.

John Stein is Professor of Physiology, Fellow of Magdalen College, University Laboratory of Physiology, University of Oxford, and is particularly interested in the auditory and visual perceptual impairments suffered by dyslexic children.

Robert J. Sternberg is IBM Professor of Psychology and Education and Director of the Center for the Psychology of Abilities, Competencies, and Expertise at Yale University. His PhD is from Stanford and he has been the recipient of five honorary doctorates. Sternberg's main interests are in intelligence, creativity, wisdom, leadership, and thinking styles.

Mark Tennant is Professor of Adult Education and Dean of the University Graduate School at the University of Technology, Sydney. His academic focus has been on developing a critical understanding of psychology in its application to pedagogy, with an emphasis on the interface of pedagogy, self and work in adult education contexts.

Roger Twelvetrees completed post-graduate research in electrical engineering at Nottingham University. He has worked in defence electronics, concentrating on the development of a new family of magnetic field sensors. To develop the analysis side of the technology further he formed a research group to perform the magnetic and electric field studies. In recent years, the research group has become the acknowledged world leader in the analysis and reduction of the magnetic and electric disturbances associated with warships. He is Research Manager for Ultra Electronics, Signature Management Systems.

Julie Viens has been for the past sixteen years with Project Zero, an educational research and development project located at the Harvard Graduate School of Education, USA. Over those years she has had the opportunity to participate in a number of multiple intelligences theory-related efforts, from preschool through adult education levels. Julie has consulted internationally regarding the theory and application of MI theory and has co-authored several MI-related publications, including: *Multiple Intelligences and Adult Literacy: A Sourcebook for Practitioners* (with Silja Kallenbach, Teachers College Press, 2004), *Multiple Intelligences: Pathways to Thoughtful Practice* (with Susan Baum and Barbara Slatin, in consultation with Howard Gardner; Teachers College Press, forthcoming) and *Building on Children's Strengths*, a three-volume collection from Project Zero's Project Spectrum (Teachers College Press, 1998). Currently Julie is Education Manager for HGSE's distance education initiative, WIDE World (http://wideworld.harvard.edu). Julie lives with her husband and two young daughters in Cambridge, Massachusetts.

R. E. Y. Wickett is a professor of educational foundations at the University of Saskatchewan in Canada. He teaches in the areas of adult education and religious education. His previous writings include the books, *Models of Adult Religious Education Practice* (Religious Education Press, 1991) and *How to Use the Learning Covenant in Religious Education* (Religious Education Press, 1999).

Mary Alice Wolf is Professor of Human Development and Gerontology and Director of the Institute in Gerontology at Saint Joseph College, West Hartford, Connecticut, USA. She is a graduate of Boston University, Sorbonne, University of Paris, and holds a Master's degree from Columbia University. Her doctorate is from the University of Massachusetts where her research was in the process of life review and the older learner. She is the author of over eighty journal articles and several books, including *Connecting with Older Adults: Educational Responses and Approaches* (Krieger, 1996), *Adults in Transition* (American Association for Adult and Continuing Education, 1998) and *Using Learning to Meet the Challenges of Older Adulthood* (Jossey-Bass, 1998). She is the Book Editor of *Educational Gerontology, An International Journal*, a Charter Fellow of the Association for Gerontology in Higher Education, and a Fellow of the Gerontological Society of America. She is interested in areas of lifespan development, learning and gerontological issues. Currently she is working on methods for the study of life course narratives and moments of transition in adulthood.

Li-fang Zhang is Associate Professor in the Faculty of Education at the University of Hong Kong. As a young scholar, she has become an internationally recognised leader in the field of intellectual styles and has received several key research grants for her work. She has published extensively on intellectual styles, student development and giftedness in academic journals. In addition, she has been invited to contribute to several edited books and special issues of journals in the areas of intellectual styles and of student development. She also has produced a widely acclaimed book (edited with Robert J. Sternberg), entitled *Perspectives on Thinking, Learning, and Cognitive Styles* (Lawrence Erlbaum, 2001).

Preface

As individuals, human beings are complex biological organisms, each interacting and existing within at least one or more social groups. The ability to operate and manoeuvre within and between the multifaceted aspects of human social groups is a characteristic of human nature and this ability, in turn, is dependent upon learning. Learning thus underpins the nature of our humanity and it is a driving force of our humanity. Academics wishing to gain an understanding of the nature of human learning are faced with a complex topic that spans the spectrum of the disciplines from the sciences to the humanities. The academic study of human learning has therefore tended to focus on discrete areas contained within disciplinary boundaries, each area contributing to an understanding of a part of the whole. This approach has tended to produce a distorted picture of human learning, with some aspects being clearly delineated and others less so. One of the consequences arising from this inaccurate picture is that learning becomes split into fractions, so that learning the physical (or manual) is seen as different to learning the abstract. An artificial divide opens up between learning associated with hand and brain or with mind and body. Learning theory based on this foundation reflects the split, so that we have (for example) theories of learning based on cognition or on behaviourism. Educational systems reflect this division too, with vocational education and liberal education being two examples. What we are trying to do in this book's collection of chapters, which represent several different disciplines, is to demonstrate that they complement rather than oppose each other, and together each can contribute to a holistic view of human learning.

The study of human learning is the study of complexity, and arguably it could be regarded as simplistic to view (one at a time) the ideas on human learning emanating from the different disciplines, as we do in this book. Currently there is (in some academic circles) an emphasis on more qualitative, descriptive treatments of complex phenomena, and so this begs the question: can an understanding of human learning be derived from examining what a collection of disciplines has to say about the matter? In reality, we would argue that neither a piecemeal approach nor a complex-whole approach can provide a truly accurate picture of the phenomenon of human learning. As an example of the piecemeal approach, we would argue that Psychology has claimed, traditionally, that the topic of learning falls within its ambit. But this assumes that learning is only a cognitive exercise carried on by individuals and it ignores the factors that affect learning within a social context. As an example of a more holistic approach we present the chapters in this book. Here there are a first and a final chapter that attempt to relate to the other chapters, because although each theory of learning throws light on the complex process, it does not capture it in its entirety. Even the collection here cannot do more than present a wide variety of perspectives, each complementing the others and leaving readers to construct their own understanding of the whole.

In this book, learning is regarded as a phenomenon that takes place everywhere, every day of human life. This is a view taken by many adult educators, and contrasts with some other views which are based on the notion that learning occurs only when people are taught. Because of this association between learning and formal teaching, there has been a tendency, in some circles, for teaching theory to take pre-eminence over learning theory, and this is evident in some of the chapters in this book. However, we (the editors) consider that such an emphasis has done some disservice to our understanding of learning. It is no wonder that when we ask people to describe their learning experiences they often find it very difficult, since they assume that learning takes place only within formal educational settings and the learning of everyday life becomes submerged, unconscious and taken for granted. One of the points that we hope will emerge from this book is that learning has for too long been associated only with formal education, and that it is in reality a major part of the incidentality of everyday life and of being human. We offer this symposium as an opportunity to correct this imbalance in our academic understanding of human learning.

Peter Jarvis
Stella Parker
May 2004

Chapter 1

Towards a philosophy of human learning

An existentialist perspective

Peter Jarvis

Any understanding of human learning must begin with the nature of the person. The human person is body and (and at this point philosophers differ!) mind, self and soul – or some combination of them. However, human beings are not born in isolation but in relationship, so that it is false to assume that individualism per se lies at the heart of individual learning. Since 'no man is an island' so the human person and human learning must always be understood in relationship to the wider society. It is in relationship – in the interaction of the inner person with the outer world – that experience occurs and it is in and through experience that people learn. Experience itself is a complex phenomenon since it is both longitudinal and episodic, and the latter relates to levels of awareness, perception, and so on.

It is this philosophy that we try to capture in this book: chapters cover a very wide range of different academic disciplines, all try to throw light on the very complex processes of learning. Perhaps one of the major lessons we can learn from this exercise is not only that every chapter is an over-simplification of the reality: even combined they still do not capture the complexity of this taken-for-granted process. Human learning is the preserve of no single discipline; definitions that fail to recognise it are incorrect, and governmental and inter-governmental policies about lifelong learning that do not include reference to the whole person are incomplete and do not do justice to the whole.

This chapter offers a philosophical understanding of these processes and one that illustrates that thinking emanating from the work of Descartes is misleading. Thereafter, we explore both physical and social perspectives on learning, examining both the physical and the individual/social aspects of human living.

A philosophical basis for learning

The human being is the existent, but the essence of humanity lies in what emerges from the existent and the process of emerging is driven by the outcomes of that interaction between the inner and the outer. Human learning

– the combination of processes whereby the human person (knowledge, skills, attitudes, emotions, values, beliefs and the senses) enters a social situation and constructs an experience which is then transformed through cognitive, emotional and practical processes, and integrated into the person's biography – is the driving force behind the emerging humanity, and this is lifelong. Human beings are, therefore, both being and becoming, and these are inextricably intertwined, since growth and development in the one affects the growth and development of the other. Learning is, therefore, existential and experiential. An experiential model of learning will be presented in this chapter (based on empirical research and subsequent reflection). It will be analysed and some of the implications of this approach, including the idea of developing multiple intelligences and the hidden benefits of learning, discussed.

We all frequently hear teachers saying, 'I teach philosophy' or 'I teach sociology', etc. It is an easy thing to do, especially as this has become a taken-for-granted form of educational language. But we do not do this! We teach students philosophy or sociology. On the surface this might appear a trivial correction, almost to the point of pedantry, but it is actually far from being of no consequence since it reflects a fundamental difference in philosophies and, for our purposes, the philosophy of learning. In this chapter, I first want to explore this philosophical basis for learning; in the second part I intend to discuss briefly my own ongoing research into human learning, and in the third section I want to illustrate an existentialist perspective on learning.

'I teach philosophy' puts the academic discipline at the centre of the discussion – it puts knowledge at its heart and the purpose of education is seen fundamentally as learning academic knowledge. This reflects a Cartesian philosophy which, ultimately, led Descartes to argue that 'I think, therefore I am', whereas I want to argue that it is the person who is at the centre. There are many weaknesses in the Cartesian position, such as we only are when we are thinking, and so on, and yet it has persisted as the most fundamental starting point for a great deal of Western philosophy. In the Cartesian argument, existence is objective, proven by thought. It is as if knowledge is objective, a finished product, out there to be acquired and, therefore, something that can be transmitted (even sold) to others. It is as if the mind were separate from the body and the sole recipient of information. However, at the very least, the person consists of body and mind, but these are not separate or distinct entities, as Ryle (1963) so forcefully argued many years ago and as neurological research has more recently verified (Greenfield 1999), and which is discussed later in this book. Mind, as this research indicates, is a construct illustrating the cognitive content of the neurological activities that brain research has demonstrated. As such it does not exist, but the brain does. Mind in some way transcends brain and enables us to know ourselves as persons, in relation to the external world. Body and mind are at least an internal dualism in relation to the external world, as Marton and

Booth (1997: 122) have suggested. By contrast, it is the Cartesian dualistic philosophy which is rejected here.

It is also quite significant that while there have been many books about the philosophy of education and even the philosophy of adult education there have been far fewer about the philosophy of learning. By learning here I want to emphasise the process of learning and not the way that the term is used contemporaneously in such phrases as 'adult learning' and 'lifelong learning'. Nevertheless, it is perhaps surprising that there are so few books since we are said to live in a learning society. However, there is one notable exception to this: Winch (1998) wrote *The Philosophy of Human Learning*. Significantly, he started his study (pp. 1–2) with four laudable aims:

- He wished to rescue learning from the social sciences and to defend its distinctive philosophical perspective.
- He wished to challenge many of the dominant ideas about learning.
- He was concerned to explore those aspects of learning commonly neglected, such as religion and aesthetics.
- He wanted to emphasise the social, practical and affective nature of human learning.

Clearly his concerns are very valid, especially when we recognise how learning has wrongly been regarded as falling within the domain of psychological study, which is itself based on Cartesian dualism. Additionally, he was concerned that the insights of Wittgenstein should not be lost to our understanding of this human process. Almost predictably, however, he began his study with a look at Descartes and the empiricists, all of whom start with 'the solitary individual as the source of knowledge' (Winch 1998: 12), and thereafter he explored other historical philosophers. In a sense, he appears to be seeking to reform a contentious approach rather than to look at other schools of thought which might have been more promising to his enterprise. However, if we do not start here with trying to prove our existence, where do we start? Trying to prove our existence is a rather circular argument and one which is in some ways solipsistic. But we know that we exist – this is a matter of given-ness – which is a better starting point for this discussion, and so Macquarrie (1973: 125) suggests that we might turn the Cartesian dictum around and argue that 'I am, therefore I think'. Macquarrie (ibid.) goes on to write:

> But what does it mean to say, 'I am'? 'I am' is the same as 'I exist'; but 'I exist', in turn, is equivalent to 'I-am-in-the-world', or again 'I-am-with-others'. So the premise of the argument is not anything so abstract as 'I think' or even 'I am' if it is understood in some isolated sense. The premise is the immediately rich and complex reality, 'I-am-with-others-in-the-world'.

In fact this is a similar starting point to one that Macmurray (1991) worked out very carefully when he came to the conclusion that we know about our own existence by participating in it. It is action that lies at the heart of our knowledge of our being – we are agents in relation to others. For him (p. 27), therefore, the premise begins with 'I act' rather than 'I think', or in other words, 'I do, therefore I am'. Macmurray (p. 86) goes on to demonstrate that 'knowledge is the negative dimension of action' – the positive one being the development of the self as agent. In other words, underlying every action is knowledge and actors cannot separate their behaviour from their knowledge about it.

> The knowledge which is involved in action has two aspects, which correspond to the reflective distinction between means and end. As knowledge of means, it is an answer to the question, 'What, as a matter of fact, is the means to a given end?'; as knowledge of end, it is the answer to another question, 'Which, of the possible ends, is the most satisfactory end to pursue?' This second question is concerned with value, not with matter of fact. It initiates a reflective activity which seeks to arrange an order of priority between possible ends. Action itself involves the integration of these two types of knowledge. To act is to choose to realize a particular objective, in preference to all other objectives, by an effective means. In reflection, however, these two questions are necessarily separated, because they require two different modes of reflective activity for their solution.
>
> (Macmurray 1991: 173)

This is also a point made very forcibly by Ryle (1963: 50) when he argued that when a person is doing something:

> He is bodily active and he is mentally active, but he is not being synchronously active in two different 'places', or with two different 'engines'. There is the one activity, but it is one susceptible of and requiring more than one kind of explanatory description.

To separate mind from body, and therefore from action, is a false dualism; indeed, in experiencing the world we are both doing something and thinking about it. Experience is a personal awareness of the Other, which occurs at the point of intersection between the inner-self and the outer world, and it is through experience as a result of being an agent that we both grow and develop. For Macmurray, an isolated agent is self-contradictory. Persons exist only in relation to others: there could be no birth without the parents, no growth without human interaction, no self without others. Individual experience is always with that which lies outside of the self. It is in interaction with the Other that I am. In other words: I do, therefore I am. In my doing, that is being an agent, I am a person.

However, there is at least one other significant factor that needs consideration: when we are agents, there is a combination of thought and movement, and when we are thinking about our actions we are thinking about the future – planning, envisaging – yet when we think about what has occurred we are still doing but we are also reflecting, or analysing the past. While this might also appear obvious, it is epistemologically very significant. Rarely when we are planning an action, or when we are carrying it out, do we think that we need a little bit of philosophy, a little bit of psychology, sociology, and so on. No, our thinking is in the form of everyday, or practical, knowledge – integrated and without academic disciplines – and when we plan that action we reflect upon previous experiences and the memories we have of them, and what we did in those situations. However, if we want to analyse events, then we might employ different perspectives or academic disciplines to show a consistent and sustained process. In a recent book (Jarvis 1999) I argued that theories, especially those arising from the study of facts and events, are always *post facto*, and can never be applied to future events since each event is unique and can never be repeated within the processes of our experience. In some ways, analytical reflection within the framework of academic disciplines is always about the past or a present phenomenon about which we are thinking, and not about planning for the future. Nevertheless, we can and do learn from this analysis. But it is in initiating action with the world, experiencing it, that we are – and it is from this that we can learn. Consequently, we are both being and becoming. Even so, this discussion about self-development and thought and action points us very clearly in the direction of the processes of human learning, and it is to these that I want to turn now.

The process of human learning

From the above discussion we can begin to understand why knowledge, which has been regarded as objective truth, could be taught and learned, so that 'I teach philosophy' or 'sociology' and so on – objective knowledge – makes sense within a Cartesian dualism, where the mind is distinct from the body. Here the learner is a passive recipient of an objective phenomenon and the body need not be considered within the process. But this is a position which needs now to be rejected. When we experience the outer world, the Other, we are doing so with both mind and body. When we experience, we are doing as well as thinking – our body is affected as well as our mind. Through experience we are aware of both ourselves and the Other as differentiated from us.

There are many theories of human learning which have been summarised in a number of books (see Jarvis *et al.* 2003; Illeris 2002) and in the following chapters of this book. But in traditional studies of learning two theories stand out in relation to the above discussion: behaviourism and experientialism. From the time of Pavlov, it has been recognised that learning is associated with behaviour. Indeed, Borger and Seaborne (1966: 14) suggested that from a behaviourist perspective, learning is 'any more or less permanent change in behaviour which is the result of experience'. Skinner (1971) not only recognised this to be learning, but he regarded his own work as a 'technology of behaviour' and so denied the dualism of body and mind. His approach has been described as the 'psychology of the empty organism' (Borger and Seaborne 1996: 77), and while there are many reasons to reject this crude behaviouristic approach, its failure to understand the nature of the person-in-the-world is perhaps the most fundamental. Even so, its emphasis on behaviour is still very important, as Macmurray's assertion that 'I do, therefore I am' demonstrates. More recently, learning theory has focused on human experience (see Weil and McGill 1989 *inter alia*), and there have been many studies from an experientialist perspective. Perhaps the most influential has been that by Kolb (1984), upon which many studies, including my own, have been based. He defines learning as 'the process whereby knowledge is created through the transformation of experience' (1984: 41). Immediately, we can see that knowledge is still at the centre of his thinking rather than the person. Indeed, in his famous learning cycle (Figure 1.1 is a simplification of his cycle; Kolb 1984: 42) the person is missing.

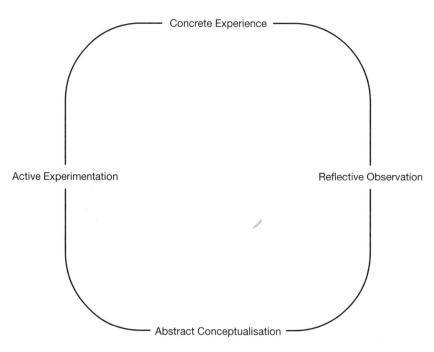

Figure 1.1 Kolb's learning cycle.

This simple figure suggests that learning can start from experience or from an abstract idea or theory. However attractive the cycle, it does not actually tell the whole story of learning, but perhaps its simplicity has been one of its major strengths. Nevertheless, it was the starting point for my own investigations into human learning which began with empirical research in the 1980s and has continued with both further empirical testing and considerable reflection ever since. Indeed, there is a certain paradox about researching learning, since any reflection on the processes of learning – including one's own – is part of one's ongoing research project. My empirical research, based on workshops in which adults were asked to describe a learning experience which they then used to try to understand the processes of human learning more broadly, was first published in 1987 (Jarvis 1987), and I began to philosophise about learning a few years later (Jarvis 1992), although I was still entrapped by Cartesian dualism. My early definition of learning (Jarvis 1987: 8) was 'learning is the transformation of experience into knowledge, skills and attitudes', and my learning diagram extended Kolb's quite considerably; it illustrated both the different approaches to learning and the different types of learning that occurred, including non-learning, non-reflective learning and reflective learning. By 1992, however, I was beginning to see that my understanding of learning was still too simple and that I also needed to break away from Cartesian dualism. I began to recognise that learning is an existential process, although I was unhappy with my own philosophical understanding of the learning processes. From that time onwards, I continued my research by testing out my emerging theory in many workshops with educators and adapting my thinking as a result of what they were describing about their own learning. In addition, I became more conscious of my own processes of learning, which reflects my existential understanding of the phenomenon. In many publications (Jarvis 1999, 2001 *inter alia*) I began to modify my initial understanding of learning. Now I see learning as *the combination of processes whereby the whole person – body (genetic, physical and biological) and mind (knowledge, skills, attitudes, values, emotions, beliefs and senses) – is in a social situation and constructs an experience which is then transformed cognitively, emotively or practically (or through any combination) and integrated into the individual's own biography.* This definition is summarised in Figure 1.2.

While there are considerable modifications in this diagram, we can see that there is also a logical progression in the way that I was both experiencing and understanding learning, since I combined the cognitive (Box 5) and the practical (Box 7) and inserted the emotive (Box 6). The arrows (→ Box 1, Box 4 → and Box 8 →) represent the passing of time, while the arrows from Boxes 4 and 8 back to Box 1 represent the ongoing nature of learning. Learning is an existential phenomenon and one which requires a philosophical understanding, albeit one which is strengthened since it is also based upon ongoing practitioner research. It is now necessary to attempt to understand learning from this perspective.

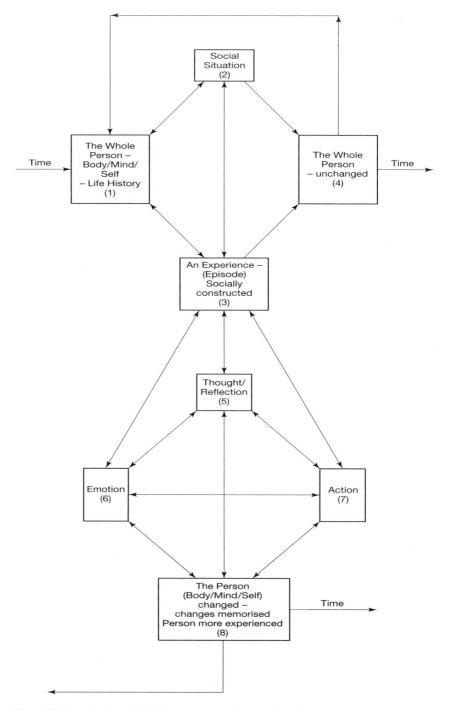

Figure 1.2 A revised model of the processes of human learning.

Towards an existential understanding of human learning

It might be claimed that existentialists are more concerned with inner data than they are with empirical fact, and my research contains both my own inner understanding of human learning and also that of many other individuals who have participated in the workshops on learning that I have conducted. Throughout all of the workshops I relied on people discussing their own experiences of learning and trying to depict them diagrammatically. I have adapted the diagrams over the years as different experiences of the participants and my own experiences suggest modifications, so that the changing diagrams are not meant to be empirical data written on tablets of stone and unchangeable, but record my current understanding of this extremely complex human phenomenon. Indeed, the diagrams are constantly developing as my own understanding of the complex human processes changes and deepens. In another sense, these diagrams are pragmatic, reflecting processes that appear to be meaningful and successful to the participants who describe and discuss them in the workshops, and they are also meaningful to my own understanding of the processes through which I go when I learn. Fundamentally, learning is seen as a human process, one in which people's existence is assumed and in which they are thinking agents, in precisely the same way as Macquarrie and Macmurray described and as we discussed in the first section of this chapter.

I now briefly want to discuss Figure 1.2 in order to demonstrate both the processes of learning and their complexity, and without trying to describe all the different forms of learning I want to try to capture the fundamental characteristics of the processes. The description is necessarily an over-simplification of the complex reality of human growth and development and it will be discussed briefly under seven sub-sections.

Being-in-the world

The person is body and mind, and both are constituted in extremely complex ways (Box 1). They are not separate but inextricably intertwined, so that there is no Cartesian dualism. Here we see (in Boxes 1 and 2) that the person is always being-in-the-world in the sense that Macquarrie described above. The person is always the agent, always interacting with the Other, since the situation is always social. The person is always Being, the existent, which grows and develops biologically as well as in every other way (Becoming) and these cannot be separated.

I have stressed the whole person, since we experience the world through our bodies (senses), through our minds (cognitively, attitudinally, ideologically and evaluatively), through our actions (practice and skill) and emotionally. Gardner's (1983) ground-breaking work pointed the way to this when he posited a theory of multiple intelligences, although Rogers (1983) had for many years been writing about the whole person. Being-in-the-world is whole person's being.

Time (Boxes 1, 2 and 4)

Being-in-the-world automatically implies existence in time and that it is impossible to step outside of it. Time is another contentious phenomenon: it is something that knows no boundaries and in which there is always emergence of newness – a sense of becoming. It is, in a sense, external to us and is a flow of ever-changing reality which Bergson (Lacey 1989) called *durée*. This is the experience of being, but within the context of *durée* being is always in the process of becoming: it is more of a subjective phenomenon – or at least our experience of it is. But our subjective experience of time is not of an unchanging phenomenon, for how often do we hear people saying, 'How time flies!' or 'Isn't time dragging?' When time flies we are hardly conscious of its passing, usually because we are doing other things, and so we tend to move from Boxes 1 and 2 to Box 4. But when time drags we become very conscious of the world in which we live, and this is important to our understanding of experience. When time flies, our biography is in harmony with our situation and we do not consciously learn. While we are acting in the world, we are not aware of the world beyond our actions, although our body continues to age through the ravages of time. In other words, we can take the world, as we experience it, for granted, as Schutz and Luckmann (1974: 7) explain:

> I trust the world as it has been known by me up until now will continue further and that consequently the stock of knowledge gained from my fellow-men and performed from my own experiences will continue to preserve its fundamental validity ... From this assumption follows the further and fundamental one: that I can repeat my past successful acts. So long as the structure of the world can be taken as constant, so long as my previous experience is valid, my ability to act upon the world in this and that manner remains in principle preserved.

Awareness of the world (Boxes 1, 2 and 3)

But we know that both the world and we ourselves are constantly changing, so that we are constantly faced with novel situations which we cannot take for granted. We are confronted with unknowns – we do not know what to do, how to act, and so on. This is the situation which in my previous writings I have called disjuncture – when my experience of a social situation and my biography are no longer in harmony and time seems to freeze. We are also confronted with situations within which we were once happy to act but, as a result of the changes that have occurred within us, we are no longer happy to act in the same manner. We become aware of the world and in a sense are aware that in some way we are separate from it. This also occurs when 'time drags'.

We are confronted with disjuncture because the outside world has changed or because a teacher has presented us with information that we did not know, and so on – something we can regard as Other-initiated, or even, because we ourselves have changed, self-initiated. But we can also have visions or hopes for the future and these also create situations of disjuncture – these may be self-induced, or some leader/teacher might have inspired us with a vision or aspiration, and so on. Other-induced situations, except those which are visionary, usually mean that we are reflecting back on a previous event, but self-initiated ones usually point to the future. For the sake of convenience we can call these two types of thought retrospective and prospective – both of which can be reflective – although much learning theory has concentrated on reflective thinking as retrospective, to the detriment of theorising about learning from analytical and creative thought planning future actions: that is, from the perspective of time itself. Reflective thought, retrospective and prospective, is a function of the self as agent.

When disjuncture occurs, we are aware of our separation from others, aware that we are, in a sense, isolated from the world in which we are, and we feel the need to re-establish harmony and connection.

Experience (Boxes 1, 2 and 3, and Box 8)

As we pointed out previously, the concept of experience is extremely complex and I will not try to discuss it in full here. Nevertheless, I want to highlight a number of things about it:

> *Intersection of the inner and outer worlds* Experience occurs at the intersection of the self-in-the-world and the world-itself, which paradoxically is created in part by the self. It is something that individuals have, but also something that is created as a result of the way that they perceive the world, as a result of their previous experiences. Consequently, experience is always a construction, both individually and socially, and this is built into my definition of learning.

> *Lifelong and episodic experience* Experience can either be episodic or lifelong – and this is reflected in the fact that in Boxes 1, 4 and 8 we see the whole person who is the result of all previous experiences. In this sense experience is lifelong (our biography) but when we suddenly become aware of the world it is usually for a brief period of time, which I call episodic experience (Box 3).

Awareness Episodic experience is created as a result of awareness of the external world which I have called disjunctural. While disjuncture implies that we 'freeze time' to experience, we have also to recognise that there are differing levels of awareness, so that we can 'see things out of the corner of our eye' or we are 'half aware' of some event while we are concentrating on something else. Consequently, we may learn things without being consciously aware of them all – this I called pre-conscious learning in my previous writing.

Multi-dimensional nature of experience Experiences occur cognitively, physically and emotionally (Goleman 1996, and see Hall's chapter later in this book) and usually they are so intertwined that it would be diffi-cult, if not impossible, to disentangle them in the way that rationalist thought has done. Disembodied rationality is most problematic, although by making this claim I am not disavowing the rules of logic.

Primary and secondary experience Experience may be primary or secondary (mediated). Primary experience is immediate, and is that which we experience in the situation we are in, in the world, although we still construct it since our mind is not a camera and we have to give meaning to the external world of facts that have no meaning in themselves. Secondary experience is mediated to us – through a teacher, another person, information media, and so on. Secondary experience is initially somebody else's primary experience which is then transmitted to us. Much of our understanding of the world is through mediated experience.

Approval or disapproval We may either approve or disapprove of what we experience and this relates to the way that both our belief and value systems, and also our emotions, affect our learning.

Acceptance or rejection We may accept or reject that experience. When we reject the experience we reject the potential learning that goes with it: there are two such types of experience which I have previously called non-consideration (we have not the time to consider) and rejection. We previously considered them to be non-learning experiences, but we may well learn about the self-in-the-world from them incidentally.

However, brief comments like this do not do justice to this complex phenomenon about which many volumes have been written.

Transformation of experience (Boxes 5, 6 and 7)

The transformation of the experience lies at the heart of learning, and perhaps this is why a number of theorists (e.g. Mezirow 2000; O'Sullivan

1999) have focused upon it. However, this is a complex phenomenon since the experience can be transformed by thought, action and feelings, or any combination of them. Learning, then, is taking into the self through processes of transformation of that which is experienced as a result of being-in-the-world.

Learning, then, involves thought, action and feeling, all of which are complex phenomena in themselves about which many books have been written. It would, therefore, be unwise to attempt to do anything more than note some of the complexities of the processes. Thinking itself can be prospective, reflective, non-reflective, critical, creative, analytical, innovative, contemplative, evaluative, and so on. Additionally, it can be affected by such phenomena as tacit knowledge and suppressed and repressed feelings and knowledge. These also relate to attitudes, emotions and actions.

In a real sense, it is the whole person who is transformed because learning is about the whole person rather than one part. As time progresses and experiences are transformed, human beings are always in the process of becoming. Their human essence continues to develop from within their existence.

The person changed and more experienced (Box 8)

The person is always becoming, always growing and developing in every sense of the word – bodily, mentally and emotively – the human essence is always emerging. This is our life experience, and so it is no wonder that researchers are beginning to focus on life history.

However, there are certain implications of this that must be recognised. First, if we learn to respond differently to our situations in the world as a result of our learning from our experiences, then we are behaving more intelligently! In other words, once we have rejected the Cartesian dualism, we are also forced to reject the simple idea of cognitive intelligence (and intelligence tests), as Gardner has also shown and which is discussed below. We can grow in intelligence through our learning, which indicates we can learn to be intelligent, and this has profound implications for traditional education. Second, there are hidden benefits of learning: for instance, improvement in physical activity improves our mental functioning and mental functioning may well improve our health, and so on. There is now considerable research, especially from the Centre for Research on the Wider Benefits of Learning, that points us in this direction (Cusack and Thompson 1998; Preston and Hammond 2002 *inter alia* – this is the first report of a number produced by the Centre and it is only recorded here as an example). Third, since we now recognise that the mind and the body are inextricably joined and that changes in the one affect the other, we must also see that this is true for the whole ageing process, including later life (Jarvis 2001) and so we should ensure that opportunities exist for both learning and physical exercise in later life.

Lifelong learning (→ Box 1, Box 4→ and Box 8→)

The person exists in-the-world and learns throughout the whole of life. While the physical body matures through the process of ageing, so the other processes in conjunction with the ageing one in the world ensure the continuing development of the whole person. Learning must be related to time and to people's awareness of their relationship with the world – Macmurray calls this 'the rhythm of withdrawal and return' – and the person comes into harmony with and then separates from the world. It is this rhythm that I called disjunctural and harmony seeking (Jarvis 1992) – it lies at the heart of learning.

Conclusion

'I teach philosophy' or 'sociology', and so on, now seems little more than just lazy language! Individuals learn – not only minds. We all teach people who learn through many different ways. Education is fundamentally about individuals who learn, grow and develop, and not about merely transmitting knowledge. Learning is lifelong, life-wide, and it plumbs the depth of human existence-in-the-world. We are always both being-in-the-world and becoming, developing, growing, maturing. As I now understand it, learning is an existential phenomenon – the combination of processes whereby the whole person, body (genetic, physical and biological) and mind (knowledge, skills, attitudes, values, emotions, beliefs and senses), is in a social situation and constructs an experience which is then transformed cognitively, emotively or practically (or through any combination) and integrated into the individual's own biography.

References

Borger, R. and Seaborne, A. (1966) *The Psychology of Learning*, Harmondsworth: Penguin.

Cusack, S. and Thompson, W. (1998) 'Mental Fitness: Developing a Vital Aging Society', *International Journal of Lifelong Education* 17 (5): 307–17.

Gardner, H. (1983) *Frames of Mind*, New York: Basic Books.

Goleman, D. (1996) *Emotional Intelligence*, London: Bloomsbury.

Greenfield, S. (1999) 'Soul, Brain and Mind' in M. J. C. Crabbe (ed.) *From Soul to Self*, London: Routledge, pp. 108–25.

Illeris, K. (2002) *The Three Dimensions of Learning*, Roskilde: Roskilde University Press.

Jarvis, P. (1987) *Adult Learning in the Social Context*, London: Croom Helm.

—— (1992) *Paradoxes of Learning*, San Francisco: Jossey-Bass.

—— (1999) *The Practitioner Researcher*, San Francisco: Jossey-Bass

—— (2001) *Learning in Later Life*, London: Kogan Page.

Jarvis, P., Holford, J. and Griffin, C. (2003) *The Theory and Practice of Learning* (second edition), London: Kogan Page.

Kolb, D. (1984) *Experiential Learning*, Englewood Cliffs, NJ: Prentice Hall.

Lacey, A. (1989) *Bergson*, London: Routledge.

Macmurray, J. (1991) *Persons in Relation*, New Jersey: Humanities Press.

Macquarrie, J. (1973) *Existentialism*, Harmondsworth: Penguin.

Marton, F. and Booth, S. (1997) *Learning and Awareness*, New Jersey: Lawrence Erlbaum Associates.

Mezirow, J. (2000) 'Learning to Think Like an Adult' in J. Mezirow and Associates, *Learning as Transformation*, San Francisco: Jossey-Bass.

O'Sullivan, E. (1999) *Transformative Learning*, London: Zed Books.

Preston, J. and Hammond, C. (2002) *The Wider Benefits of Further Education: Practitioner Views*, London: University of London, Centre for Research on the Wider Benefits of Learning.

Rogers, C. (1983) *Freedom to Learn for the 80s* (second edition), New York: Merrill.

Ryle, G. (1963) *The Concept of Mind*, Harmondsworth: Penguin; first published by Hutchinson, London, 1949.

Schutz, A. and Luckmann, T. (1974) *The Structures of the Lifeworld*, London: Heinemann.

Skinner, B. (1971) *Beyond Freedom and Dignity*, Harmondsworth: Penguin.

Valberg, J. (1992) 'The Puzzle of Experience Objects' in T. Crane (ed.) *The Contents of Experience*, Cambridge: Cambridge University Press.

Weil, S. and McGill, I. (eds) (1989) *Making Sense of Experiential Learning*, Buckingham: Open University Press and Society for Research in Higher Education.

Winch, C. (1998) *The Philosophy of Human Learning*, London: Routledge.

Chapter 2

The biology of learning

Stella Parker

Introduction

Why a biology of learning? Mainly because an understanding of the nature of human learning is best perceived from as many different viewpoints as possible. The biological sciences provide one of these viewpoints, and recent work from this discipline indicates that learning is human nature and it is human nature to learn. A second reason is that much of the academic literature exploring the nature of human learning draws on disciplines that include the social sciences, psychology and the humanities. Therefore, although educationalists have a plethora of literature about learning drawn from these areas, they have little drawn from the biological sciences. This chapter, together with the other science-based ones in this book, attempts to plug this gap.

The dearth of educational literature referring to a science-based understanding of human learning reflects my own personal experience of discussing the biology of learning with colleagues from arts or humanities backgrounds. Generally such discussions have met with blank faces and, in some cases, even hostility to the topic. In contrast there are others who accept that a biological basis can add to our understanding of learning and appear to conclude that everything about humanity can be explained by our biology. Each of these views represents the opposite ends of a spectrum; at one end there is a denial of a biological basis for humanity and at the other end there is an uncritical acceptance of it. I consider that both views are deficient, and a more balanced view lies somewhere in the middle.

The evidence upon which I shall draw in this chapter comes mostly from studies that are relevant to an understanding of the physical and mental characteristics of human beings, particularly with respect to their evolutionary development. My reason for choosing this approach is that I consider we cannot know about ourselves as a species unless we know where we have come from and how we got here. The chapter is not long enough to go into these questions in any detail, so only a brief résumé will be included here. Suggestions for further reading are given at the end of the chapter.

This chapter starts with a brief opening discussion of the meaning of learning based on the work of many authors, and refers to the learning that takes place both within and without education systems. This broad meaning of learning is probably more familiar to adult educators than to those who specialise in the learning that takes place within the organised context of education systems. The broad meaning taken here reflects that proposed by a myriad of adult educators, but in particular Illeris (2002), Jarvis (1992) and Merriam and Caffarella (1999). Drawing upon the work of authors such as these, human learning is here considered from three different perspectives, which are:

- a process or cognitive perspective, based on learning as a function of the brain;
- a perspective of the learner as an individual, arising from her/his particular circumstances of gender, developmental stage, age, experience, context, and so on;
- a contextual or social/cultural perspective, based on learning as a result of the effects of the social/cultural context on learners.

Although learning can be considered from these three different perspectives for the purposes of academic study, for the individual learner all three are inextricably linked. Each perspective provides such a rich vein of study that research into human learning often concentrates on only one or maybe two. From whatever perspective it is considered, biological processes that have their origins in the brain but which affect other parts of the human body also underpin human learning. If learning is viewed from a biological stance, then an explanation for what happens during the process of learning can be reduced to one word: change. The biological nature of change and its dynamics are the subject of this chapter, but before going any further it is important to foreshadow the themes that run through the chapter.

Change is at the heart of learning and dealing with change is at the heart of the nature of humanity. In this chapter the nature of humanity is not discussed as a topic in its own right, but because human nature is so inextricably bound up with learning it is important to explain how I view it. Human nature has a meaning which is twofold, the first being observable manifestations of genetically determined capacities. These are the capacities that give rise to physical attributes such as height, so men in general are genetically predisposed to be taller than women; some people inherit a capacity to run faster or for longer than others; there is a genetically determined and absolute division between men and women in terms of child-bearing capacities; children inherit the ability to master the complexities of language even at an early stage of their intellectual development; and so on. This first meaning refers only to predetermined capacities which are programmed in the genetic material (deoxyribonucleic acid, or DNA) of our genes. Genetic material is passed on from one generation to the next in an egg and a sperm when they fuse to produce a human embryo. The embryo contains information (coded in its inherited DNA) about how to grow and develop into a new human being. The DNA can be regarded as a recipe rather than a blueprint because the information it contains will be manifest only if the external environment in which it develops is enabling. For example, someone who has inherited genes for tallness can suffer from poor nutrition during childhood, so may not grow as tall as she or he could; in other words, they may not achieve their genetic potential because the environment is not sufficiently enabling. The outcome is a result of the interaction between genes and environment and this is always the case; the external environment and genes always interact, and this affects the way physical characteristics are expressed.

If the first meaning of human nature refers to physical characteristics, then the second meaning refers to individuals: to their temperaments, beliefs, prejudices, their talents and their interests – in other words, their behaviour. The minutiae of behavioural patterns are not predetermined genetically, although there are some who would argue that there are genetically determined aspects of behaviour (see Cosmides and Tooby 1992). There are no genes for (say) a bundle of behaviour patterns that could be regarded as 'feminine behaviour' (whatever that may be!) and there is no evidence at all to indicate that complex behaviour patterns in humans are determined by single genes (Jones 2002). Attempts to find identifiable biological characteristics that underpin a common 'human nature' or 'behaviour' have been fruitless, and any individuals who exhibit similar behaviour patterns are likely to have had shared or similar conditions of upbringing.

To summarise, the 'nature of humanity' refers to the physical makeup and behaviour patterns of humans, who (in biological terms) are bipedal, relatively hairless, medium-sized mammals with large brains and a capacity for learning. Both the physical form of this mammal and how it functions on many different levels are influenced by its biology, but many aspects of behaviour are not determined absolutely by biology. This argument (when applied to human learning) means it is influenced by biology but not determined by it.

Learning as process or cognitive process, based on learning as a function of the brain

In the introduction to this chapter, it was proposed that the first of three perspectives for considering learning is that of process. Much of the literature about learning that focuses on the processes or cognitive dimensions of learning comes from Physiology or Psychology, and the latter includes studies that are behaviourist in approach, or take a developmental stance, and so on. These studies tend to be based on manifestations of learning associated with variables (such as sound, images, etc.) that are manipulated under controlled conditions. When (say) a child associates a particular sound with a visible object, observable changes in behaviour are underpinned by micro changes deep down in the tissues of the human brain. Here in these tissues are locations of the physiological processes that underpin learning. Human brain tissue consists of trillions of nerve cells, and in newly born babies brain tissue appears to be relatively undifferentiated, with few connections between adjacent nerve cells. As a baby increases its interaction with its environment, the nerve cells in its brain begin to connect up into neural networks. The driving force behind these connections is the biochemistry that occurs when brain cells are stimulated as a result of interaction with the external environment. The brain is connected to this environment by sense organs, so when a baby's eyes are stimulated by her mother's face, electrochemical impulses are generated which pass down a nerve tract behind the eyes to the brain. If this stimulation is repeated, a site in the brain eventually changes permanently to become the site of recognition for the mother's face. In other words, the baby's brain has become rewired. This change or rewiring is the biological basis of learning.

At the level of process, the biological basis of learning is the production of electrochemical impulses, but these do not take place at random. They take place in specific nerve cells when specific parts of the brain are stimulated. The nerve cells are arranged according to a genetically inherited and specifically human pattern, with the brain being divided up into different functional sections. So (for example) one functional section controls physical functions such as appetite, another controls limb movement, and so on. The sites for the processes that govern the higher functions of the human brain such as cognition are less clearly identified. Basically, brain scientists have two different approaches as to the locations of the cognitive faculties of the human brain. One approach can be regarded as being 'modular' and the other 'unitary' (Donald 1991). Modular theories propose a separate location for aspects of cognitive ability, so (for example) mathematical ability or non-verbal thought would each be located separately. In contrast, unitary theories propose that the higher cognitive functions are an overall property of the highly developed and refined memory system of the brain. Whichever of these two theories is correct is debatable, and in fact neither one excludes the other as an explanation for cognitive abilities. However, the cognitive abilities of the human brain do fall into two main camps, one being things all of us are good at and the other being things that all of us are not so good at.

Because all human beings find certain cognitive tasks easy, then it is highly possible that we all use the same mental faculties to do these tasks. In terms of things we are good at, I include here all the activities that healthy human beings learn very quickly and easily, such as how to talk, how to recognise people, how to make friends, how to influence people, and so on. All of these are so easy to learn and so universally part of the nature of humanity that we take them for granted. They are learned intuitively, implying in biological terms that we have innate cognitive structures in the human brain that govern the development and execution of these behaviours. In terms of things we are not so good at, I refer to activities that (for most people) do not 'come naturally' but require the intensive focus on learning provided by formal education. Examples include reading, writing, some aspects of mathematics and subjects such as modern physics, cosmology, genetics, evolution theory and economics – all of which are taught (but not necessarily learned) in educational establishments. The process of formal education can be regarded as a technology or a tool we have invented for making up for the innate deficiencies of human cognitive abilities. If we view the process of education through a biological 'lens', then we can see that it is more likely to succeed if it builds on something that is already there: in other words, our inherited, intuitive faculties.

The work of evolutionary psychologists such as Pinker (2002) and cognitive scientists such as Gardner (1999) indicates that there are a limited number of these faculties and they are common to all humankind. They are thus genetically determined and provide ways of knowing about the world. They are considered to have remained virtually unchanged since they developed in our prehistoric ancestors around 200,000 to 150,000 years ago, when the world was a very different place. These faculties are rooted in the neural circuits of our brains and were sufficient to enable the survival of a non-literate people living in small groups, using their wits and exploiting their external environment for food and shelter. Cognitive scientists have not agreed exactly what these faculties are, but the list that follows is defensible (Pinker 2002). There is a faculty that leads to an intuitive understanding of physical objects and their movement through space and time; this is equivalent to an intuitive physics. Similarly, there are other faculties that give rise to intuitive understandings of natural history and the belief in an 'essence' of living things; an understanding of tools and their purposeful design; of people and their behaviour; of spatial navigation; of number, quantity and amounts and of pattern recognition; of the probability of events; of reciprocal exchange; of cause and effect. Finally, there is an intuitive understanding of spoken language. Language is our major mode of communication and is based on rules that are very complex, but which children learn intuitively although their intellectual powers are relatively poorly developed at the time. These eleven faculties are considered common to all healthy human beings and are controlled by data processing systems in the brain.

The eleven faculties are sometimes referred to as the basis of multiple intelligences and can be equated roughly with academic disciplines. The second of these (natural history) relates approximately to the biological sciences; the third approximately to engineering, and so on. However, academic disciplines are very recent developments and there is no evidence that people show any intuitive grasp of them whatsoever. In fact, academic disciplines provide views of the world that can sometimes contradict the naïve views emanating from 'the multiple intelligences'. An example would be the naïve view that two objects of different weights, if dropped from the same floor on the tower of Pisa, will hit the ground at the different times. It was Galileo who (at the beginning of the seventeenth century) was able to demonstrate that this is not the case, and later he suffered for attacking the then widely held but naïve belief that the sun goes around the earth. The breakthroughs in thinking by geniuses such as Albert Einstein, Charles Darwin, Freud and others are the result of great leaps of imagination and insight beyond the boundaries of naïve ways of looking at the world. Once these pioneers had 'broken out of the box' and carved new ways of thinking, others could learn to follow. But following new ways of thinking can be hard, especially if the learning involved goes against 'the grain' of intuition.

These eleven or so intuitive faculties were all that were needed for our prehistoric ancestors' way of life. As far as we know they had no cognitive tools for any counter-intuitive ways of understanding the world. Today, counter-intuitive ways of understanding the world have led to the development of the science and technology that underpins contemporary lifestyles. Counter-intuitive ways of understanding the world have to be learned, but before this learning can take place, intuitive understanding needs to be unlearned. This unlearning has important implications for teaching – for example, how can a child understand evolution by means of natural selection if she believes that all design is purposeful? The issue of unlearning becomes even more important when teaching adults, because not only may they still rely on intuitive understandings of the world, but also they are likely to have additional ideas and concepts derived from those intuitions. A sound educational theory would thus start from what learners understand and work collaboratively with them to open the routes to non-intuitive theory. There are several authors whose educational theories stress the importance of finding out what learners know about a topic before starting out on a new learning journey (Brookfield 1996; Bruner 1968; Laurilland 1993; Rogers 1996). In biological terms, the end point of successful learning would be change in the 'wiring' of the brain.

The perspective of the learner as an individual, arising from her/his particular circumstances of gender, developmental stage, age, experience, context, and so on

The second perspective for considering learning is from the point of view of the individual, both in terms of the similarities and in terms of the differences between individuals. Much of the traditional literature about learning that focuses on the individual learner comes again from Psychology and focuses on differences in individuals in terms of personality, psychoanalysis, motivation, and so on. Other contributions come from the life experiences of learners, from the effects of life changes on learning and other variables. Contributors to this perspective of learning include Havinghurst (1972), Mezirow (1991), Tennant (1997) and many others. Perspectives on the learner as an individual can come from biology too, and the ones that are discussed here focus on what makes us all the same but different at the same time.

In many respects, individuals are more similar than they are different. Starting at the most basic level, all of us are composed of exactly the same chemical materials as each other (and every other creature on planet earth). The mixture of chemicals that makes us human is slightly different from the mixture that makes (say) insects or seaweeds. The similar chemicals give rise to similar chemical processes of life inside our bodies and release energy to digest our food, reproduce the species and so on. The importance of this point about similarities is that it provides evidence of our relationship to other life forms on the planet, all of which are governed by the same biological rules. If we are similar at a deep and cryptic level, we are certainly different at observable levels.

The obvious differences in the observable physical appearances of living things are used to classify animals and plants into distinctive groups; this classification is known as taxonomy. According to biological taxonomy, humans belong to a group called mammals which is further subdivided into another group called primates, which includes lemurs, monkeys and apes. Primates share certain physical and behavioural characteristics, including a capacity for learning. The human capacity for learning is the greatest among primates and the most distinctive. Despite its singularity, it can be regarded as part of a spectrum of primate ability to learn, with perhaps lemurs at one end and humans at the other. Therefore, human learning is, at the same time, both a common biological phenomenon and a unique biological phenomenon.

The apparent contradiction in being the same and yet different can best be understood by looking at where our species has come from. Current evidence from human palaeontology and genetic studies indicates that human beings have a long evolutionary history that began around 6 million years ago in Africa (Olson 2002; Renfrew 2003). At that time, two distinct species of apes arose, one of which (through many intermediate stages) eventually developed into human beings. The second group (through many intermediate stages) became chimpanzees. Humans and chimpanzees are so very, very different in terms of their physical appearance, their mental abilities and so on, but they have 98 per cent of their genetic material in common! In other words, they share very much at the basic level of chemistry and physiology, but despite this they are different anatomically and in many other ways too. Only 2 per cent of genetic material is needed to make all the difference between being human and being an ape. Despite their divergence 6 million years ago, the genetic makeup of each species has barely changed. It has not changed much because the main function of genetic material is to store information safely and then to pass it on from one generation to the next. So if change in genetic material does not occur frequently, what is responsible for the evolutionary changes that do occur? Charles Darwin proposed the answer, in terms of the theory of evolution by means of natural selection. This theory accounts for the evolution of all life forms (including human beings) on this planet and it is explained briefly in the next few paragraphs.

Charles Darwin's theory of the evolution of species by natural selection proposes that natural forces (e.g. disease, the availability of food or water, the proximity of predators, and the occurrence of fire, earthquakes or floods) act as selective agents on living things, and determine whether they live or die. Those that survive into adulthood despite the onslaught of natural forces such as disease, predators, etc. have, in effect, been subject to selection for survival by these natural forces. These survivors are the only ones that are able to reproduce. Darwin described the survivors as 'fit' – the survival of the fittest. If those who are 'fit' differ from their peers by having some particular physical characteristic that enables them to survive and then go on to produce offspring, then their offspring may inherit the particular characteristic of their parent(s). 'Fit' offspring are more likely to survive similar onslaughts than are others who do not have the advantage of the survival characteristic. In this way, the characteristics for 'fitness' are passed on from one generation to another. There are so many examples of 'fitness' that it is difficult to choose one, but the spotted coat of leopards (which allows them to blend in with their background) is an example of the fitness that enables these animals to survive.

Darwin's view was that the process of natural selection could account for the evolution of living things from simple forms to more complex. It works on the basis that all living things are similar and yet different, the differences being the raw material on which selection acts. Darwin's theory (at the time) drew upon evidence from the fossil record and from his observations on his experiments with selective breeding in pigeons. It is not yet possible to trace every fossil link in (say) the gradual evolution of groups such as birds, of the horse, or of the species of *Homo sapiens* to which we all belong. However, there is ample evidence that demonstrates that life forms of the past were at first very similar and then, over billions of years, became very different because of their interactions with the environment.

The theory of evolution by natural selection can account for the evolution of the human species too. According to current evidence, human ancestors were ape-like but became bipedal about 4 million years ago, and around 2 million years ago they began to use tools. Both of these changes in habit could not have happened unless there had been changes in the wiring of the brain. Two million years ago early hominids began to change their environment by chipping away at it, to create sharp-edged tools for hunting and the preparation of food. They were the forebears of the genus *Homo*, our earliest ancestors, and had much bigger brains than did their predecessors. The brains of early tool-making forebears were about twice the size of those of apes and about two-thirds the size of those of present-day humans.

These physical features, the enlarged brain and changes in gait, can be accounted for by natural selection. The fossil record provides evidence that the skills of tool-making that were learned aeons ago were passed on from one generation of early hominid to the next. We have no evidence as to how this was done, but it must have required some form of communication. The ability of an individual to communicate to others what has been learned is not unique to humans, as there is ample evidence to suggest that it occurs in other animals too (Laland and Brown 2002). This communication is the basis of social learning, meaning that it involves interactions between individuals within and between groups. While tool-making provides evidence of early teaching and learning by means of social learning, it is not until around 200,000 years ago, according to archaeological and fossil records, that a new species of *Homo* appeared with a much bigger brain, a lightly built body and a new form of cognitive flexibility. This was *Homo sapiens*, and this is the species to which all humans on this planet now belong. At the same time, according to the fossil and archaeological record, there is evidence of the development of human culture. By culture, I mean here a cohesive set of mental representations, together with ideas, beliefs and values that are shared among individuals. Culture is undoubtedly an outcome of social learning, and social learning in humans is different compared with that of other animals. In other animals, social learning is neither as rich nor as stable as it is in human beings, where it gives rise to beliefs, attitudes and values. In humans these can be transmitted laterally across different groups and horizontally down the generations in the form of traditions. There is no evidence that other animals can do this.

The ability of *Homo sapiens* to walk, talk and share the fruits of learning depends on structures in the brain; these structures are the result of natural selection just as are other bodily structures. The prehistory of human beings is thus a saga of interaction with the external environment during which some mental faculties were more favourable for survival than were others. Over time, individuals who had the favourable characteristics were more likely to survive than others and passed these on to their offspring. This process of natural selection works because of the differences between individuals. In *Homo sapiens* these differences are both obvious and not so obvious. Whereas all human beings are built according to a common pattern they do exhibit observable variations in physical appearance. This is probably because, sometime in the past, *Homo sapiens* migrated from the ancestral homelands to different geographical locations and then became subject to the effects of different climates and different diseases and developed different ways of living (Olson 2002). However, the evidence from the Human Genome Diversity Project (HGDP) is that all modern humans are descended from one common African source (Sykes 2001). This common origin means we all have the same basic cognitive framework with the same chemical processes underpinning our learning. There is no evidence that some groups of humans (for example, some nationalities or ethnic groups) have inherently different cognitive frameworks or mental faculties than do other groups. In essence this means that any differences in learning outcomes and achievement between individuals or groups are likely to be the result of differences in upbringing and environment, both of which affect human capacities for learning.

But, within groups, how much of the difference between individuals is due to nature and how much is due to nurture? There is evidence to indicate that some of the individual differences in personality and cognitive abilities have an inherited component. This does not mean that genes are in control of personality and cognitive ability. If this were the case, then personality and cognitive ability would be at the mercy of genetic determinism. Genetic determination as the basis for human differences is wrong for three reasons. The first is that most inherited traits are the product of many genes, each with a small effect and each modified by other genes. Second, the manifestation of a gene is a probability; even identical twins with their identical genes have only a 50 per cent chance of exhibiting the same traits. Third, their environment affects the expression of genes, and in the case of humans the environment has two components. One is the shared environment and consists of home life, family and so on. The second social environment is outside of the home, where we learn to fit in (or not!) to society. The expression of individual differences in terms of personality and intellectual ability is the result of complex interactions between an individual's genetic makeup and interactions with others (Harris 1998). The old adage of nature versus nurture can be rephrased as nature via nurture (Ridley 2003). A generally acceptable ratio for nurture and nature is that genes probably contribute up to 30 to 50 per cent of an individual's characteristics and the environment (including social environment) contributes a balance of 50 to 80 per cent.

The contextual or social/cultural perspective, based on learning as a result of the effects of the social/cultural context on learners

This third perspective for viewing learning is from a contextual or social/cultural dimension. This dimension has two parts; the first is how learning is affected by the immediate context of the individual and the second is how learning is affected by the wider social context. The stance taken here in this third perspective is slightly different from the two preceding ones because it enters the territory of human affairs, involving an understanding of how the structures and functions of society affect the learning of individuals or of groups. These issues are in the realm of the social sciences; authors on these issues are numerous and their studies include the effects of social class on learning (and on education), the effects of gender, of culture, of participation, of achievement, of policy. This section of the chapter summarises what biologists can say about the effects of the external, social environment on human learning. Perhaps the first thing to say is that this social environment is considered to be one of the factors responsible for the incredibly rapid development of humankind from its first emergence as *Homo sapiens* between 200,000 and 100,000 years ago. In evolutionary terms, this represents a very rapid transition from behaviour patterns associated with bare subsistence to those associated with agriculture, settlement and urbanisation. The changes necessary for this are likely to have been brought about by factors other than biology, and the most likely driver for such rapid change is human culture. Culture is the product of the human brain and our capacity for culture is considered the major adaptation driving our transition from the so-called 'primitive' lifestyles of early *Homo sapiens* to the modern day.

The second thing to say is that because culture is essentially concerned with human affairs, science in general can have little to say about it. This is because currently there is no branch of science that can satisfactorily explain human society or the beliefs, knowledge and values underpinning culture. Despite science's inability to throw much light on human affairs, the popular press often carries 'scientific' explanations for (say) human behaviour, based on the work of prominent scientists. These press reports, together with some television programmes (certainly in the UK), frequently present science as an absolute explanation for human affairs (Appleyard 2003). Such explanations, because they appear to be supported by some members of the scientific community, lay the foundations for an ideology of scientism. This ideology holds that science and the methods of science are all-powerful and can be applied to human affairs. There are several reasons why this cannot be the case, and these are explored below.

First, the ideology of scientism rests upon a general misconception about scientific results, which are often presented as if they are absolute statements of fact, whereas in reality they are not. Scientific results are generally provisional and couched in terms of probability. Scientific explanations do not necessarily provide a definitive explanation for a phenomenon or an issue, but they are a way of stating (for example) that the chances of such and such being the case are 999 in 1,000. In other words, there is always the possibility that a scientific result may be incorrect.

Another major reason why science cannot provide a framework for an understanding of human affairs is that the methods of science are not designed to deal with human affairs. They are designed to deal with stable, non-changing, material subject matter. When the methods of science are applied to appropriate science-based questions, the answers are objective, generalisable and universal. Objectivity and generalisability can apply only if the subject matter is non-changing and material. In contrast, the subject matter of human affairs is constantly changing. Answers to questions or problems about human affairs are thus generally subjective, not generalisable from one context to the next, and thus are not universal. Questions about human affairs are the opposite to those of science.

The third reason for the inability of science to cast much light on human affairs is that the scientists who attempt to do so do not speak with one voice. The major group of scientists working on issues related to human affairs are involved in research that was stimulated by the work of Edmond Wilson (1975) in his book *Sociobiology: The New Synthesis*. This book was a major work that reviewed the evolution of behaviour in social animals and included a chapter that treated *Homo sapiens* in the same way as other animal groups. One of Wilson's main aims for the book was to provide some common ground between the social sciences and the biological sciences, but at the time it did the opposite. The book, although a major work of biological scholarship, reflects Wilson's (then) political naïveté in using a scientific framework to explain human affairs. The book earned Wilson many critics, drawn not just from the social sciences but from the biological sciences too. The debates that followed over the years were acrimonious and now, almost thirty years later, sociobiology per se is not so much of an issue, but around five sub-fields have been spawned by it.

These five sub-fields (Laland and Brown 2002) focus on possible relationships between human affairs and human biology, and they range from those that consider genes to have only a limited influence over human behaviour to those that consider that human behaviour is influenced strongly by genes (human sociobiology). At the human sociobiology end of the spectrum is the view that the conduct of human affairs is based on inherited cognitive structures that have evolved to maximise Darwinian fitness; at the other end there are the views that Darwinian fitness can be overruled by culture.

None of the views held by these five sub-groups is exclusive, and all may have some validity. For example, there is empirical evidence suggesting that human culture is not necessarily congruent with the external physical environment and that cultural traditions may be maintained despite the environment (Guglielmino et al. 1995). Other studies show that even if individuals are divided into arbitrary groups, a group 'culture' generally emerges (Knowles and Knowles 1972), indicating that the need to develop a culture is at the core of humanity. Culture is based on information that passes between individuals and is transmitted freely, quickly and easily across groups (horizontally), down groups (vertically) and between groups (obliquely). This information is frequently modified and adapted so that it changes very quickly, and people can adapt their culture (their beliefs and values and behaviour) in very short periods of time. In contrast, genetic material (which is information) is transmitted much more slowly, and only in one direction (vertically); it does not change very quickly and remains unmodified for long periods of time. As a conveyor of information, it is a good vehicle for basic biology, but that is its limit. It is neither sufficiently malleable nor sophisticated enough to account for the rapidity of human behavioural evolution, but culture is.

Although the sub-groups agree that human learning mechanisms have been moulded by natural selection, the question that divides them is how humans learn from each other. Undoubtedly social learning is the key process, but is this learning entirely dependent upon evolved predisposition or is it free of these? The answers to such questions will be dependent on the results of empirical research, and obviously such data cannot be easy to obtain. However, among the five sub-fields there is one that attempts to explore any common ground between human affairs and human biology by modelling mathematically the interaction between culture and genes. The sub-field known as gene-culture co-evolutionists is considered by some (Laland and Brown 2002) to be capable of producing results that may find common ground between human affairs and human biology.

The five sub-fields of human evolutionary thought can appear to be virtually indistinguishable to the lay person and anyone could be forgiven for thinking that they are one and speak with one voice. The reality is that they do not, and while this is evident in academic circles it does erupt into the public arena too (Ridley 2003). Indeed, it is possible that the divisions between the sub-fields could hinder the future of any studies on the evolution of human affairs. However, whatever the differences between the sub-fields, they all agree that for the past 200,000 years or so, the development of human affairs has been dependent upon the information passed between individuals through learning.

Conclusions

This chapter started out by exploring what the biological sciences can add to our understanding of human learning. First, human learning is a product of our physical makeup and in particular of our brains. The human brain is the site of our emotions, our intelligence, our perceptions and our humanity, all of which makes up the human spirit, but in reality this spirit is the product of the material world. Charles Darwin's theory of natural selection provides an explanation for how living things on this planet could have evolved from a material world. The theory applies to the evolution of human beings so the 'footprints' of our early evolutionary prehistory are likely to remain in our brains, just as the 'footprints' of our prehistory remain elsewhere in our bodies too (for example, humans have the rudiments of a tail at the base of the spine). There is some evidence to indicate what these cerebral 'footprints' might be (see the section on individuals as learners, above) and they appear to be the cognitive structures we all possess for making sense of the world.

Second, human learning is unique. Although it is part of a spectrum of behaviour that is found in other animals, and particularly in highly intelligent social animals, human learning is much more complex, rich and intricate than that of any other living creature on this planet. Uniquely, humans are able to pass on the fruits of their learning through culture, which stores or encodes it for the benefit of others.

Finally, because human learning is at the heart of the nature of humanity, then an understanding of the nature of humanity can help us grapple with the most fundamental questions about human freedom, morality and ethics. These questions are traditionally the preserve of philosophy and the social sciences, and I do not suggest that these disciplines should make way for the biological sciences. However, I do suggest that an understanding of where we came from can help us to decide where we want to go, and (importantly) how to get there. Certainly, it seems as if the forces of natural selection drove the prehistory of hominids, but the latter phases of the development of *Homo sapiens* were driven by something additional. So whereas human genes are largely identical to those of chimpanzees, human cognitive structures are entirely different. These structures enable us to learn and function as humans, and human learning has no parallels in the animal kingdom (Donald 1991). The forces of natural selection do not bind us and so our future is in our hands. This immense responsibility requires all of us to use our powers of reason collectively, as we have done so many times in the past (Dennett 2003). But the moral choices that may underpin our reasoning cannot be derived from a 'survival of the fittest'.

This does not mean that we should reject Darwinian evolutionary theory as being irrelevant to human affairs. Those who do reject it fall into two camps. One camp denies Darwinian theory as the basis for understanding the evolution of all life on earth, and instead accepts accounts drawn from religion. These include creation stories with their accounts of how life came to be. The second camp accepts Darwinian theory as an explanation for the evolution of life on earth, but excludes human beings from the process. Arguments from this second camp imply that humans are somehow 'special' and arrived on this planet by some route other than evolution. The views from both camps are difficult to sustain in the light of all the available evidence about our material origins. However, more importantly, both views are difficult to sustain when pitted against proponents of the scientism and biological determinism as propagated in the mass media. The appeal of both biological determinism and scientism is that they appear to offer definitive answers to the big questions about the nature of humanity. Their answers are that we came from animals, we are animals and so human behaviour that includes atrocities is somehow excusably 'natural'.

Those who argue against these views of so-called 'natural' human behaviour can (of course) do so by denying any evidence of our animal origins. The problem is that these arguments are likely to be ignored or considered ill-informed, particularly in the light of so much evidence to the contrary. An alternative is to be aware that there is a body of evidence that can explain the evolution of human beings. This evidence indicates that *Homo sapiens* has used learning as a tool to break away from the inevitability of nature 'red in tooth and claw' for the past 200,000 years, and there is every indication that this can continue.

References

Appleyard, B. (2003) *Understanding the Present: An Alternative History of Science*, London: Tauris Parke.

Brookfield, S. D. (1996) *Understanding and Facilitating Adult Learning*, Milton Keynes: Open University Press.

Bruner, J. S. (1968) *Towards a Theory of Instruction*, New York: W. W. Norton.

Cosmides, L. and Tooby, J. (1992) 'Cognitive Adaptations for Social Exchange' in J. H. Barkow, L. Cosmides and J. Tooby (eds) *The Adapted Mind: Evolutionary Psychology and the Generation of Culture*, Oxford: Oxford University Press, pp. 163–228.

Dennett, D. C. (2003) *Freedom Evolves*, London: Allen Lane.

Donald, M. (1991) *Origins of the Modern Mind*, Cambridge, MA: Harvard University Press.

Gardner, H. (1999) *Intelligence Reframed: Multiple Intelligences for the 21st Century*, New York: Basic Books.

Guglielmino, C. R., Viganotti, C., Hewlett, B. and Cavalli-Sforza, L. L. (1995) 'Cultural Variation in Africa: Role of Mechanism of Transmission and Adaptation', *Proceedings of the National Academy of Sciences USA* 92: 7585–9.

Harris, J. R. (1998) *The Nurture Assumption. Why Children Turn Out the Way They Do*, New York: Free Press.

Havinghurst, R. J. (1972) *Developmental Tasks and Education*, New York: Mckay.

Illeris, K. (2002) *The Three Dimensions of Learning*, Roskilde, Denmark: Roskilde University Press.

Jarvis, P. (1992) *The Paradoxes of Learning*, San Francisco; Jossey-Bass.

Jones, S. (2002) *The Descent of Men*, London: Little, Brown.

Knowles, H. C. and Knowles, M. (1972) *Introduction to Group Dynamics*, Chicago: Association Press/Follet.

Laland, K. N. and Brown, G. R. (2002) *Sense and Nonsense*, Oxford: Oxford University Press.

Laurilland, D. (1993) *Rethinking University Teaching*, London and New York: Routledge.

Merriam, S. B. and Caffarella, R. S. (1999) *Learning in Adulthood*, San Francisco: Jossey-Bass.

Mezirow, J. (1991) *Transformative Dimensions of Adult Learning*, San Francisco: Jossey-Bass.

Olson, S. (2002) *Mapping Human History*, London: Bloomsbury.

Pinker, S. (2002) *The Blank Slate*, London: Allen Lane.

Renfrew, C. (2003) *Figuring It Out*, London: Thames and Hudson.

Ridley, M. (2003) *Nature via Nurture*, London: Fourth Estate.

Rogers, A. (1996) *Teaching Adults*, Buckingham: Open University Press.

Sykes, B. (2001) *The Seven Daughters of Eve*, London: Bantam Press.

Tennant, M. (1997) *Psychology and Adult Learning*, London and New York: Routledge.

Wilson, E. O. (1975) *Sociobiology: The New Synthesis*, Cambridge, MA: Harvard University Press.

Chapter 3

The brain and learning

John Stein

Introduction

The human brain is the largest organised structure in the universe – an extravagant claim, but true. It contains 100,000 million (10^{11}) neurones and four times that number of supporting 'glial' cells. Each neurone makes on average 10,000 connections with other neurones. In other words, there are 1,000 million million connections in the brain (10^{15}). This means that the brain can make more possible combinations of connections than there are particles in the whole universe. So the human brain is indeed the largest organised structure in the universe. Yet all these connections are fundamentally organised to perform only the three vital behavioural functions of all animals: finding food and water, self-preservation and procreation.

The organisation of the brain arises from interaction of genetic control and environmental influences, not only during development but throughout all the experiences of life. The most basic biochemical processes, such as control of protein synthesis, are dominated by the genes, but higher cognitive functions such as speech, language and visuospatial ability result from a roughly equal mix of genetic control and intrauterine prenatal and postnatal environmental influences throughout life. A most important contribution to this postnatal development is of course education.

In the last twenty years neuroscience has advanced so rapidly that, despite some doubting Cassandras, we can now begin to think that its discoveries will soon really help teachers to develop new, evidence-based techniques, rooted in understanding the biology of learning, for improving the way we educate our children. In particular, we are now beginning to understand how individual differences in higher cognitive functions arise, so that we should be able soon to develop educational programmes that target each child's strengths and weaknesses. It must be admitted, however, that unfortunately we have not quite yet reached that happy position. Neuroscience findings cannot yet be transferred directly to the improvement of educational techniques. Understanding the biological basis of memory, learning and higher cognitive functions has not turned out to automatically lead to ways of improving them. In fact, there is already a backlash of those who claim that, really, neuroscience will never offer teachers very much that will actually help their classroom practice.

For example, although clear structural differences have been found in the brain between individuals, these do not automatically tell us what functional differences they represent, nor does the stage at which they develop tell us when is the optimum time to introduce particular kinds of education for different individuals. Likewise, knowing the biochemical mechanisms that alter the strength of nerve connections that underlies learning does not tell us directly how to help children learn.

However, I am an optimist. Recently techniques have been developed that enable us to look at functional differences between individuals. So they offer the hope that we will soon be able to adapt our teaching methods to match the learning needs of individual children. In this chapter, therefore, I want to briefly describe the structural and functional changes that occur in the brain during development, and how understanding how these vary between individuals may enable us to target educational approaches to individual learning needs.

Finally I will show, using the particular example of reading, how understanding individuals' different brain strengths and weaknesses is already being exploited to improve the teaching of reading. This shows how potentially we will be able to target our educational methods to individual children's functional brain differences, hence match them to individuals' different learning needs.

Brain development

The brain is made up of 100,000 million (10^{11}) separate cells, 'neurones', that gather information from diverse sources through their 'dendrites' (Figure 3.1), integrate them in the 'cell body' and send the outcome of their processing to be passed on to the next neurone via their elongated axons which make 'synapses' with the next neurone in the chain. The most rapid period of brain development occurs during development of the foetus in utero from the sixth week to the sixth month of pregnancy. During this time, a million million (10^{12}) new neurones are generated; in fact, an amazing 250,000 new neurones are added every minute. However, only 10 per cent (still 10^{11}) of these neurones are destined to survive after birth. The other 90 per cent are programmed to self-destruct ('apoptose') because they fail in a lethal competition with other neurones to make useful functional connections. This is an example of a general principle of brain function that persists throughout life: 'use it or lose it'. The main function of each neurone is to communicate with other neurones via synapses made with its dendrites and axons, either close by or at great distances. In an adult the axons of neurones connecting touch receptors on the toe with the brain are up to 2 metres in length. But unless a connection or contact serves a functional purpose, it will lose out in a cut-throat competition and be removed.

Thus the connections that grow between neurones only survive if they perform a useful service. Genetic control specifies the general ground plan of the brain, but even at this early stage which neurones survive is determined by current environmental influences according to how effective each neurone is in communicating with other neurones. If the connecting synapses between neurones give rise to correlated electrical activity between them, this

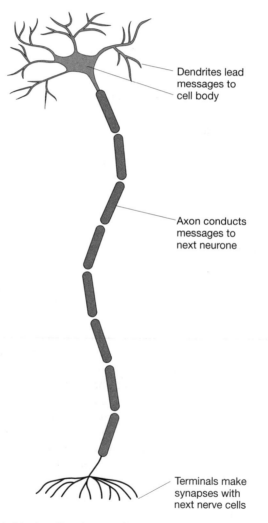

Dendrites lead
messages to
cell body

Axon conducts
messages to
next neurone

Terminals make
synapses with
next nerve cells

Figure 3.1 A typical brain cell – a 'neurone'.

enables them to switch on the synthesis of essential growth factors. These rescue the neurone from self-destruction, consolidate and strengthen existing synapses and even promote sprouting of new axon terminals to make more synapses with neighbouring neurones. The other great principle of brain development is therefore: 'neurones that fire together wire together'. Only the most successful neurones and synapses survive this lethal competition.

Postnatal growth

At birth the brain contains almost all the neurones it ever will. But at this time the baby's brain is only a quarter the size of an adult's. Even giving birth to a brain that size stresses the female pelvis greatly. However, after birth the brain grows over fourfold in size, not by producing more neurones but by further division of supporting 'glial' cells and also, crucially, in the first few years after birth by increasing the number of connections between neurones. This huge increase in connectivity is the main reason why our brains are so much more powerful than those of our closest primate relatives, the chimpanzees. Their brains are only 25 per cent smaller in size than ours are. They have almost the same number of neurones, but they only have about a quarter the number of interconnecting synapses that we enjoy.

The peak number of these connections is reached between one and three years after birth. It has therefore been suggested that it is during this very early period when these connections are forming that education should be concentrated. Some have even wondered whether there is any point at all in education after this time. This growth in connections in infancy is also adduced to explain the 'Mozart effect', that playing Mozart to baby in the cradle increases her intelligence.

But these ideas are based on a misunderstanding. The crucial period for development of the function of the brain occurs not during but after this period. In the visual system, for example, 50 per cent of the connections formed in the first three years of life are pruned out over the next ten years. This process remodels the brain in response to external stimuli. It follows the same general principles of 'using it or losing it' and 'firing together wiring together' as in utero, but now the correlated activity between neurones is generated by external stimuli. Synapses are only retained and strengthened if they achieve correlated activity of both pre- and post-synaptic neurones. And this will only occur if they respond to a visual feature that is seen in the outside world sufficiently often, and is therefore ecologically relevant. Seen often enough, this will generate enough correlated electrical activity to allow the neurones to synthesise their synapse-saving growth factors. Thus synapses and connections that correspond to salient external features are reinforced, whereas those that do not regress. Thus the network comes to 'represent' in the brain visual features that are encountered sufficiently often in the outside world. This mechanism explains why it is so important to provide lots of visually stimulating objects in the environment. It was shown thirty years ago that the visual cortex of rats reared in a plain cage without any interesting objects retained 50 per cent fewer synapses than their genetically identical litter mates reared in the same type of cage but enriched with other rats and many pipes, tubes, boxes and hoops to play in and explore.

Note that this process of selective pruning of connections continues until puberty, at 12 to 13 years old in humans. In fact the highest rate of pruning does not occur until early in puberty. No wonder that puberty is so stressful for all concerned! But what this long period means is that exposure to environmental influences, such as education, is going to strongly influence which synapses are pruned. Thus education has an important effect on the very structure of the brain, at least until puberty. But actually, we now know that restructuring the architecture of synapses in the brain in this way continues throughout life.

Learning and memory

This remodelling occurs throughout life because the mechanism by which we learn and lay down memories is an extension of the same developmental processes that have been going on in childhood. There is no clear biological distinction between how the brain develops and how learning experiences throughout later life modify its structure. Whereas development of the brain in utero mainly involves culling of neurones, and in childhood mainly involves pruning of excess connections, the laying down of memories mainly involves adjustment to the strength and numbers of the synapses that have already been formed.

Altering the strength of synapses (synaptic modulation) occurs by interaction of two basic processes, known as long-term potentiation (LTP) and long-term depression (LTD). LTP facilitates synapses between two neurones when they discharge together, helping them to wire together. Millions of events of this sort modulate networks to represent events and knowledge stored in memory. But LTD is equally important to remove unwanted and unuseful associations.

LTP and LTD have been most studied in two 'model' systems in animals. The hippocampus is the brain structure that plays a crucial role in associative, episodic memory, and it has proved ideal for investigating LTP, whereas LTD has been mainly studied in the cerebellum. The main function of this structure behind and below the cerebral hemispheres is to mediate another form of learning, the acquisition of automatic motor skills for the co-ordination and optimisation of movement. But both LTP and LTD occur throughout the whole brain, particularly in the association areas of the cerebral cortex, which are the areas that mediate the cognitive functions that interest educationalists most.

Synapses not only change their strength. They can also switch to new positions, and new ones can sprout as well. During learning, synaptic spines on neuronal processes seem to search around randomly to find useful contacts. Once found, these consolidate and stabilise, embodying the learnt material. No one synapse represents a single memory, 'an engram', however. Slight alterations are made to a whole network of millions of synapses. For example, written words are represented over a very extensive network of cortical areas in the left cerebral hemisphere. Not only are representations of its sound, its visual written form and its meaning included in the network, but importantly also how you would speak the word, together with how you would act it, are all involved. The network includes the planum temporale in the temporal lobe and the fusiform gyrus in the occipital lobe, the angular and supramarginal gyri in the posterior parietal lobe, together with the motor speech area in the inferior frontal gyrus and even the motor cortex in the precentral gyrus of the frontal lobe. All these areas and several million synapses are therefore involved in representing just one word, and these overlap extensively with the representation of other words.

Active learning

One important lesson that has emerged from study of these networks is that they always involve motor as well as sensory areas of the cortex. The rats mentioned earlier, which were brought up in an enriched environment and retained more synapses in their visual cortex, not only explored the tubes, pipes and boxes with their eyes, but also ran among them and poked their noses into them. In a classic experiment, pairs of kittens were reared differently to see the effect of active and passive visual experience. The passive kitten was confined to a basket hanging from the end of a pole so that it could not move much, but it could see everything around it. The other kitten was harnessed to the other end of the pole so that it had the same visual experience, but it actively pulled the passive one round in a circle. After a few weeks the visual skills of the pair were compared. Despite almost identical visual experience, the performance of the passive kitten was severely impaired in a variety of visual tasks compared with that of the active one.

These results transfer directly to the teaching situation. Children made to sit and listen passively to teacher without active involvement in teaching themselves have consistently been shown to lag behind children who are encouraged to actively find things out for themselves. Learning by doing turns out to be a much more effective teaching technique than learning by passive listening or viewing, and this can be traced directly back to the active participation of motor areas in the memory networks of the cerebral cortex. These areas will be much more efficiently activated by acting out the motor component of the memory than by passive listening or viewing.

Brain plasticity

The combination of growth and alteration of neural synaptic connections with modulation of their strength underlies neural 'plasticity'. This causes environmental influences and experiences to be captured and represented in the detailed, microscopic, 'ultra' structure of the brain. The most striking example of this is demonstrated by the response of the brain to injury.

Immediately after a stroke, which blocks the blood supply to a part of the brain, this area is completely destroyed. For example, a patient may be immediately paralysed and incapable of speech. But very often in the weeks and months that follow s/he will recover almost all these functions. Modern functional imaging techniques have shown that this occurs because neighbouring and connected parts of the brain are able to take over the functions of the damaged area. This return of function is mediated by unmasking and strengthening latent, very weak, pre-existing synaptic connections and by the sprouting of new connections to surviving structures. This plasticity in the face of injury makes use of the same underlying mechanisms that mediate the learning of new memories, and it demonstrates that they are still potentially powerful even in adults. Who knows what talents we could unleash if we could learn how to exploit it properly for educational purposes?

Neuroscience in the classroom?

Studying the biological basis of memory has generated several Nobel Prizes and we now understand the underlying mechanisms reasonably well. The details need not concern us here. But has it helped education? Has our hard-won understanding contributed materially to educational practice? The answer is 'Not yet'. So far our knowledge is too basic to be transferred directly to the classroom because the cognitive functions that educationalists are interested in are so many levels higher than what goes on at each synapse. Thus, for example, drugs that affect these processes have far too extensive effects to be any good for selectively improving just the cognitive functions desired.

However, one advance in education that all this new knowledge has provided is settlement of the old 'nature vs nurture' argument. Not only do we now know that both are equally important for the development of the brain, but also it is now clear that it is simply not possible to determine what component of personality, intelligence or athletic talent is genetically innate and what is dependent upon upbringing and environment. Theoretically it is still possible to conceive them as being separable and to statistically apportion their contribution to individual differences, for example by means of twin studies. But it is quite clear that they are so inextricably interlinked when one gets to the level of cognitive differences that it is utterly impossible to separate their contributions to any of the mechanisms that are of interest to education, e.g. how people differ in personality, intelligence, etc.

This conclusion is heartening because it supports neither the right-wing view that justifies the status quo by claiming that all individual differences are hereditary, preordained and immutable, nor the left-wing view that genetics plays no part in individual differences, so that they can all be eliminated by sufficiently radical teaching changes. Nevertheless, the strong influence of environment means that genetics need not consign people to an unalterable fate, as many people seem to fear. Properly targeted education and remediation ought to be able to compensate for much hereditary weakness, as I shall show later in the case of reading problems.

Structural changes in the brain continue in response to experience throughout life, though at a diminishing rate after puberty. What this implies, therefore, is that education really does matter a great deal, because it actually helps to determine the structure of the pupil's brain. Each thing a child learns does indeed alter his brain a little bit. Therefore we should worry even more about the 1 in 5 people who reach adulthood and say that they gained little or nothing from their education. We should think hard about this indictment of modern education. Why do current educational practices serve so many people so poorly?

Individual differences

Another thing that neuroscience has clarified is how different individual 'normal' brains are. We always knew this at a psychological and personality level. Now we know it at the level of brain structure and function as well. Modern magnetic resonance imaging has shown, for example, that the anatomical structure of people's brains differs much more, for example, than the differences between people's faces. Even very basic structures in the brain, such as, for instance, the brain fissure where the primary visual cortex is situated, can differ from individual to individual in its position with respect to the centre of the back of the skull by as much as 1 cm.

Functional magnetic resonance imaging has made this even clearer, and shown that experience changes brain structure as well. For example, if you learn two languages simultaneously as a child, the area in the temporal cortex which is activated for one language is indistinguishable from that employed by the other. But if you learn one in childhood and the other, just as fluently, later in life, the two activate clearly different, though adjacent, regions.

Large differences can also be seen when testing people's sensory sensitivities. For example, although people's visual acuity varies only over a narrow three-fold range, their sensitivity to a slightly higher level function, visual motion, varies over a ten-fold range. These individual differences then impact on much higher cognitive levels – for example, their reading or visual spatial abilities, as we shall see.

Hemispheric specialisation

Another important source of differences between individuals that is of potentially great relevance to education is the degree to which the two sides of the brain are specialised to perform different functions. In 97 per cent of people, including two-thirds of left-handers, the left hemisphere is relatively specialised for speech and language, whereas the right is more important for visuospatial analysis and emotional expression. These differences are not absolute: the right hemisphere is important for some aspects of language, such as its emotional tone, and the left hemisphere plays a part in some visuospatial functions such as helping to determine the relative position of letters in a word.

Now we know from magnetic resonance imaging in live humans that these functional differences are associated with structural differences between the hemispheres. Most brains are twisted anticlockwise as seen from the top, so that the front of the right hemisphere protrudes further forwards than the left, whereas the back of the occipital lobe in the left hemisphere sticks out backwards more than the right (see Figure 3.2). Thus the right frontal lobe is larger than the left, but the left temporal lobe is larger than the right.

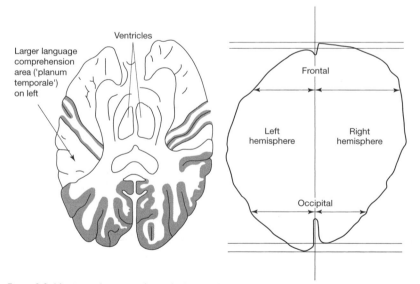

Figure 3.2 Horizontal section through the cerebral hemispheres showing anticlockwise twist favouring back of left hemisphere, front of right hemisphere.

Left hemisphere language

The twist seems to be mainly caused by the language comprehension area known as the planum temporale being much larger on the left. The degree to which the left planum temporale is larger on the left tends to correlate with individuals' language abilities, suggesting that this structural difference somehow underlies different degrees of language skill. Recently it has become possible, using magnetic resonance 'diffusion tensor' imaging, to measure in living subjects the thickness of the nerve fibres joining different parts of the brain to one another. Their thickness tells us how rapidly they can conduct messages between them, because fibre diameter determines conduction velocity. It turns out not only that the fibres are larger in the left hemisphere, but also that the diameter of these fibres in individuals correlates with that person's language skills. The larger they are, the faster can their owner find words to describe a situation, or learn new words in a foreign language.

However, the situation is complicated by sex differences. Females tend to have less marked hemispheric specialisation, with more cross-talk between the left and right temporal lobes. This may explain why females have, on average, superior language skills to males and why they are less likely to lose language skills after damage to the left hemisphere. But it means that the correlation between the ratio of left to right planum temporale size and left fibre diameter with language skills is much weaker in females than in males.

Right hemisphere

As mentioned earlier, the right hemisphere does play some part in language. It is now clear that important aspects are the responsibility of the right side. The right hemisphere seems to pick up the emotional valence of a sentence by analysing not the detailed phonology of its constituent words, which is the job of the left hemisphere, but its overall intonational shape and prosody. This function of sensing emotional signals is not confined to language, but extends also to sensitivity to the emotional content of music, facial expressions and even colours and odours.

The emotional skills of the right hemisphere derive from a difference in its structure that is not yet fully understood. It seems to be adapted in some way to capture holistic rather than sequential detail. This explains its visuospatial dominance. It provides us with a view not of the fine ordering of visual detail but of the overall layout of a whole visual scene or piece of music, together with the relationships of large chunks with each other. But this aspect of hemispheric specialisation has been far less studied than language. One must not think of hemispheric specialisation as being absolute. Both hemispheres play important parts in every kind of sensorimotor processing. But the left hemisphere contributes sequencing of fine detail in time and space. This is most suited to communication by ordered gesture, speech and writing. In contrast, the right hemisphere provides a larger holistic overview which is suited to visuospatial and emotional processing and non-verbal communication. To the extent that the degree of specialisation varies in different individuals, this is another parameter that ought to be taken into account when considering different individuals' learning needs and designing educational programmes for them.

Reading

I now want to turn to a particular example where neuroscience has begun to elucidate a higher cognitive process, and thereby has begun to impact on techniques to improve its teaching. Ten per cent of children have serious difficulties learning to read and are defined as 'dyslexic'. But a further 10 per cent barely learn to read, so that 20 per cent of young people leave school functionally illiterate (Moser 1999). These are the 1 in 5 adults who say they gained almost nothing from their ten years of schooling. But this illiteracy has far-reaching effects: a child's early loss of self-esteem leads to heart-rending misery and despair, or to frustration, anger and violence. Seventy-five per cent of imprisoned criminals are illiterate. Failure to learn to read is thus a major cause of psychological, social and economic problems, and it is an indictment of our educational systems that it remains so common. Measures to improve our understanding of the reading process and how to improve it should therefore receive much greater support than they currently enjoy. I study eye movement disorders, not only in dyslexics but also in diseases such as Parkinson's. Parkinson's affects 2 per cent of people over 65, i.e. for perhaps fifteen years; dyslexia causes misery to 10 per cent of children for their whole lives. Yet I've always found it easier to raise money for my research on Parkinson's disease, and it receives roughly 100 times the funds that dyslexia does.

Orthographic and phonological analysis

Reading is probably the most complicated skill that most of us ever acquire. It is difficult because it requires the analysis of small, visually sparsely detailed letters and their order, their conversion into sounds, and then association with the word's meaning, all this at the rate of two to three words a second.

The process begins with vision. The visual system scans the print in order to put letters and words in their correct order and thus to identify them. For familiar words we recognise the whole word at once and this allows us to grasp its meaning straight away from its visual form; this is the lexical/orthographic route for reading. We do not have to painstakingly sound out 'd', 'o', 'g' each time we read that word. But for unfamiliar words, and remember that most words are unfamiliar to a child learning to read, a further phonological process is required. Each letter has to be converted into the sound it stands for; then the auditory sequence has to be blended together to give its spoken form, thence its meaning. The visual orthographic route is clearly faster, but it will only work for words that are already in your 'sight vocabulary'. The auditory/phonological route, although slower, will work for any regular word, however unfamiliar. Clearly, the whole-word route will mainly rely on visual orthographic processing, whereas the phonological route will also require accurate auditory processing.

Visual/orthographic analysis

Although the spatial ordering of letter features and letters in a word sounds a perfectly simple process, in reality it requires a highly complex series of visuomotor operations. This is because only the centre of gaze has sufficiently high acuity to analyse print, so that we can only identify about seven letters accurately during each fixation of the eyes. Each fixation lasts for only about a quarter of a second. The eyes then have to move along the line of print to precisely fixate the next word, one at a time. It is therefore particularly important that the eyes move accurately to each fixation point and remain stationary there while the letters are being taken in. In fact, poor readers have little difficulty with identifying separate letters; both their visual acuity and their visual memory for individual letters is satisfactory. Instead, their main visual problem seems to be ocular-motor: in particular, they are poor at keeping the eyes steadily fixated on each word. This unsteady control leads the letters to appear to move around, so many dyslexics confuse letter order.

The stability of ocular motor control depends upon the quality of the control signals that are fed back from the eyes. Any unwanted movements cause images to slip off the high acuity centre of the retina. Normally the visual motion generated by this slip is fed back to the ocular motor control system very rapidly, and this reverses the eye movements that caused them and brings the eyes back on target. Hence high sensitivity to such visual motion is essential for steady binocular fixation. We have found that many children with problems learning to read have low visual motion sensitivity and that this often results in very unsteady fixation, 'wobbly eyes'. This can cause letters to appear to move around and cross over each other when the two eyes' lines of sight cross over each other. Such children complain that the letters seem to blur and move over each other when they are trying to read, because their eyes are wobbling around when they are looking at small print.

We have therefore been measuring the quality of individuals' visual motion signalling systems to attempt to trace the connection between this and their reading. Visual motion is detected by a subcomponent of the visual system, termed the magnocellular system. Its large neurones are specialised for timing transient events in the visual world. Hence it is particularly sensitive to visual motion. The sensitivity of individuals' visual magnocellular system can be measured relatively easily to see whether this relates at all to reading skill. We have made use of a technique developed for assessing motion sensitivity in the early stages of the visual system in animals, using simple stimuli that have nothing to do with reading. We display a field of bright dots moving around randomly on a dark background, so that the scene looks like an untuned TV receiver. A proportion of the dots are then moved all together in the same direction so that they look like a cloud of snowflakes blown by the wind. By reducing the proportion that move together instead of randomly, until the subject can no longer see any coherent motion in the cloud, we can measure individuals' sensitivity to visual motion, hence the basic sensitivity of their visual magnocellular, transient, system.

We then compare this with their visual reading skill. We assess this by measuring their ability to spell irregular words like 'yacht', or to spell homophones: which is correct, 'rane' or 'rain'? Neither of these tasks can be solved by sounding out the words; the correct 'orthographic' visual form of the word has to be remembered. We found, as expected, that there is indeed a correlation between individual subjects' motion sensitivity measured in this way and their visual orthographic reading skill. Thus we have been able to show that a very basic low-level visual function, motion sensitivity, plays an important role in determining how well individuals can acquire the high-level orthographic cognitive skills required for reading. This has turned out to be true for everyone: children and adults, good and poor readers.

However, these correlations are not huge, and of course correlation does not prove causation. Probably visual motion sensitivity is only one of several indirect influences contributing to how well orthographic reading skills develop. We need to fill in the gaps. Therefore we have tested and confirmed that visual motion sensitivity predicts subjects' ability to fixate steadily on non-reading small targets, that individual differences in fixation stability correlate with the ability to order non-letter symbols correctly in a sequence, and finally that symbol ordering skill predicts orthographic ability.

But the best way to prove causation is to see whether changing one changes the other. Therefore we have investigated whether improving eye control helps children with reading difficulties to learn to read. There are several ways of doing this, depending on the child's particular pattern of problems. But in all instances we have found that if we can improve the steadiness with which children can fixate on the words they are trying to read, their reading improves greatly thereafter.

In fact, we can generally increase the reading progress of poor readers dramatically. If poor readers receive no special help at all, their reading tends to regress with respect to their age, so that in six months on average their reading age increases by only three months. But we have been able to show that after successful treatment improving children's binocular control their reading leaps ahead, increasing on average twelve months in six months, so that many catch up with their peers in two years.

Thus our intervention studies have suggested strongly that improving binocular control improves reading in many dyslexics. Since binocular stability depends on people's visual motion sensitivity, which is an index of their visual magnocellular performance, these results support the hypothesis that visual magnocellular function helps to determine how well children can develop their orthographic reading skills through its effect on binocular stability. Likewise, it means that targeting poor binocular control can help children to avoid reading failure.

Auditory/phonological skill

But visual analysis alone is not sufficient for reading unfamiliar words; an extra phonological stage is necessary. A child confronted with the word 'bad' will need to sound out the three letters separately and then blend them together in order to recognise the word. The way in which we distinguish these different letter sounds, 'phonemes', is by our auditory system tracking the changes in frequency and amplitude that characterise them in the speech signal. For instance, the only difference between 'b' and 'd' is that 'b' has an upward frequency shift at the onset of the sound, whereas 'd' has a downwards one.

Since these transient cues are so important for identifying phonemes, we have a specialised auditory transient processing system for identifying them. Hence this plays a crucial part in the development of phonological skill. The reader will no doubt have noticed that this system is analogous to the visual magnocellular transient system, and so s/he will not be surprised to hear that auditory transient processing also seems to be mediated by a system of large magnocellular auditory neurones.

As for the visual system, we can measure subjects' basic sensitivity to acoustic frequency and amplitude transients using much simpler stimuli than speech. In this case we play a warbling sound. The warble is produced by regularly increasing and then decreasing the frequency of a tone; this is called frequency modulation (FM). We can then reduce the frequency change, the degree of warble, until the subject can no longer distinguish it from a pure tone. Again we have done this in good and poor readers, in both adults and children. As expected, we found that individuals' sensitivity to warble correlates highly with their phonological ability.

We assess children's phonological reading ability by measuring the ability to make spoonerisms, such as converting 'car park' into 'par cark', and also by assessing their reading of nonsense words. Spoonerisms require the subject to break down the words into their constituent sounds and then to exchange the initial phonemes. Nonsense words like 'tegwop' can be read perfectly well and quickly if the subject is skilled at applying the letter/sound rules, even though they are unfamiliar. Both tasks therefore depend on phonological skill. Again, therefore, we've been able to show that a very basic low-level sensory process, in this case auditory FM detection, plays an important part in determining how well individuals can develop the much higher cognitive phonological skills required for reading.

Magnocellular systems

Thus our research has demonstrated that visual transient processing is very important for the development of orthographic skill, whereas auditory transient sensitivity plays a large part in the development of phonological reading skill. Both these sensory processes seem to be mediated by large magnocellular neurones that are specialised for timing transients. Magnocells are found throughout the brain and they are important for transient processing not only for vision and audition, but also in the cutaneous, muscle, attentional and movement systems. Moreover, development of these neurones seems to be impaired in extremely poor readers, such as developmental dyslexics, so that many dyslexics display a plethora of other symptoms, such as inattention and incoordination, as well as having reading difficulties. When we compared individuals' visual, auditory and motor transient performance we found that they all tended to be closely correlated. This immediately suggests that the development of magnocellular systems throughout the brain may be under some sort of common control and that their development may be impaired in poor readers.

Genetics

The most likely candidate for such control is genetic, for the development of magnocellular neurones throughout the brain is, of course, under genetic control. Also, reading ability is probably partially genetically determined, and this may explain why reading problems tend to run so strongly in families. The genes concerned are located on the twenty-three pairs of chromosomes situated in the nucleus of every cell in the human body. The genes direct the synthesis of proteins on which life depends. Several genes are likely to be involved in any cognitive skill as complex as reading. We have been studying families with at least one dyslexic child, looking for linkage of reading ability to particular chromosomal sites, and we have been able to show that reading ability links to several sites on at least chromosomes 1, 2, 3, 6, 15 and 18.

The strongest linkage evidence so far connects reading ability with a site on the short arm of chromosome 6. This site has now been confirmed in at least seven different samples from all over the world. It was at first argued that the strongest loading was for phonological skill, therefore that the C6 site was selective for phonology. But it turned out that real word reading, orthographic skill, spelling and attention also link to the same site, and this was confirmed by principal component and multivariate analysis. These results suggest the possibility that the gene or genes concerned on C6 may affect the development of all magnocellular nerve cells throughout the nervous system since these play a part in all the auditory, visual, memory, attentional and motor processes required for reading.

The site on chromosome 6 that links to reading is in or very close to an important immunological regulation site, the Major Histocompatibility (MHC) gene complex. This might explain variation in individuals' magnocellular/transient processing functions, because it has recently been shown that the development of magnocellular neurones is actually regulated by MHC molecules. It is therefore possible that whether neurones become specialised to become magnocells, together with the quality of their eventual temporal transient processing performance, may depend on genetic control via the MHC system.

In summary, the quality of magnocellular specialisation for neural timing functions may depend on genetic regulation via the MHC system, and this in turn may ultimately determine how well each individual develops her orthographic and phonological skills for reading and spelling. Thus the well-known fact that literacy skills are inherited may be explained in part by this genetic regulation of magnocellular neuronal development.

Classroom applications

I hope that this account has given readers an insight into the way we learn from a neuroscience perspective, and that you agree that it provides a plausible explanation as to why some individuals have difficulties with acquiring literacy. But does it do what I set out to do? Can this knowledge actually help teachers in the classroom? Many people fear that if this genetic account is correct, it will consign poor readers to the literary dustbin, their fate having been dealt out to them by their genetic inheritance, and that there is nothing that neuroscientists or teachers can do to alter this.

But this is very far from being true. One of the most encouraging developments in the last ten years of neuroscience has been the finding that the brain remains so remarkably plastic and adaptable, even into adulthood. Therefore, genetic regulation of reading ability is not anything like a death sentence. Elucidating its mechanism will tell us how the brains of poor readers differ from those of good readers. Far from being immutable, this knowledge will enable teachers to assess individual children's basic sensory skills and thus show them how to develop individual training programmes that will help children to compensate for their particular weaknesses. Armed with this knowledge about individual differences, the teacher will be able to exploit the brain's wonderful plasticity to help each child personally. As we have seen, the right treatment applied at the right time can help a child enormously.

Ultimately, therefore, performing a few simple visual and auditory transient tests that do not depend on reading should enable teachers to identify their pupils' strengths and weaknesses. They will then be able to adapt their teaching strategies to match individual children's profiles. For most children, a standard mix of orthographic and phonological training will suffice; but for the identified minority special attention can then be devoted to extra training in the auditory or visual transient skills that they lack.

Conclusions

Thus I believe that now neuroscientists really are beginning to be able to help teachers understand how children learn. Although the details of recent discoveries about brain development cannot yet be applied directly in the classroom, they do lead to general principles that can and should be applied. The details of how LTP and LTD contribute to the synaptic modulation that underlies learning cannot be used directly. But now that we understand how individual differences arise from interaction of genetic and pre- and post-natal environmental influences on brain development, we are in a much better position to exploit environmental influences, such as education, to obviate any adverse genetic ones. Now that we know how memory networks involve synaptic linkage of all the different visual, auditory, language and movement areas associated with an idea, it is obvious that teachers should use all these multimodal relations, particularly involving children in active finding out for themselves, to help them understand and remember the idea. Our newer understanding of hemispheric specialisation will replace the over-simplistic idea that the left hemisphere is confined to language and the right to emotion with a more sophisticated account of how both hemispheres interact to mediate all functions. Teachers will be able to measure individual differences in the analytical performance of the left hemisphere and the holistic performance of the right, and use them to optimise their teaching.

We can now sketch a fairly convincing 'bottom up' account of the way in which cognitive reading skills depend on low-level auditory and visual sensory processing. These processes make use of the links between the visual and language areas of the cerebral cortex to piggyback on the neurological apparatus that evolved for speaking in order to associate the visual form of words with their spoken counterparts for reading.

The eyes scan each word to identify their letters and their order. The visual control of these eye movements is mainly mediated by the magno-cellular subcomponent of the visual system that is specialised for timing visual events. Hence this system can detect any unwanted motion of the eyes and thus enable the ocular motor system to correct them. Therefore impaired development of the visual magnocellular system is associated with unsteady fixation on words during reading, hence visual confusion and slow reading progress.

Analogous processes seem to be important for hearing. Unfamiliar words are read by translating the letters into their sounds, then assembling them into the auditory form of the word which gives its meaning. The distinctions between different letter sounds are conveyed by changes in the frequency and amplitude of the acoustic speech signal. These are picked up by large auditory neurones specialised for sensing auditory transients. Hence people with high auditory transient sensitivity find it easy to acquire phonological skill, whereas poor readers tend to have low sensitivity to acoustic transients and end up with poor phonological skills.

Thus both visual and auditory transient sensitivity, hence orthographic and phonological skills, are mediated by magnocellular systems in the brain which are specialised for tracking temporal changes. Hence the acquisition of reading skills depends on genetic control over the development of magnocellular neurones, which explains why literacy skills are so strongly inherited.

However, showing that cognitive difficulties have a genetic neurobiological basis does not mean that teachers can do nothing to help children with these problems. Armed with knowledge of how auditory and visual transient sensitivity determines the development of reading skills, and of the profile of a particular pupil in each of these areas, teachers can design programmes targeted to each individual's strengths and weaknesses. Taking advantage of the incredible plasticity of the developing brain, we now know that cognitive weaknesses can be bypassed and compensated for by appropriate training. Thus our increasing understanding of the neuroscience behind cognitive processes is already beginning to benefit teachers in their classrooms, directly and practically, to help children acquire the literacy skills required in modern life. And this understanding will accelerate in the future.

Further reading

Moser, C. (1999) *A Fresh Start,* London: Department for Education and Science.

Stein, J. F. (2001) 'The Magnocellular Theory of Developmental Dyslexia', *Dyslexia* 7: 12–36.

—— (2003) 'Why Did Language Develop?' *Journal of Paediatric Otorhinology* (in press).

Stein, J. F. and Walsh, V. (1997) 'To See, but Not to Read: The Magnocellular Theory of Dyslexia', *Trends in Neuroscience* 20: 147–51.

Chapter 4

Multiple intelligences theory in adult literacy education

Julie Viens and Silja Kallenbach

Introduction

The long-standing common view of intelligence describes it as a singular entity that is applied to all tasks we undertake, whether it is programming a computer, reading a book or creating a work of art. This traditional view also claims that intelligence is measurable by a relatively short paper-and-pencil intelligence quotient (IQ) test. Howard Gardner introduced the Multiple Intelligences (MI) theory to counter the IQ view, which he found wholly inadequate (Gardner 1993). MI theory describes intelligence as pluralistic, as being about solving problems, and as being qualitatively, not simply quantitatively, different from one individual to the next. While the IQ view asks, "How smart are you?" MI theory asks, "How are you smart?"

The differences between MI theory and the traditional view of intelligence do not stop at the theoretical level, of course. MI theory's educational implications are typically at odds with educational practices that find their roots in the IQ view. While the traditional view of intelligence has given us an over-reliance on standardized testing and uniform approaches to teaching, MI theory suggests diverse approaches aligned with the diverse and distinctive intelligence profiles any given group of individuals brings to bear in the learning environment.

This chapter presents the divergent implications of MI theory for educational practices against the backdrop of the traditional view of intelligence. We share the work of the Adult Multiple Intelligences (AMI) Study, the first systematic research and development project concerned with MI theory at the adult literacy level. The AMI Study helped evolve implications into applications of MI theory in and for the adult basic education context in the USA. In the process, we learned a great deal about how this theory can serve as a powerful and effective tool to develop teaching and learning approaches that address each learner as a uniquely intelligent individual.

Describing intelligence

The IQ view

Intelligence has been equated with Intelligent Quotient (IQ) since the early twentieth century. In 1911, at the request of the French Ministry of Education, Alfred Binet and Theodore Simon developed a test that identified children at risk for school failure. The test was effective for that purpose, but it was soon used to measure individuals' general capabilities or intelligence. In 1912, German psychologist Wilhelm Stern came up with the Intelligence Quotient, or "IQ," which represents the ratio of one's mental age to one's chronological age, as measured by the tests. In the early 1920s, Lewis Terman, an American psychometrician, introduced the Stanford-Binet IQ tests, the first paper-and-pencil, group-administered versions of the test.

The intelligence test quickly became a standard part of the US educational landscape. Since that time, most people have equated intelligence with the IQ measurement. The early IQ work, particularly Terman's, played a significant role in the development of two common beliefs about intelligence: that it is unitary, fundamentally inherited and largely static and unchangeable (Gardner 1993; Gould 1981).

MI theory

In his work with three different populations – normally developing children, stroke victims, and gifted children, Gardner believed the traditional definition of intelligence was woefully inadequate at describing intelligence. He found that normally developing children demonstrated different rates of development for different domains (e.g. language, scientific understanding). His work with stroke victims illustrated that the loss of certain kinds of abilities, say language, occurred without loss of others, suggesting that these abilities work autonomously. And he found the gifted children to be gifted in one area while being average or even below average in other areas, suggesting separately operating and qualitatively different abilities at work.

In response to his observations among these and the general population, Gardner developed a new definition of intelligence: the biological potential to process information in certain ways that can be activated in a cultural setting to solve problems or make products that are valued in a culture or community. Through his subsequent research, Gardner claimed seven relatively independent intelligences when he first introduced the theory. An eighth intelligence, naturalist, was introduced in 1995.

The eight intelligences

Linguistic
Logical-mathematical
Spatial
Musical
Bodily-kinesthetic
Naturalist
Interpersonal
Intrapersonal

MI theory's central feature claims that intelligence is pluralistic: There are at least eight different types of intelligence. Two other central features of MI theory with major implications for education include its definition of intelligence as problem solving and that every individual possesses a unique profile of intelligence strengths and preferences.

How our view of intelligence shapes educational practices

IQ's reach in formal education

In the USA, actual IQ testing nowadays is primarily limited to special situations, such as when a learning disability is suspected or when selecting entrants into a gifted program (Gardner 1999). But the line of thinking to which intelligence testing gave rise maintains a powerful presence that underlies how education, including adult literacy learning, is designed and delivered in the USA. Still, the traditional view of intelligence has had inordinate influence on determining standard school fare, including worksheets and other passive seatwork, with the same narrow set of language and math skills that hearken back to intelligence test items. There is an underlying assumption that a uniform approach works with all students (given that they all possess the same "kind" of intelligence), in curriculum and assessment.

Implications of MI in education

The features of MI theory suggest diverse, authentic, and differentiated instructional approaches (Gardner 1993, 1999; Kornhaber and Krechevsky 1995). MI theory's definition of intelligence as problem solving and product-making implies learning that is authentic and active. That there are eight intelligences or more suggests offering different and distinctive ways to learn a given topic, idea or subject matter. Finally, if individuals possess unique collections of strengths and preferences, as MI theory suggests, then instructional approaches and activities can be differentiated according to the proclivities that exist in a given group of students.

MI in practice

The Adult Multiple Intelligences Study

Background

In 1996 ten English for Speakers of Other Languages (ESOL), Adult Basic Education (ABE) and Adult Secondary Education (ASE) teachers from five New England states embarked on the Adult Multiple Intelligences (AMI) Study, an effort to understand what the MI theory offered teaching and learning in their settings. The AMI Study incorporated two qualitative research projects. The first involved ten individual studies conducted by the AMI teachers in their classrooms, supported by the study's directors. The second was a study across those ten contexts, conducted by the co-directors (for more about the AMI Study, go to our website: http://pzweb.harvard.edu/ami).

The AMI Study asked, "How can Multiple Intelligences (MI) theory support instruction and assessment in Adult Basic Education (ABE), Adult Secondary Education (ASE) and English for Speakers of Other Languages (ESOL)?" Conducted under the auspices of the National Center for the Study of Adult Learning and Literacy, the AMI Study recruited and supported a small group of the educators as teacher researchers. With the support of the study directors (the authors), these educators were asked to consider and develop MI-based practices[1] for their own settings, according to their best professional judgment.

The adult literacy field's prevailing methods of instruction show the same constraints as those in the education of children and youth, primarily emphasizing workbook exercises, comprehension questions, and written responses to prompts. Beder (2001) found that teaching in ABE is by and large teacher-directed. Adult literacy students often struggle with the uniform, narrowly defined teaching approaches that are used, and many have a low sense of self-efficacy when it comes to mastering literacy. We identified MI theory as a theoretical and pedagogical framework with which to enhance adult literacy teaching and learning.

AMI Study activities

Several AMI teachers interpreted MI theory's main feature – that intelligence is pluralistic – as a call for new ways of teaching that tap into a variety of intelligences, to increase the likelihood of reaching all students. Suggesting that any given group of students will bring to bear all the intelligences to varying degrees, the AMI teachers used MI theory as a way to plan and develop activities that called on and/or explored a range of intelligences. Most of the AMI teachers first analyzed their instruction informally through an MI lens. That is, they analyzed which intelligences they were inviting students to use, and to what extent, through the learning experiences they offered. Based on that analysis, they used MI theory as a conceptual framework to develop learning activities that filled the self-identified gaps in their offerings.

Drawing on MI theory's claim that we each have our own unique collection of strengths, some teachers prioritized creating student profiles: identifying and describing each student's particular collection of intelligences. Others took to heart MI theory's definition of intelligence as problem solving and focused on problem-centered instructional applications. How and to what extent the major features of MI theory contributed to the teachers' practices varied. The teachers' pre-existing beliefs about teaching and learning, their previous training and experience, and the type of class they were teaching (Adult Basic Education, Adult Secondary Education and English for Speakers of Other Languages) also contributed to their decisions about how to use MI theory in their settings.

MI-Inspired Instruction and MI Reflections

In our analysis we identified two categories of teachers' interpretation of MI theory to practice, which we termed MI-Inspired Instruction and MI Reflections. These categories are distinguished by their distinct sets of pedagogical goals. Goals under the MI-Inspired Instruction umbrella focused on developing classroom practices and materials. Under the MI Reflections umbrella, goals focused on using MI to engage students in reflections about their own strengths and preferences as learners.

MI-Inspired Instruction

Three ideas figure prominently in AMI teachers' application of MI theory as MI-Inspired Instruction: choice, learner-centeredness, and student enjoyment. We identified three central findings related to the AMI teachers' MI-Inspired Instructional approaches:

Learning activities that drew on MI theory and its central tenets were characteristically authentic
Researchers have concluded that learning is enhanced when instructional materials reflect the real world and students' current and prior experiences (Fingeret and Drennon 1997; Purcell-Gates *et al.* 2000). Purcell-Gates *et al.* (2000) found that using authentic, real-life literacy materials (such as schedules, menus, forms, business letters, and notices) increased students' use of

literacy skills outside of the classroom. In other words, authentic materials and activities increased the transfer of learning in the instructional setting to students' lives outside of the classroom.

Authentic and real-life learning activities tend to be learner-centered. Of all the lessons the AMI teachers documented, those most engaging to students included content that reflected student interests and realities. Lessons that offered an authentic audience and an opportunity for students to apply activities to make real-life improvements were seen as best of all. Studies have indicated that the motivation to learn increases when students feel that their learning activities are helping others (Bransford, Brown and Cocking, 2000; Pintrich and Schunk, 1996; Schartz, Lin, Brophy and Bransford, 1999).

One way that English for Speakers of Other Languages (ESOL) teacher Terri Coustan increased the authenticity of her beginning-level classes was through a gardening project. Knowing that most of her students had been farmers in their native country, Laos, Terri developed a project that built on her students' naturalist abilities. The students constructed an indoor greenhouse and prepared seed trays. They maintained outdoor garden plots. Terri integrated a number of related activities into her ESOL class such as planning gardens, choosing seeds, and discussing topics such as dividing and sharing the gardening space.

Learning activities that drew on MI theory and its central tenets were typically relevant and meaningful to students
Using materials or real experiences from students' daily lives in literacy instruction is not always possible. When students are preparing to pass the US high school equivalency test, known as the GED test, the content and skills that must be mastered are dictated by this multiple-choice test that covers several subject areas. Adult Basic Education and GED teachers in the AMI Study found MI theory was a useful framework for developing learning activities that helped students connect content from outside their experience, such as reading historical fiction or learning about the planets, to their own lives. In effect, MI practices served to make instruction learner-centered by creating relevance or meaning to students where, on face, none existed.

AMI teacher Martha Jean developed a set of MI-informed activities to help her students learn about planets. "Planets" is a GED test topic, but it is hardly a pressing topic of concern to these homeless adults. Martha prepared a packet of readings from different sources and made other reference materials available. She also included practice GED questions. After reviewing the information, students worked on their understanding of the planets through a "Choose 3" lesson, in which students chose three of several activity options around that topic. Like all of Martha's Choose 3 activities, the options were based on Martha's understanding of how various intelligences could be tapped for this content.

Her students' comments suggest that the learning experiences Martha developed became more meaningful to them when the students were invited to select activities compatible with their intelligence strengths or preferences. Some of their comments highlight how the students were positively and actively engaged by Martha's choice activities. Students made different choices and felt they learned because they had fun. They had fun because the activities were hands-on, which they repeatedly emphasized was unlike their prior school experiences. We believe that using MI theory as a framework for developing curriculum results in more and more diverse hands-on activities, which in turn increase student engagement in the learning experience, particularly when these activities map onto intelligences with which students feel at ease and able.

MI-informed classrooms became increasingly less teacher-directed and more learner-directed
Providing a greater variety of entry points, or ways into the topic or skill area at hand, is perhaps the most common MI-informed practice, resulting from the most generative of the theory's features, that there is a plurality of intelligences. Lesson formats that gave students choices that correspond to the eight intelligences and use them in different combinations (across different domains) were popular among AMI teachers and their students. Perhaps the AMI teachers' MI-based activities provided students with a broader array of choices, and therefore gave them even greater control in the learning process. When teachers give students choices in how they learn and demonstrate what they have learned, they effectively are giving some control to students.

It is possible that the act of validating students' strengths, interests, and preferences is an important first step that helps build the students' self-confidence and enables them to take control over their own learning and the curriculum. Furthermore, when students examine their strengths, they are likely to deepen their self-knowledge, giving them a firmer foundation from which to direct their learning. As they implemented MI-based practices, the AMI teachers developed a keener understanding and appreciation of their students' strengths. Lezlie Rocka's comment illustrates this point:

> Originally, I thought that I saw my students' strengths no matter what kinds of lessons I did. But after reviewing all my data, especially comparing that of last year to this year, I see that through choice of expression and projects, I am able to see a wider variety of strengths. And the students are able to see their own strengths and the strengths of each other.
>
> (Rocka 1997)

The AMI teachers perceived a noticeable shift in the teacher-to-student power relations as a result of their MI-based practices. MI-based practices such as choice activities helped to ease students into a shift in the balance of power. Over time, as students experienced diverse MI-based learning activities, they began taking more initiative and control over the content or direction of the activities. In effect, this shared decision-making made the classroom more learner-centered. The AMI teachers found themselves relinquishing some control by giving their students choices and respecting individual ways of learning and knowing.

Reviewing her lesson plans from the two years prior to the AMI Study, Terri Coustan discovered she had doubled the number of choices in learning activities she gave to her students in the course of her AMI involvement. She found that as students began to express preferences through choice-based activities, they also became more assertive in other ways, slightly shifting the balance of power in the classroom (Kallenbach and Viens 2001: 74). She wrote:

> My experience over the past few years had shown me that these students were reluctant to share their preferences with me. I had almost given up hope of ever being able to learn their preferences and had decided that this behavior was related to learners with limited English. Now, the students appeared to have reached a benchmark or milestone … More students made choices. And those choices reflected both what the students liked and did not like about the activities I suggested.
>
> (Coustan 1998)

Likewise, Lezlie Rocka comments:

> My class became more interactive and student-directed as I experimented with MI theory. Before this research project, I did most of the leading and dictated the order of the activities.
>
> (Kallenbach and Viens 2001: 215)

When the MI-based activity encouraged group work, students began to look to each other as sources of knowledge and ideas. With the teachers' encouragement and faced with challenging learning projects, they looked less to the teachers, and more to one another, for information and direction through the steps of the project. Although she did not use the Choose 3 format, Jean Mantzaris made room for many different entry points that touched upon several intelligences through two activities she developed: Memory Lane activity and Jobopoly game. Jean wrote:

> Once I started to diversify my lesson plans, I began to look to the students for more input. As time went on, students took over decision-making for activities such as the career board game. For example, they wrote all the Chance cards for the game. Their ideas were quite different

from mine in that they focused more on the kinds of assistance they would need, whereas I would have included some luxury items such as a trip to a warm island, new car, jeweler, etc. They added two new squares: on-the-job training and Ph.D. programs. They developed the MI show for teachers on their own. I became a guide and participant in these activities designed by the students. As Julie [a student] commented, "It was a lot of fun and showed how much a bunch of people could accomplish if they got together."

(Kallenbach and Viens 2001: 142)

MI Reflections

MI Reflections is the term we coined to refer to approaches and activities through which students learned about MI theory and, more to the point, that used MI theory for self-reflection and to identify their particular intelligence strengths. To implement MI Reflections, the AMI teachers designed different ways to uncover and identify students' strengths, as well as to have students identify and acknowledge their own and each other's intelligence strengths. Each AMI teacher came to her particular version of MI Reflections based on different learning objectives, contexts, and student populations. Our data analysis yielded three forms of MI Reflections adopted by the AMI teachers:

Using MI theory as content can help resistant students

It is the rare adult educator who has not experienced students hesitating, if not resisting, a non-traditional lesson or unit. Perhaps because of its hands-on nature, role play, music, drawing, or movement may strike some students as juvenile and not appropriate for adult learning. Moreover, these sorts of learning activities do not match many students' notions of activities appropriate for English for Speakers of Other Languages, Adult Basic Education and Adult Secondary Education classes. Most likely based on their previous school experiences, students understand appropriate classroom activities in ways that reflect the more traditional, paper-and-pencil-based approaches.

The more traditional approaches may be a good fit with some students' learning preferences. For many others, however, the preference for workbooks and other passive learning methods is an unexamined assumption based on a lack of exposure to other ways of learning. Furthermore, based on their negative learning experiences in academic settings, some students incorrectly assume that learning cannot be enjoyable or fun – no pain, no gain. If a learning activity is fun, it is automatically suspect. The AMI experience suggests that adult educators interested in introducing MI-based lessons need to anticipate and plan for these responses. Many AMI students who were initially hesitant or, in some cases, quite negative toward MI-informed activities came to embrace them relatively quickly. The AMI experience demonstrates that an explicit introduction to MI theory and its relationship to unfamiliar, non-traditional activities can work to overcome students' bias against these new learning experiences.

An added potential benefit of having conversations about intelligence with students is countering any unhelpful, even detrimental, concepts of intelligence or of their own abilities that they may hold. Bransford *et al.* (2000) state:

> Students' theories of what it means to be intelligent can affect their performance. Research shows that students who think that intelligence is a fixed entity are more likely to be performance-oriented than learning-oriented – they want to look good rather than risk making mistakes while learning. These students are especially likely to bail out when tasks become difficult. In contrast, students who think that intelligence is malleable are more willing to struggle with challenging tasks; they are more comfortable with risk.
>
> (p. 23)

Conversations about multiple intelligences or the concept of intelligence are not typically a part of the curriculum in English for Speakers of Other Languages, Adult Basic Education and Adult Secondary Education instruction. As there are few resources for teaching about intelligence, AMI teachers who chose to go down this path had to create their own lessons. They created presentations, handouts, and hands-on activities, and paused to identify intelligences students were using during classroom activities. These activities introduced students to MI theory's major tenets. In a few instances, they also engaged students in debating the concept of intelligence.

Lessons about MI theory did not resonate with all learner groups. Students can perceive MI theory as extraneous, confusing, or irrelevant to their learning goals. The ESOL teachers found success with MI-informed activities and reflections about the lessons without connecting them explicitly to MI theory or using the MI "lingo." All but one of the AMI secondary-level teachers and the one career counselor, on the other hand, found talking about MI theory quite useful for increasing students' acceptance and appreciation of non-traditional activities. The talk about MI theory provided a rationale for MI-inspired lessons. Ultimately, of course, the success of the non-traditional learning activity that followed had as much to do with the lesson itself: how engaging and relevant it felt to students.

MI Reflections enhance students' perceptions of their abilities and career aspirations
Understanding the link between students' perceptions of their abilities and their actual academic performance, several AMI teachers set out to create opportunities for students to recognize and experience their abilities as

defined and described by MI theory. They wanted to use MI theory to help students feel positive about their abilities, recognizing that "of the various self-perceived causes of achievement, ability is seen as the most significant influence on academic performance" (Covington 1989: 86). Covington notes, "Those students who ascribed an earlier failure to lack of ability experienced shame, which in turn inhibited subsequent performance."

Almost every AMI teacher documented similar student comments about more positive feelings toward their abilities and themselves as learners. Our data suggest that MI Reflections prompted these adult learners to see themselves as learners in a more positive light after identifying and reflecting on their own abilities. This was particularly the case when they were able to apply their abilities to successful learning strategies in the classroom. Perhaps, in those cases, seeing was believing.

As in the case of learning about MI theory, MI self-assessments did not reach students in the two beginning-level ESOL classrooms. By and large, they proved more frustrating than productive to the beginning-level ESOL students and their teachers. We do not know how more advanced ESOL students would have responded.

Not all the Adult Basic Education or secondary-level students saw the relevance of self-reflection to their goals or to learning in general. Some students' objections and unwillingness to engage in MI self-reflection seemed to come more from unfamiliarity and lack of experience with metacognitive practices – that is, thinking about their thinking and learning. It was not that they came in with a firm position *against* MI Reflections but, rather, this was unfamiliar to them. The data indicate that students shifted their paradigm about intelligence and its relevance to them based on the teacher's persistence in helping them develop the necessary metacognitive skills.

MI Reflections are useful for identifying learning strategies for students

Research suggests that those who know themselves as learners and are able to monitor and change their learning strategies accordingly are better able to transfer their learning to new contexts (Bransford *et al.* 2000). Further, the teaching of metacognitive skills should be integrated into the curriculum in different subjects rather than taught as a separate set of skills. In the AMI Study, MI theory served as a tool for developing the learners' metacognitive abilities. In virtually every class, this was a challenging undertaking that required the teacher's skill and persistence.

For the majority of AMI teachers, MI self-reflection with students was an important preliminary step to identifying learning strategies. Four of the ten teachers helped their students develop learning strategies based on what they could observe about the students' intelligence strengths. Yet it would be misleading to suggest that translating information about a student's intelligence strengths into learning strategies for literacy or numeracy is straightforward or easy. In taking on this task, the AMI teachers ventured into a territory with few guideposts.

Work with MI theory led ESOL teacher Diane Paxton to engage her students in ongoing reflections about what they did or did not like about the lessons and which activities they considered the most beneficial to learning English. In one class, several students resisted even the reflection process because they were not used to it and did not see its value. However, Diane concluded that the reflection process itself proved an important factor in gradually decreasing students' resistance to non-traditional learning activities. She wrote, "Participation in oral assessments exposed students to a rich diversity of opinions about effective ways to learn and about what is beneficial for an ESOL student" (Kallenbach and Viens 2001: 164). Many students from this group voiced the opinion that the diversity of non-traditional activities Diane offered to them was central to their improving English. She found that building trust and a safe learning environment over time also contributed to their paradigm shift (p. 169).

MI close up: one teacher's AMI journey

Meg Costanzo joined the AMI Study in her twenty-seventh year in education. During the AMI Study, Meg taught an adult secondary-level class. At any one time, the class had three to six students. It met twice a week for a total of four hours. Meg wanted to focus her AMI work on developing MI-based teaching approaches to math and writing because these were her students' most challenging areas.

By her own account, Meg was used to teaching through different senses, using manipulatives to teach math, and doing talk-aloud protocols with her middle-school students. However, she had shied away from using these kinds of non-traditional teaching techniques, fearing they would appear juvenile to her adult students. MI theory gave her license to try some of those techniques – most notably project-based learning – with her adult students and increased her use of math manipulatives.

Definition of intelligence as the touchstone

The definition of intelligence served as Meg's touchstone for thinking about MI-based instruction and assessment. Meg reasoned that if intelligence involves solving problems and making products, instruction should create opportunities for students to use their intelligence strengths to do that. Moreover, Meg engaged her students in thinking about what intelligence means to them. For example, she wrote the word "intelligence" on the board and asked students to say the first thing that came to mind. In that way, she drew out students' conceptions of intelligence and created an early opportunity for them to compare their views with MI theory.

Strong emphasis on students' unique intelligence profile and self-reflection

Meg's understanding of MI theory was equally grounded in valuing each person's unique intelligence profile. Meg relied on her strong intrapersonal intelligence and understanding of herself to understand MI theory. She asserts that "my own understanding of MI came about through my experiences in applying the theory in practice and my attempts to understand my own intelligences as well as the intelligences of others whom I know well" (Kallenbach and Viens 2001: 31). She reflected on her childhood and the types of toys and activities she liked. She also analyzed how she learned a skill that was not her strength, i.e. skiing. She felt that relating MI theory to her own life was crucial to her understanding of the theory. Meg's self-reflection confirmed to her the value of having students reflect on their own intelligences.

Meg developed an AMI survey of her own to "encourage students to go through the same type of reflective process I had just experienced" (Kallenbach and Viens 2001: 32). She also developed other pathways to self-assessment, such as a writing assignment in which students were asked: If you had 24 hours to yourself to plan anything you wished, what would you do? She instituted dialogue journal writing as a regular part of every class to help her students reflect on their learning processes and preferences. She noted that students started staying longer after class to write their journals and continue discussions. This reinforced Meg's commitment to implementing self-reflection activities with her students.

Above all, Meg viewed self-reflection as a means for her students to develop more suitable learning strategies for themselves. After four months of encouraging and expecting her students to do this, she acknowledged that she was expecting students to make the leap to self-reflection too quickly and that this skill "needs more cultivation and guidance ... I have to provide numerous opportunities for students to analyze their problem-solving capabilities" (Costanzo 1997, April). Rather than abandon her efforts, Meg redoubled them and changed her expectations about the students' pace of change regarding new learning strategies.

The interpersonal and intrapersonal intelligences became important components of Meg's instruction. By the end of the AMI Study eighteen months later, Meg concluded, "I'm quicker to teach students self-assessment and monitoring of understanding. Right from the start, I get them involved in planning their own course of action in the classroom" (Costanzo 1998, January).

Many ways of being smart

Project-based learning was the primary means by which Meg interpreted MI theory in her instructional strategies. For Meg, projects offered many opportunities for students to apply their unique profiles of intelligences.

To determine the topic for her first project-based unit, Meg had her students complete an interest inventory. She also considered informal conversations with her students in selecting Vermont's changing nature as the topic reflecting student interest. She began the unit by asking students to list how Vermont had changed in their lifetime and to rate the changes based on how they felt about them: positive, negative, or neutral. As part of this project, students analyzed a political cartoon about development in Vermont, read articles, and listened to a guest speaker, a photographer Meg had invited as a way to encourage students to explore their intelligences. She had purchased a disposable camera and offered it to anyone who would like to take pictures of Vermont's changing nature.

Meg found that the class discussions about MI and her willingness to respect and honor different intelligences made students more receptive to non-traditional teaching approaches. In that sense, the MI Reflections activities reinforced the success of MI-based lessons.

Meg's growth as a teacher

Although Meg entered the AMI Study an experienced, "MI savvy" educator, her work with MI theory caused her to expand her repertoire and take risks. Meg reflected on her experience:

> My work involving the application of MI theory at the adult learner level has given me a new lens with which to view adult students. This experience has also given the adult learners with whom I worked the opportunity to contemplate on how they learn best and a vocabulary to express their reflections. I had the chance to develop or modify teaching strategies that work best with adult learners, allowing them to demonstrate a variety of strengths and talents. Because the students accepted and acknowledged their intelligences, they were more willing to respond to these non-traditional teaching strategies and take on the responsibility of discovering for themselves how they learn best. I expanded my methods of assessment to allow students to demonstrate their knowledge of the subject matter in alternative ways.
>
> Because of my involvement in the AMI Study, I have come to recognize a new dynamic that emerged in my class. I come away from my research with a revised model for an effective Adult Basic Education classroom, one that is less teacher-centered and which gives the students a greater voice in what they study. It is a classroom that emphasizes personal growth as well as academic development. It is a model that encourages students to solve real life problems and develop a variety of skills they will find useful in the future.
>
> (Kallenbach and Viens 2001: 56)

To conclude

The AMI Study illustrated the potential of MI theory and its central features in the development and implementation of pedagogical practices that reach out to and engage individual adult literacy learners in meaningful ways. We also saw that practices in the spirit of MI theory, drawing from the same set of features of intelligence that MI theory claims, can be – and are – quite distinct from one another, depending on the context and content (Baum *et al.* in press; Kornhaber and Fierros 2000). We learned that program and teacher goals, time, student population and numbers, as well as the idiosyncrasies of individual classrooms, play significant roles in shaping how MI theory is interpreted and used. In short, there is no *one* way to apply MI theory in instruction, just as there is no single kind of learner. True to the theory, MI practices are as diverse as the learners they are meant to serve; and that is as it should be.

Note

We use the following terms interchangeably: MI-based, MI-inspired, MI-informed, and in the spirit of MI theory.

References

Baum, S., Viens, J. and Slatin, B. (forthcoming, 2005), *Multiple Intelligences in the Elementary Classroom: A Toolkit for Teaching*, New York: Teachers College Press.

Beder, H. (2001) *Teaching in Adult Literacy Education: Learner-centered Intentions, Teacher-directed Instruction. Proceedings of the 42nd Annual Adult Education Research Conference*, East Lansing: Michigan State University.

Bransford, J., Brown, A. and Cocking, R. (eds) (2000) *How People Learn*, Washington, DC: National Academy Press.

Costanzo, M. (1997, April) AMI Study journal entry. Unpublished.

—— (1998, January) AMI Study journal entry. Unpublished.

Coustan, T. (1998, June) Progress Report for AMI Study. Unpublished.

Covington, M. (1989) "Self-esteem and Failure in School: Analysis and Policy Implications," in A. M. Mecca, N. J. Smelser and J. Vasconcellos (eds) *The Social Implications of Self-esteem*, Berkeley, CA: VC Press, pp. 71–124.

Fingeret, H. and Drennon, C. (1997) *Literacy for Life, Adult Learners, New Practices*, New York: Teachers College Press.

Gardner, H. (1993) *Frames of Mind: The Theory of Multiple Intelligences* (tenth anniversary edition), New York: Basic Books.

—— (1999) *The Disciplined Mind*, New York: Basic Books.

Gould, S. J. (1981) *The Mismeasure of Man*, New York: W. W. Norton.

Kallenbach, S. and Viens, J. (eds) (2001) *Multiple Intelligences in Practice. Teacher Research Reports from the Adult Multiple Intelligences Study*, Cambridge, MA: National Center for the Study of Adult Learning and Literacy.

Kornhaber, M. and Fierros, E. (2000) *Project SUMIT (Schools Using Multiple Intelligences Theory)*, http://pzweb/harvard.edu/SUMIT

Kornhaber, M. and Krechevsky, M. (1995) "Expanding Definitions of Learning and Teaching: Notes from the MI Underground," in P. Cookson and B. Schneider (eds) *Transforming Schools*, New York: Garland.

Pintrich, P. R. and Schunk, D. (1996) *Motivation in Education: Theory, Research, and Application*, Englewood Cliffs, NJ: Merrill Prentice-Hall.

Purcell-Gates, V., Degener, S., Jacobson, E. and Soler, M. (2000) *Affecting Change in Literacy Practices of Adult Learners: Impact of Two Dimensions of Instruction*, Cambridge, MA: National Center for the Study of Adult Learning and Literacy.

Rocka, L. (1997, December) AMI Study journal entry. Unpublished.

Schwartz, D.L., Lin X., Brophy S. and Bransford J.D. (1999) "Toward the development of flexibly adaptive instructional designs. pp. 183–213 in *Instructional Design Theories and Models: Volume II*, C.M. Reigeluth (ed), Hillsdale, NJ: Erlbaum.

Viens, J.T. and Hallenbach S. (2004). *Multiple Intelligences and Adult Literacy: A sourcebook for practitioners.* New York: Teachers College Press.

Chapter 5

The role of individual differences in approaches to learning

Li-fang Zhang and Robert J. Sternberg

People learn in different ways. Some learn better orally, others visually. Some learn better by listening, others by being actively involved. Learning approach, as a critical individual-difference variable in human learning, has been widely investigated over the last three decades. However, the majority of the factors relating to learning approaches that have been studied are limited to such student characteristics as age, gender, socio-economic status, self-esteem, learning motivation, as well as to the teaching/learning contexts. Other factors that might also be pivotal for students' learning approaches have barely received the attention that they deserve. Early in 1970, Biggs and his colleague (Biggs and Das 1973) tested associations between students' learning approaches and their personality characteristics. More recently, two studies (Murray-Harvey 1994; Sadler-Smith 1997) were identified as examining the relationships between learning styles and learning approaches. In this chapter, we argue that continuing efforts should be made to identify the possible effects of other individual-difference variables upon learning approaches.

Learning approach is defined in terms of two components in the process of learning: motivation for learning and strategy for learning (Biggs 1979, 1992). Early investigators (e.g. Craik and Lockhart 1972) were interested in the "duality of levels of processing in an approach to learning, which reflected either a deep or surface engagement with the task" (Rayner and Riding 1997: 16). Subsequently, both Biggs (1979) and Ramsden and Entwistle (1981) independently identified a third learning approach, which Biggs called "achieving." The studies to be described in this chapter are based on Biggs's (1979, 1987, 1992) theory of students' learning approaches. Biggs proposed three common approaches to learning: surface, which involves a reproduction of what is taught to meet the minimum requirements; deep, which involves a real understanding of what is learned; and achieving, which involves using a strategy that will maximize one's grades.

One of the instruments used to assess learning approaches among university students is the "Study Process Questionnaire" (SPQ, Biggs 1987, 1992). The SPQ is a self-report test composed of 42 items falling into six subscales:

surface-motive, surface-strategy, deep-motive, deep-strategy, achieving-motive and achieving-strategy. Both internal and external validity data are abundant. It is worth noting, however, that in the study of the internal structure of the inventory, some investigators have obtained three factors (surface, deep, and achieving, e.g. O'Neil and Child 1984), which supported Biggs's original argument for three learning approaches, whereas others have identified a two-factor (surface and deep) model (e.g. Niles 1995; Watkins and Dahlin 1997). The two-factor model is consistent with the model proposed separately by Marton (1976) and Entwistle (1981).

Studies involving the SPQ have been conducted in diverse contexts: cross-cultural comparisons (e.g. Kember and Gow 1990; Wilson 1987), the language medium of instruction (e.g. Watkins et al. 1991), teaching/learning environments (Biggs 1988), and professional and staff development (e.g. Biggs 1988). More recent studies examining these learning approaches have had as their foci one or more of the following: examining the differences between learning styles and learning approaches (e.g. Murray-Harvey 1994); investigating the relationships between learning approaches and academic performance (e.g. Rose et al. 1996); and constructing other versions of the SPQ (e.g. Albaili 1995). Some of these studies have been conducted in Asian cultures, including Hong Kong and mainland China (e.g. Tang and Biggs 1996; Zhang 2000a).

The present chapter describes four studies conducted among university students in three cultural contexts: Hong Kong, mainland China, and the United States. We examined the relationships of learning approaches to three individual-difference variables: thinking styles, career personality types, and personality traits. The role of these three constructs in learning approaches is particularly important to examine because they have been three of the more influential individual-difference variables that have occupied the minds of scholars and educational practitioners in the last three decades. A major common characteristic shared by the three constructs is the breadth of each construct (see introduction to each construct). Each of them has been shown to affect students' learning outcomes. However, we believe that it is equally important to identify the impact of these individual-difference variables upon what happens during the process of learning – in this context, students' approaches to learning. Learning process may mediate between individual-difference variables and learning outcome.

The remainder of this chapter is composed of three main parts. The first part introduces the theoretical foundation for each of the aforementioned three constructs (i.e. personality types as relevant to careers, personality traits, and thinking styles) to be examined in relation to learning approaches. Also in the first part, we describe one major assessment tool for measuring each construct. The second part provides empirical evidence for the role of each of the three individual-difference variables in learning approaches. The third part synthesizes the major research findings and discusses the implications of these findings for research and education.

Theoretical foundations and assessment tools

Each of the three constructs against which the learning-approach construct was examined has its own theoretical foundation. The thinking style construct is elaborated in terms of Sternberg's (1988, 1997) theory of mental self-government. The career personality type construct is defined in terms of Holland's (1973, 1994) theory of career personality types. Finally, the personality trait construct is conceptualized in terms of the five-factor model proposed by Costa and McCrae (1985, 1992). In the rest of this section, we describe these theories as well as one major assessment tool associated with each of the theories.

Theory of mental self-government and the Thinking Styles Inventory

The period between the late 1950s and the early 1970s saw a proliferation of theories and research on styles, which have been variously termed as cognitive styles, learning styles, and thinking styles. Recently, there has been a resurgence of interest in styles. Part of this resurgence occurred in 1988 with the publication of Sternberg's theory of mental self-government (see also Sternberg 1997). Using the word "government" metaphorically, Sternberg contended that just as there are different ways of governing a society, there are different ways that people use their abilities, or rather, different "thinking styles." According to Sternberg, there are thirteen thinking styles, which fall into five categories:

Functions As in government, there are three functions in human beings' mental self-government: legislative, executive, and judicial. An individual with a legislative style enjoys being engaged in tasks that require creative strategies. An individual with an executive style is more concerned with implementation of tasks with set guidelines. An individual with a judicial style focuses attention on evaluating the products of others' activities.

Forms Also as in government, a human being's mental self-government takes four different forms: monarchic, hierarchic, oligarchic, and anarchic. An individual with a monarchic style enjoys being engaged in tasks that allow a complete focus on one thing at a time. On the contrary, an individual with a hierarchic style likes to distribute attention to several tasks that are prioritized. An individual with an oligarchic style also likes to work toward multiple objectives during the same period of time, but may not like to set priorities. Finally, an individual with an anarchic style enjoys working on tasks that would allow the greatest possible flexibility as to what, where, when, and how one works.

Levels As with governments, human beings' mental self-government is at two different levels: local and global. An individual with a local style enjoys being engaged in tasks that require work with concrete details. On the contrary, an individual with a global style would pay more attention to the overall picture of an issue and to abstract ideas.

Scopes Mental self-government can deal with internal and external matters. An individual with an internal style enjoys being engaged in tasks that allow one to work independently. In contrast, an individual with an external style likes to be engaged in tasks that provide opportunities for developing inter-personal relationships.

Leanings Finally, in mental self-government, there are two leanings: liberal and conservative. An individual with a liberal style enjoys engaging in tasks that involve novelty and ambiguity, whereas a conservative person tends to adhere to the existing rules and procedures in performing tasks.

These thinking styles are, in principle, value-free, for any particular thinking style that can serve one person positively in one situation may fail the same person in another. However, in their various studies, Zhang and her colleagues (e.g. Zhang and Postiglione 2001; Zhang and Sternberg 2000) have found that these thinking styles can be loosely classified into three groups. The first group, comprising what we call Type I thinking styles, is composed of styles that tend to be creativity-generating and that denote higher levels of cognitive complexity, including the legislative, judicial, hierarchical, global, and liberal styles. The second group, which we refer to as Type II thinking styles, comprises styles that suggest a norm-favoring tendency and that denote lower levels of cognitive complexity, including the executive, local, monarchic, and conservative styles. The remaining four thinking styles (i.e. anarchic, oligarchic, internal, and external) belong neither to the Type I group nor to the Type II group. However, they may manifest some of the characteristics of the styles from both groups, depending on the stylistic demands of a specific task. These four styles have recently been labeled as "Type III thinking styles" (Zhang, in press-a).

The theory of mental self-government has been tested through a number of related inventories, with the Thinking Styles Inventory (TSI, Sternberg and Wagner 1992) being the most frequently used. The TSI is a self-report test consisting of 65 statements. Each of the 13 thinking styles is assessed by 5 statements. For each statement, the participants rated themselves on a 7-point Likert scale, with 1 indicating that the statement does not at all describe the way they normally carry out tasks, and 7 denoting that the statement characterizes extremely well the way they normally carry out tasks. The inventory was translated and back-translated between Chinese and English in 1996. In one of the four studies to be discussed in this chapter, the English version was used for two university student samples in the USA, while the Chinese version was used for Hong Kong and mainland Chinese students.

Both the internal and external validity of the theory have been supported by numerous studies conducted among students and teachers from a number of cultures, including those of Hong Kong, mainland China, the Philippines, Spain, and the United States (e.g. Dai and Feldhusen 1999; Cano-Garcia and Hughes 2000; Grigorenko and Sternberg 1997; Zhang and Sternberg 1998, 2000, 2002). Finally, the thinking style construct has proved itself to be a broad style construct in that it encompasses styles proposed in many other theories of styles (see Zhang, in press-a).

Theory of career personality types and the Self-Directed Search

According to Holland (1973, 1994), people can be characterized by six personality types corresponding to six occupational environments: realistic, investigative, artistic, social, enterprising, and conventional. The realistic type of person likes to work with things and enjoys outdoor activities, but may lack social skills. People with the investigative type of career personality like to be engaged in investigative and scientific kinds of work, but often lack leadership ability. The artistic type of person likes to deal with tasks that provide one with opportunities to use his/her imagination, but often lacks clerical skills. The social type of person likes to work in situations in which one can interact and cooperate with other people, but may lack mechanical and scientific ability. Like the social type of person, the person with an enterprising career personality also enjoys working in environments in which he or she can interact with people; however, the enterprising type of person likes to take leadership roles. Finally, the conventional type of person likes to work with data under well-structured situations, but often lacks artistic ability.

The Self-Directed Search (SDS, Holland 1985, 1994) is the inventory that has been used most frequently to assess these six career personality types. The SDS has been widely used in studies carried out in both Western and non-Western cultures (e.g. Bickham et al. 1998; Glidden and Greenwood 1997). Apart from being used as a career counseling tool, the SDS also has been examined in comparison with people's individual differences in other attributes, such as competencies, values, and cognitive styles.

A short version of the SDS (Short-Version Self-Directed Search, SVSDS, Zhang 1999) was particularly constructed for Zhang's (2000b) study of Hong Kong university students. The inventory is based both on Holland's (1973, 1985) theory of career personality types and on part of his Self-Directed Search (Holland 1994). Comprising two parts, it is a 24-item self-report test, with each part containing 12 items. In Part One, two statements are used to measure each of the six career personality types. A sample item in this part is: "I like to work with people – to inform, help, train, or develop them; I am skilled with words" (Social). The 12 items in the second part are drawn directly from the "self-estimate" section in Holland's (1994) SDS, each two items assessing one of the six career personality types. For each item, participants rated themselves on a 7-point scale.

So far, apart from having been used in Zhang's (2000b) study of the Hong Kong students, the SVSDS has also been tested among university students from Nanjing, mainland China (Zhang 2001). Both studies indicated that the SVSDS is a reliable and valid inventory for assessing Holland's six career personality types. In one of the four studies delineated here (Zhang, in press-b), the inventory was used to test against the learning approach construct.

Five-factor model of personality traits and the NEO Five-Factor Inventory

The five-factor model (FFM) of personality traits resulted from several decades of factor analytic research centering on trait personality. Early in 1981, Goldberg stated that the five dimensions of rating personality could serve as a framework for many theories of personality at the time, including the theories of Cattell (1957), Norman (1963), Eysenck (1970), and of Guilford (1975). Earlier empirical work (e.g. Fiske 1949; Tupes and Christal 1992) indicated that there existed five fairly strong and recurrent personality factors. These are surgency (termed as "extraversion" by many others), agreeableness, dependability (including such dimensions as responsibility and conscientiousness), emotional stability, and culture. More recent empirical investigations have demonstrated the stable existence of the five personality domains (e.g. Digman 1994; Goldberg 1990), which have been given slightly different names. These five personality dimensions are neuroticism, extraversion, openness to experience, agreeableness, and conscientiousness.

Neuroticism is the opposite of emotional stability. People high on the N scale tend to experience such negative feelings as emotional instability, embarrassment, guilt, pessimism, and low self-esteem. People scoring high on the Extraversion scale tend to be sociable and assertive. Openness is characterized by such attributes as open-mindedness, active imagination, preference for variety, and independence of judgment. People high on the Agreeableness scale typically are altruistic, sympathetic, and readily helpful. Moreover, they value and respect other people's beliefs and conventions. Individuals who are high on the Conscientiousness scale are, in general, purposeful, strong-willed, responsible, and trustworthy (see Costa and McCrae 1992 for more details).

The FFM has piqued the interest of many personality psychologists. The work of Costa and McCrae (1985, 1992; see also McCrae and Costa 1997) is especially noteworthy. According to the review of Taylor and MacDonald

(1999), the NEO Personality Inventory (Costa and McCrae 1985, 1992) has not only demonstrated good psychometric properties; it also has been successful in accommodating constructs that are already measured by existing tests, including the Eysenck Personality Inventory (Eysenck and Eysenck 1964), one of the most widely used tools in research on personality. Moreover, the NEO-PI has been successfully used in investigating the relationships of personality to other important variables, including creativity and divergent thinking (e.g. McCrae 1987), achievement motivation (e.g. Busato *et al.* 1999), and career decision making (e.g. Shafer 2000).

A short version of the NEO Personality Inventory is the NEO Five-Factor Inventory (Costa and McCrae 1992). Composed of 60 statements, the NEO Five-Factor Inventory is considered a brief and comprehensive measure of the five personality dimensions. Each of the five dimensions is assessed by 12 statements. For each statement, the participants rated themselves on a 5-point Likert scale from 0 to 4, with verbal anchors of strongly disagree, disagree, neutral, agree, and strongly agree. The statements are scored in both directions. The total score for each personality dimension is the summed score from the 12 statements of each scale.

The NEO Five-Factor Inventory has been successful in reliably measuring the five personality dimensions (e.g. Courneya and Hellsten 1998; Saucier 1998). The inventory was translated and back-translated between Chinese and English in the year 2000. The Chinese version of the inventory has been tested among both Hong Kong and mainland Chinese students (Zhang 2002a, 2002b; Zhang and Huang 2001). Results indicated that the NEO Five-Factor Inventory is reliable and valid for assessing the five personality traits. The study (Zhang 2003) to be reviewed in this chapter adopted the Chinese inventory.

Do the three individual-difference variables matter in learning approaches?

In order to find out if the three individual-difference variables indeed play a role in learning approaches, we conducted a series of four studies between the years 1997 and 2002. Across the four studies, research participants were from five higher educational institutions in three cultures: Hong Kong, mainland China, and the United States. The total number of participants was 1,824, with 700 of them male students, and 1,124, female students.

In all four studies, the reliability and validity of all relevant inventories were examined. Moreover, in all studies, statistical procedures were used to control the possible effects of age, gender, university class level, and academic discipline. Across the four studies, there were three major objectives. The first was to explore the relationships between thinking styles and learning approaches (Studies 1 and 2). The second was to investigate the predictive validity of career personality types for learning approaches (Study

3). The third was to examine if the Big Five personality traits would predict learning approaches (Study 4). In the following, we recapitulate the parts of each study that directly address the thesis of this chapter.

Thinking styles and learning approaches – Studies 1 and 2

Our initial interest in learning approaches arose from our investigation of the relationship between thinking styles and learning approaches. This relationship became important for us to study because whereas the two constructs have been individually shown to be critical to student learning, nothing was known about how the two constructs were related to each other.

Therefore, in a first study (Zhang and Sternberg 2000), we investigated the relationships between thinking styles and learning approaches among 854 (362 male and 492 female) entering students from the University of Hong Kong and 215 (114 male and 101 female) undergraduate freshmen from two universities in Nanjing, mainland China. The participants responded to the Study Process Questionnaire and the Thinking Styles Inventory.

As expected, results (see Table 5.1) indicated that, in general, students who indicated a stronger preference for Type II thinking styles tended to report a surface approach to learning, whereas students who scored higher in Type I thinking styles tended to report a deep approach to learning. Although most of the correlations between the (sub)scales of the two inventories were low, they were statistically significant. In addition, these results largely supported our own hypotheses about the relationships between the two inventories. Therefore, we believe that these correlations, although weak, revealed true relationships between the two constructs. Nevertheless, it is important that the study be replicated in other cultural contexts.

Therefore, in a second study (Zhang 2000c), the relationships between thinking styles and learning approaches were further explored. The participants for this study were two independent samples of university students from the United States. In 1997, 67 (19 male and 48 female) students studying in an introductory psychology class from a mid-western university participated in the research. In 1998, the study was replicated among a different cohort group of students (14 males and 51 females) registered in the same class in the same university.

The correlation coefficients between the (sub)scales in the two inventories, also shown in Table 5.1, confirmed the results from the previous study. Moreover, the majority of the correlations were greater in magnitude than were those obtained from the first study.

Thus, results from these two studies have led us to conclude that thinking styles and learning approaches are closely associated with each other. Although these significant relationships do not guarantee any causal

Table 5.1 Pearson Correlation Matrix for the scales in the Study Process Questionnaire and Thinking Styles Inventory

Scale	SM HK	SM NJ	SM USA-1	SM USA-2	DM HK	DM NJ	DM USA-1	DM USA-2	AM HK	AM NJ	AM USA-1	AM USA-2
Leg	0.04	-0.09	-0.09	-0.19	0.28*	0.24*	0.41*	0.49*	0.21*	0.20	0.16	0.23
Exe	0.24*	0.23*	0.20	0.44*	0.17*	0.08	0.20	0.04	0.20*	0.20	0.43*	0.28
Jud	0.00	-0.02	-0.09	-0.09	0.39*	0.31*	0.42*	0.48*	0.17*	0.15	0.33*	0.20
Global	0.17*	0.05	0.12	0.04	0.24*	0.04	0.33*	0.20	0.18*	0.13	0.37*	0.14
Local	0.17*	0.18	0.00	0.16	0.24*	0.15	0.02	0.40*	0.21*	0.14	0.18	0.27
Liberal	0.07	-0.15	0.01	-0.24	0.37*	0.31*	0.41*	0.50*	0.20*	0.08	0.17	0.01
Con	0.25*	0.36*	0.22	0.39*	0.07	0.00	0.15	-0.04	0.19*	0.19	0.36*	0.23
Hier	-0.01	-0.13	-0.06	-0.08	0.32*	0.35*	0.44*	0.49*	0.13*	0.23*	0.34*	0.38*
Mon	0.22*	0.20	0.20	0.17	0.28*	0.23*	0.14	0.20	0.26*	0.30*	0.30	0.43*
Oli	0.18*	0.23*	0.12	0.29	0.13*	0.23*	0.16	0.14	0.10	0.24*	0.36*	0.19
Ana	0.04	0.14	-0.11	-0.17	0.25*	0.26*	0.46*	0.45*	0.10	0.28*	0.31	0.21
Internal	0.07	-0.02	-0.26	-0.01	0.24*	0.13	0.33*	0.22	0.24*	0.36*	0.29	0.14
External	0.02	-0.02	0.12	-0.01	0.22*	0.07	0.28	0.43*	0.02	-0.06	0.14	0.09

Notes
N=854 for Hong Kong; N=215 for mainland China; N₁=67 for USA; N₂=65 for USA
SM=Surface motivation, DM=Deep motivation, AM=Achieving motivation,
SS=Surface-strategy, DS=Deep-strategy, AS=Achieving-strategy
Leg=Legislative, Exe=Executive, Jud=Judicial, Con=Conservative,
Hier=Hierarchical, Mon=Monarchic, Oli=Oligarchic, Ana=Anarchic

*indicates that correlation is statistically different from zero at 0.01 level.

SS HK	SS NJ	SS USA-1	SS USA-2	DS HK	DS NJ	DS USA-1	DS USA-2	AS HK	AS NJ	AS USA-1	AS USA-2
-0.02	-0.12	-0.13	-0.10	0.25*	0.33*	0.39*	0.48*	0.10	0.02	0.27	0.30
0.26*	0.34*	0.43*	0.39*	0.17*	-0.04	-0.01	0.03	0.20*	0.20	0.26	0.14
-0.13*	-0.11	0.05	-0.03	0.38*	0.49*	0.33*	0.36*	0.26*	0.18	0.47*	0.20
0.13*	0.02	0.10	0.00	0.25*	0.13	0.19	0.18	0.13*	0.00	0.11	0.06
0.17*	0.23*	0.29	0.10	0.26*	0.10	-0.04	0.43*	0.30*	0.23*	0.38*	0.45*
-0.03	-0.31*	-0.22	-0.26	0.37*	0.53*	0.37*	0.45*	0.19*	0.18	0.26	0.37*
0.36*	0.47*	0.41*	0.42*	0.07	-0.16	-0.07	-0.05	0.19*	0.07	0.24	0.02
-0.04	-0.14	0.08	-0.10	0.36*	0.39*	0.34*	0.52*	0.39*	0.49*	0.44*	0.47*
0.22*	0.18	0.18	0.34*	0.24*	0.21	0.05	0.15	0.29*	0.31*	0.13	0.32
0.19*	0.23	0.48*	0.27	0.13*	0.14	0.06	0.09	0.12	0.25*	0.17	-0.02
0.08	0.08	0.02	-0.03	0.24*	0.27*	0.38*	0.50*	0.18*	0.30*	0.45*	0.36*
0.05	-0.02	-0.12	0.11	0.20*	0.30*	0.22	0.12	0.07	0.10	0.15	0.12
-0.02	0.02	0.07	-0.06	0.24*	0.09	0.10	0.45*	0.20*	0.22*	0.44*	0.20

relationship, they do imply that change in one variable would lead to change in the other. Therefore, from the viewpoint of examining the effect of thinking styles upon learning approaches, we may argue that thinking styles contribute to the development of learning approaches.

Then, the question that arose was: "Would a different style construct also relate to one's approaches to learning?" There are many style constructs. We chose Holland's theoretical construct of career personality type, which was classified as a personality-centered style construct within Sternberg's model of three approaches to the study of styles. Holland's construct appeals to us because it is one that has demonstrated a great extent of universality, as discussed earlier.

Career personality types and learning approaches – Study 3

Therefore, in a third study (Zhang, in press-b), the predictive validity of career personality types for learning approaches was investigated among 203 (146 female and 57 male) students from a large comprehensive university in Shanghai, P. R. China. The participants responded to the Study Process Questionnaire and the Short-Version Self-Directed Search.

One of the fundamental questions of this study was "Which career personality types statistically contribute to each of the three learning approaches?" Using hierarchical multiple regressions, we found that five of the six career personality scales (all but the social scale) statistically contributed to the prediction of learning approaches beyond age. The unique contributions (see Table 5.2) of particular career personality types to each of the three learning approaches are as follows: First, the R scale contributed negatively to the surface learning approach by 6 per cent. Second, the I and A scales together contributed positively to the deep learning approach by 31 per cent. Finally, the I, A, E, and C scales together contributed positively to the achieving approach by 20 per cent.

Therefore, these data have shown that learning approaches are predictable from an additional individual-difference variable – one's career personality type. Such significant findings from the previous three studies made us wonder if a more general attribute, such as personality trait, would contribute to the development of learning approaches. In literature, one of the long-standing debates has been over whether or not styles need to be measured in addition to the measurement of personality traits, for personality traits, as a much broader human attribute, have been proved to overlap with styles (e.g. Furnham 1996; Riding and Wigley 1997). Because styles have shown predictive validity for learning approaches, we anticipated that personality traits, as a broader human attribute than styles, would also have predictive value for learning approaches. Thus, it was under this assumption that the final study was conducted.

Table 5.2 Predicting learning approaches from career personality types

Variables in the equation	Variable summary	Model summary	
	ß weights	R^2	F Value
Surface approach			
Age	0.17*	0.02[a]	$F_{(1, 201)}=5.18$[a]*
Realistic	-0.23**	0.08[bs]	$F_{(2, 200)}=8.59$[bs]***
Deep approach			
Age	-0.18**	0.06[a]	$F_{(1, 201)}=13.80$[a]***
Investigative	0.50***	0.34[bd]	$F_{(2, 200)}=50.59$[bd]***
Artistic	0.19**	0.37[cd]	$F_{(3, 199)}=39.28$[cd]***
Achieving approach			
Age	-0.16*	0.04[a]	$F_{(1, 201)}=9.33$[a]**
Investigative	0.21**	0.14[ba]	$F_{(2, 200)}=16.87$[ba]***
Artistic	0.18**	0.20[ca]	$F_{(3, 199)}=16.34$[ca]***
Enterprising	0.15*	0.23[da]	$F_{(4, 198)}=14.69$[da]***
Conventional	0.14*	0.24[ea]	$F_{(5, 197)}=12.72$[ea]***

Notes
*$p<0.05$
**$p<0.01$
***$p<0.001$
[a] Predictors: (Constant), age
[bs] Predictors: (Constant), age, realistic
[bd] Predictors: (Constant), age, investigative
[cd] Predictors: (Constant), age, investigative, artistic
[ba] Predictors: (Constant), age, investigative
[ca] Predictors: (Constant), age, investigative, artistic
[da] Predictors: (Constant), age, investigative, artistic, enterprising
[ea] Predictors: (Constant), age, investigative, artistic, enterprising, conventional

Table 5.3 Predicting learning approaches from personality traits

Learning approach	Surface motive	Deep motive	Achieving motive	Surface strategy	Deep strategy	Achieving strategy
R^2_{Total}	0.14	0.22	0.23	0.14	0.25	0.24
R^2_a	0.10	0.13	0.10	0.08	0.15	0.23
R^2_b	0.13	0.22	0.16	0.13	0.23	0.24
R^2_c	0.14		0.19	0.14	0.25	
R^2_d			0.23			
β_1	***0.44$_{Neuroticism}$	***0.30$_{Conscientious}$	***0.42$_{Conscientious}$	***-0.27$_{Openness}$	***0.36$_{Conscientious}$	***0.51$_{Conscientious}$
β_2	***0.21$_{Extraversion}$	***0.30$_{Openness}$	***-0.22$_{Agreeableness}$	***0.31$_{Neuroticism}$	***0.29$_{Openness}$	**-0.14$_{Agreeableness}$
β_3	*-0.11$_{Openness}$		***0.33$_{Neuroticism}$	*0.13$_{Extraversion}$	**-0.13$_{Agreeableness}$	
β_4			***0.26$_{Extraversion}$			
F	22.05***	58.77***	30.86***	22.93***	45.29***	66.92***
df	3, 416	2, 417	4, 415	3, 416	3, 416	2, 417

Notes
Conscientious = Conscientiousness
a First predictor
b First and second predictors
c First, second, and third predictors
d First, second, third, and fourth predictors
*p<0.05
**p<0.01
***p<0.001

The Big Five personality traits and learning approaches – Study 4

In this study (Zhang 2003), 420 (286 female and 134 male) university students from a large research-oriented university in Shanghai, P. R. China, responded to the Study Process Questionnaire and the NEO Five-Factor Inventory.

Results indicated that each of the six learning approach subscales was significantly predicted by particular personality dimensions. The degree of prediction of learning approaches by personality dimensions ranged from 14 per cent (surface-motive and surface-strategy) to 25 per cent (deep-strategy). For each learning approach subscale, at least two personality dimensions served as predictors. For example, the surface approach to learning was positively predicted by neuroticism and extraversion, but negatively by openness. Moreover, the deep approach was positively predicted by conscientiousness and openness, but negatively by agreeableness (see Table 5.3). Therefore, like the previous two human attributes examined, students' personality traits are also significantly associated with their learning approaches.

General discussion and implications

This chapter has reviewed a series of four studies that focused on investigating the nature of learning approaches, a critical aspect in human learning. It has been established that people's learning approaches not only are associated with their learning environments and personal characteristics, as has been demonstrated in previous investigations, but also vary as a function of their thinking styles, career personality types, and personality traits. However, the question that arises is: "How do these findings make substantive sense?" In our original writings, we have addressed this question. In the following, we summarize our explanations to our major research findings.

We start by offering our view on the significant relationship between thinking styles and learning approaches. Conceptually, both theories concern the manners in which tasks are perceived and performed. For example, someone who is motivated to understand the learning material and use a deep strategy to learn would use all possible means, including using innovative and nontraditional strategies (i.e. using Type I thinking styles), to solve the puzzles in their mind. Vice versa, someone who prefers to use Type I thinking styles would be dealing with their tasks by creating their own ways of doing things and by using complex thinking – a manifestation of a deep approach to learning. Consequently, it is fair to say that thinking styles and learning approaches seem to have an overlapping conceptual role.

Practically, it is conceivable that students who take a surface approach to learning and those who prefer to use Type II thinking styles share a similar way of dealing with tasks. That is, they would want to get things done with given structures and to "play it safe." Similarly, students who take a deep approach to learning and those who prefer to use Type I styles also share a major characteristic in dealing with tasks. That is, they would be inclined to make up their own minds and use their own judgments in learning and work situations in which their creativity and imagination would be allowed free rein. Thus, both empirical data and conceptual argument support that thinking styles play an important role in learning approaches.

We now reiterate our rationale for our belief in the substantive sense made by the significant relationship between career personality types and learning approaches by offering the following examples. First, the negative relationship between the surface approach and the realistic career personality type makes substantive sense because the surface learning approach and the realistic career personality type entail very different characteristics and behaviors. The surface learning approach is characterized by a simple reproduction of what has been taught. For the purpose of simply reproducing what one has been taught, one would have no motivation/need for (or interest in) obtaining hands-on experiences. On the contrary, the realistic career personality type is characterized by one's strong interest in gaining direct knowledge about the subject matter being dealt with and by a preference for using the trial-and-error method, rather than merely by trying to memorize what has been taught.

Second, the positive relationship of the deep approach to learning to both the artistic and investigative types could be explained by the fact that deep learners and people of artistic and investigative types tend to be engaged in similar kinds of learning. The deep approach to learning is characterized by learning that involves intrinsic motivation or curiosity. In order to satisfy one's curiosity about the issues being dealt with, an individual will use all possible means of examining the related issues – a manifestation of the investigative career personality type. The individual has to think creatively both in trying to find ways of investigating the issues and in making sense of the results obtained from the investigations – a manifestation of the artistic type of personality type with regard to career preferences.

Similarly, we could argue for the authenticity of the existence of the significantly positive relationships of the achieving approach to the investigative, artistic, enterprising, and conventional career personality types (see Zhang, in press-b). The message is that, together with empirical evidence, these conceptual arguments and our discussion of common sense have demonstrated that career personality types also play a critical part in students' learning approaches.

Finally, we discuss the substantive sense in the significant relationship between personality traits and learning approaches. As in their relationships to thinking styles and career personality types, the relationships of learning approaches to personality traits are also easily observed. For example, the positive relationships of conscientiousness and openness to the deep approach to learning can be explained as follows: Conscientiousness is characterized by a sense of purposefulness and strong will, whereas openness is clearly characterized by open-mindedness and active imagination. To gain a deep understanding of what is learned (i.e. to use a deep approach to learning), the characteristics of conscientiousness and openness would be desirable, if not necessary. Therefore, it makes sense that an individual with high degrees of conscientiousness and openness would have the motivation to understand what he/she learns (deep-motive) and would use a deep strategy to learn.

A second example is the surface approach's positive relationship to neuroticism, as well as its negative relationship to openness. It is conceivable that students who are emotionally unstable and who suffer from low self-esteem (characteristics of neuroticism) would tend to avoid taking the risk of making mistakes. Instead, they tend to feel more comfortable with performing learning tasks that require them to reproduce what they are taught (i.e. that involve the surface approach to learning). By the same token, students who do not keep an open mind and who do not use their imagination (the opposite characteristics of openness) might also seek refuge in the surface approach to learning. Therefore, we have succeeded in contending, through both presenting empirical data and providing theoretical conceptualization, that students' learning approaches are also associated with their personality traits.

Then, a further question that one would ask is: "What are the implications of these findings for research on human learning and for educational practice?" First, we discuss the implications for research on human learning, in particular, for the investigation of learning approaches. Given that the findings suggested that each of the three constructs examined (i.e. thinking styles, career personality types, and personality traits) was significantly related to learning approaches after students' age, gender, university class level, and their academic discipline had been taken into account, scholars should keep in mind that learning approach is a construct that is intricately entwined with other constructs. Therefore, in conducting research on learning approaches, one should look into the complex nature of the learning-approach construct. Furthermore, a heuristic model for individual differences and learning approaches should be developed so that new individual-difference variables in learning approaches can be identified, and thereafter be given the attention that they rightfully deserve. Finally, in order to gain a deep understanding of the nature of different learning approaches, future studies should adopt more sophisticated research methods such as using experimental and longitudinal designs as well as taking a qualitative approach. The questions that we ought to be asking and answering are the ones that start with the "whys" and the "hows." Results from such research procedures would be very useful in supplementing our existing knowledge about the nature of human learning.

For educational practice, although the findings do not warrant arguing for any causal relationship between the constructs under investigation, the fact that they were significantly correlated with or predictive of each other suggests that change in one construct will likely lead to change in another. Thus, in educational settings, teaching faculty and university counselors could facilitate student learning and development by using the relationships of learning approaches to career personality types, personality traits, and to thinking styles. For instance, assuming that changes in students' career personality types may affect their learning approaches, as has been indicated by the data, university counselors may exert an impact on students' learning approaches through the types of career environments to which they expose students. Data suggested that engaging students in the realistic types of tasks would discourage students from taking a surface approach to learning. Also, for example, in making use of the predictive relationships of personality traits to learning approaches, teachers may educate students about the value of being conscientious and open-minded in their learning tasks so that students may acquire a deep approach. Moreover, in capitalizing on the relationships of thinking styles to learning approaches, teachers may use assessment methods that would encourage the use of Type I thinking styles. Through using Type I thinking styles, students may also develop a deep approach to learning. Finally, going beyond what we have presented in this chapter about the role of the above three individual-difference variables in learning approaches, we believe that there is a great need for educators to be well informed about new educational research findings so that they could make their educational practice more theoretically and scientifically based.

References

Albaili, M. A. (1995) "An Arabic Version of the Study Process Questionnaire: Reliability and Validity", *Psychological Reports* 77 (3): 1083–9.

Bickham, P. J., Miller, M. J., O'Neal, H. and Clanton, R. (1998) "Comparison of Error Rates on the 1990 and 1994 Revised Self-directed Search", *Perceptual and Motor Skills* 86 (3, Part 2): 1168–70.

Biggs, J. B. (1979) "Individual Differences in Study Processes and the Quality of Learning Outcomes", *Higher Education* 8: 381–94.

—— (1987) *Student Approaches to Learning and Studying*, Hawthorn: Australian Council for Educational Research.

—— (1988) "Assessing Student Approaches to Learning", *Australian Psychologist* 23 (2): 197–206.

—— (1992) *Why and How Do Hong Kong Students Learn? Using the Learning and Study Process Questionnaires*, Education Paper No. 14, Hong Kong: Faculty of Education, University of Hong Kong.

Biggs, J. B. and Das, J. P. (1973) "Extreme Response Style, Internality–Externality and Academic Performance", *British Journal of Social and Clinical Psychology* 12: 199–210.

Busato, V. V., Prins, F. J., Elshout, J. J. and Hamaker, C. (1999) "The Relation between Learning Styles, the Big Five Personality Traits and Achievement Motivation in Higher Education", *Personality and Individual Differences* 26 (1): 129–40.

Cano-Garcia, F. and Hughes, E. H. (2000) "Learning and Thinking Styles: An Analysis of Their Relationship and Influence on Academic Achievement", *Educational Psychology* 20 (4): 413–30.

Cattell, R. B. (1957) *Personality and Motivation Structure and Measurement*, New York: World Books.

Costa, P. T., Jr., and McCrae, R. R. (1985) *The NEO Personality Inventory*, Odessa, FL: Psychological Assessment Resources.

—— (1992) *The NEO-PI-R: Professional Manual*, Odessa, FL: Psychological Assessment Resources.

Courneya, K. S. and Hellsten, L.-A. M. (1998) "Personality Correlates of Exercise Behavior, Motives, Barriers and Preferences: An Application of the Five-factor Model", *Personality and Individual Differences* 24 (5): 625–33.

Craik, F. I. M. and Lockhart, R. S. (1972) "Levels of Processing: A Framework for Memory Research", *Journal of Verbal Learning and Verbal Behavior* 11: 671–84.

Dai, D. Y. and Feldhusen, J. F. (1999) "A Validation of the Thinking Styles Inventory: Implications for Gifted Education", *Roeper Review* 21 (4): 302–7.

Digman, J. M. (1994) "Historical Antecedents of the Five Factor Model", in P. T. Costa and T. A. Widiger (eds) *Personality Disorders and the Five Factor Model of Personality*, Washington, DC: American Psychological Association, pp. 13–18.

Entwistle, N. (1981) *Styles of Teaching and Learning: An Integrated Outline of Educational Psychology for Students, Teachers, and Lecturers*, New York: John Wiley and Sons.

Eysenck, H. J. (1970) *The Structure of Human Personality* (third edition), London: Methuen.

Eysenck, H. J. and Eysenck, S. B. G. (1964) *Manual of the Eysenck Personality Inventory*, London: Hodder and Stoughton.

Fiske, D. W. (1949) "Consistency of the Factorial Structures of Personality Ratings from Different Sources", *Journal of Abnormal and Social Psychology* 44: 429–444.

Furnham, A. F. (1996) "The Big Five Versus the Big Four: The Relationship between the Myers–Briggs Type Indicator (MBTI) and NEO-PI Five Factor Model of Personality", *Personality and Individual Differences* 21 (2): 303–7.

Glidden, R. C. and Greenwood, A. K. (1997) "A Validation Study of the Spanish Self-Directed Search using Back-translation Procedures", *Journal of Career Assessment* 5 (1): 105–13.

Goldberg, L. R. (1981) "Language and Individual Differences: The Search for Universals in Personality Lexicons", in L. Wheeler (ed.) *Review of Personality and Social Psychology*, Beverly Hills, CA: Sage, vol. 2, pp. 141–65.

—— (1990) "An Alternative Description of Personality: The Big Five Factor Structure", *Journal of Personality and Social Psychology* 59: 1216–29.

Grigorenko, E. L. and Sternberg, R. J. (1997) "Styles of thinking, abilities and academic performance". *Exceptional Children*, 63 (3), 295–312.

Guilford, J. P. (1975) "Factors of Personality", *Psychological Bulletin* 82: 802–14.

Holland, J. L. (1973) *Making Vocational Choices: A Theory of Careers*, Englewood Cliffs, NJ: Prentice-Hall.

—— (1985) *Making Vocational Choices: A Theory of Vocational Personalities and Work Environments* (second edition), Englewood Cliffs, NJ: Prentice-Hall.

—— (1994) *Self-Directed Search*, Odessa, FL: Psychological Assessment Resources.

Kember, D. and Gow, D. (1990) "Cultural Specificity of Approaches to Study", *British Journal of Educational Psychology* 60: 356–63.

McCrae, R. R. (1987) "Creativity, Divergent Thinking and Openness to Experience", *Journal of Personality and Social Psychology* 52: 1258–65.

McCrae, R. R. and Costa, P. T. (1997) "Personality Trait Structure as a Human Universal", *American Psychologist* 52 (5): 509–16.

Marton, F. (1976) "What Does It Take to Learn? Some Implications on an Alternative View of Learning", in N. J. Entwistle (ed.) *Strategies for Research and Development in Higher Education*, Amsterdam: Swets and Zeitlinger, pp. 200–22.

Murray-Harvey, R. (1994) "Learning Styles and Approaches to Learning: Distinguishing between Concept and Instruments", *British Journal of Educational Psychology* 64 (3): 373–88.

Niles, F. S. (1995) "Cultural Differences in Learning Motivation and Learning Strategies: A Comparison of Overseas and Australian Students at an Australian University", *International Journal of Intercultural Relations* 19 (3): 369–85.

Norman, W. T. (1963) "Toward an Adequate Taxonomy of Personality Attributes: Replicated Factor Structure in Peer Nomination Personality Ratings", *Journal of Abnormal and Social Psychology* 66: 574–83.

O'Neil, M. J. and Child, D. (1984) "Biggs' SPQ: A British Study of Its Internal Structure", *British Journal of Educational Psychology* 54: 228–34.

Ramsden, P. and Entwistle, N. J. (1981) "Effects of Academic Departments on Students' Approaches to Studying", *British Journal of Educational Psychology* 51: 368–83.

Rayner, S. and Riding, R. (1997) "Towards a Categorization of Cognitive Styles and Learning Styles", *Educational Psychology* 17 (1 and 2): 5–27.

Riding, R. J. and Wigley, S. (1997) "The Relationship between Cognitive Style and Personality in Further Education Students", *Personality and Individual Differences* 23 (3): 379–89.

Rose, R. J., Hall, C. W., Bolen, L. M. and Webster, R. E. (1996) "Locus of Control and College Students' Approaches to Learning", *Psychological Reports* 79 (1): 163–71.

Sadler-Smith, E. (1997) " 'Learning style': frameworks and instruments", *Educational Psychology* 17 (1–2): 51–63.

Saucier, G. (1998) "Replicable Item-cluster Subcomponents in the NEO Five-Factor Inventory", *Journal of Personality Assessment* 70 (2): 263–76.

Shafer, A. B. (2000) "Mediation of the Big Five's Effect on Career Decision Making by Life Task Dimensions and on Money Attitudes by Materialism", *Personality and Individual Differences* 28: 93–109.

Sternberg, R. J. (1988) "Mental Self-government: A Theory of Intellectual Styles and Their Development", *Human Development* 31: 197–224.

—— (1997) *Thinking Styles*, New York: Cambridge University Press.

Sternberg, R. J. and Wagner, R. K. (1992) "Thinking Styles Inventory" (unpublished test, Yale University).

Tang, C. and Biggs, J. (1996) "How Hong Kong Students Cope with Assessment", in D. Watkins and J. Biggs (eds) *The Chinese Learner: Cultural, Psychological, and Contextual Influences*, Hong Kong/Melbourne: Comparative Education Research Center/Australian Council for Educational Research, pp. 159–82.

Taylor, A. and MacDonald, D. A. (1999) "Religion and the Five Factor Model of Personality: An Exploratory Investigation Using a Canadian University Sample", *Personality and Individual Differences* 27: 1243–59.

Tupes, E. C. and Christal, R. E. (1992) "Recurrent Personality Factors Based on Trait Ratings", *Journal of Personality* (Special Issue – *The Five-Factor Model: Issues and Applications*) 60 (2): 225–51.

Watkins, D., Biggs, J. and Regmi, M. (1991) "Does Confidence in the Language of Instruction Influence a Student's Approach to Learning?" *Instructional Science* 20: 331–9.

Watkins, D. A. and Dahlin, B. (1997) "Assessing Study Approaches in Sweden", *Psychological Reports* 81: 131–6.

Wilson, A. (1987) "Approaches to Learning among Third World Tertiary Science Students: Papua New Guinea", *Research in Science and Technological Education* 5 (1): 59–67.

Zhang, L. F. (1999) "Short-Version Self-Directed Search" (unpublished test, University of Hong Kong).

—— (2000a) "University Students' Learning Approaches in Three Cultures: An Investigation of Biggs's 3P Model", *Journal of Psychology* 134 (1): 37–55.

—— (2000b) "Are Thinking Styles and Personality Types Related?" *Educational Psychology* 20 (3): 271–83.

—— (2000c) "Relationship between Thinking Styles Inventory and Study Process Questionnaire", *Personality and Individual Differences* 29: 841–56.

—— (2001) "Thinking Styles and Personality Types Revisited", *Personality and Individual Differences* 31 (6): 883–94.

—— (2002a) "Measuring Thinking Styles in Addition to Measuring Personality Traits?" *Personality and Individual Differences* 33: 445–58.

—— (2002b) "Thinking Styles and the Big Five Personality Traits", *Educational Psychology* 22 (1): 17–31.

—— (2003) "Does the Big Five Predict Learning Approaches?" *Personality and Individual Differences* 34: 1431–46.

—— (in press-a) "Contributions of Thinking Styles to Critical Thinking Dispositions", *Journal of Psychology*.

—— (in press-b) "Learning Approaches and Career Personality Types: Biggs and Holland United", *Personality and Individual Differences*.

Zhang, L. F. and Huang, J. F. (2001) "Thinking Styles and the Five Factor Model of Personality", *European Journal of Personality* 15: 465–76.

Zhang, L. F. and Postiglione, G. A. (2001) "Thinking Styles, Self-esteem, and Socio-economic Status", *Personality and Individual Differences* 31: 1333–46.

Zhang, L. F. and Sternberg, R. J. (1998) "Thinking Styles, Abilities, and Academic Achievement among Hong Kong University Students", *Educational Research Journal* 13 (1): 41–62.

—— (2000) "Are Learning Approaches and Thinking Styles Related? A Study in Two Chinese Populations", *Journal of Psychology* 134 (5): 469–89.

—— (2002) "Thinking Styles and Teacher Characteristics", *International Journal of Psychology* 37 (1): 3–12.

Chapter 6

A comprehensive understanding of human learning

Knud Illeris

Since the middle of the nineteenth century many theories and understandings of how human learning takes place have been launched. They have had different angles, different epistemological platforms, and a very different contents. Some of them have been overtaken by new knowledge and new standards, but in general we have today a picture of a great variety of learning theoretical approaches and constructions, which are more or less compatible and more or less competing on the global academic market.

The aim of this chapter is to try to unite a wide selection of the best of these constructions into an overall understanding or framework which can give a general overview of the field and at the same time point out where the different contributions are situated in the field and how they relate to each other.

The understanding presented is based on two fundamental assumptions: first, that all learning includes two essentially different types of process, namely an external interaction process between the learner and his or her social, cultural and material environment, and an internal psychological process of acquisition and elaboration in which new impulses are connected with the results of prior learning. Second, that all learning includes three dimensions, namely the cognitive dimension of knowledge and skills, the emotional dimension of feelings and motivation, and the social dimension of communication and cooperation – all of which are embedded in a societally situated context. In addition, the approach specifies four types of learning and deals with what happens when intended learning does not occur.

The development of this understanding is described in detail in my book, *The Three Dimensions of Learning*, which was published in Danish in 1999 and in English in 2002 (Illeris 2002). This chapter is an elaborated version of an article in the *International Journal of Lifelong Education* (Illeris 2003).

The new interest in the concept of learning

It is striking that the concept of learning in the last years of the 1990s experienced a revival of sorts, both in public debate and in professional psychology, education and management circles. Part of the background for the new interest in learning is no doubt the increasing orientation towards education and lifelong learning as important factors in the global competition between nations and companies. This has led to growing expenses for educational measures, and therefore also to increased attention to the outcome. Politicians, administrators and managers seem at length to have realised that while what they grant money for is teaching, what they actually want to buy is learning, and that there is no simple and automatic connection between the two. The fundamental questions to be addressed again are thus: what is learning, how does it come about, how can it be promoted, and why does teaching not always result in learning?

At the same time there has been rapid development in ideas about the sort of learning that is necessary and desirable. Learning can no longer be conceived of as merely the acquisition of a syllabus or curriculum. If one examines job advertisements or interviews personnel managers, it becomes obvious that general skills and personal qualities are considered at least as important as professional qualifications. In contemporary everyday life, such skills and qualities are also essential both to manage the complex functions of modern life and to maintain the common and democratic functions of society.

Thus, what should be learned in education as well as in working and social and societal life is a complex totality of traditional and up-to-date knowledge, orientation and overview, combined with professional and everyday life skills and a broad range of personal qualities such as flexibility, openness, independence, responsibility, creativity, etc. In management, and to a certain extent also in education, the concept of competence or competencies has been used increasingly to capture this complex situation – and for learning theory and educational practice it is an evident challenge to develop a concept of learning that is able to match this concept and include the acquisition of the whole range of different competencies at stake.

The combination of the variety of learning theories into a comprehensive framework

For the purpose described, the starting point of the development of such a theory was a very broad and open definition of learning covering all processes that lead to relatively lasting changes of capacity, whether they be of a motor, cognitive, psychodynamic (i.e. emotional, motivational or attitudinal) or social character, and which are not due to genetic–biological maturation. The significance of this definition is mainly that it avoids any separation between learning, personal development, socialisation, qualification and the like by regarding all such processes as types of learning when viewed from different angles or positions.

In relation to this definition, many existing theories are of relevance whether or not they present themselves as learning theories, and the procedure in the work of establishing a comprehensive and coherent understanding of the field has been, so to speak, to scrutinise a great variety of relevant and important theories to see how each of them can contribute to an overall understanding. In this way I have tried to gradually build up a framework or model which covers the totality and places the various contributions in relation to each other.

Naturally, a process of this kind cannot be carried through in any neutral or objective manner. It is evident that when constructing the model I have had to involve my personal and professional views as to what is basic, important and significant, and to continuously employ my own interpretations and judgements and make my own additions. In this connection I believe that I have had the advantage of having a broad orientation in Nordic, Continental European, Russian, British and American approaches. Nevertheless, in no way do I believe or claim that the process or the model developed is anything but a personal construct and that other researchers could not build up other equally or perhaps more appropriate and useful understandings. I am also quite aware that developers or devotees of the many theories involved may feel their contributions or opinions intimidated by being placed in a construction which is based on a fundamental understanding and a scientific rationality different from their own.

However, learning in the broad sense, as described above and as it will be regarded in the following account, is a very complex process involving both biologically founded psychological and societally founded social elements which follow different sets of logic and work together in a complex interaction. Therefore, I regard it as a necessity to bring these different approaches together and find a way of dealing with the totality in spite of, and simultaneously in acknowledgement of, these basic differences.

The two basic processes

The first important step in the construction is to realise that all learning implies the integration of two very different processes, namely an external interaction process between the learner and his or her social, cultural or material environment, and an internal psychological process of acquisition and elaboration.

Many learning theories deal only with one of these processes, which of course does not mean that they are wrong or worthless, as both processes can be studied separately. However, it does mean that they do not cover the whole field of learning. This may, for instance, be said of traditional behaviourist and cognitive learning theories focusing only on the internal psychological process. It can equally be said of certain modern social learning theories which – sometimes in explicit opposition to this – draw attention to the external interaction process alone. (Here I am referring to types of approach such as social constructionism (Gergen 1991, 1994) and the concept of situated learning (Lave and Wenger 1991).)

However, it seems evident to me that both processes must be actively involved if any learning is to take place.

The three dimensions of learning

In my model construction of the field of learning, I start by depicting the external interaction process as a vertical double arrow between the environment, which is the general basis and therefore placed at the bottom, and the individual, who is the specific learner and therefore placed at the top.

Next I add the psychological acquisition process as another double arrow. It is an internal process of the learner and must therefore be placed at the top pole of the interaction process. Further, it is a process of integrated interplay between two equal psychological functions involved in any learning, namely the function of cognition, dealing with the learning content, and the emotional or psychodynamic function, providing the necessary mental energy of the process. Thus, the double arrow of the acquisition process is placed horizontally at the top of the interaction process and between the poles of cognition and emotion: see Figure 6.1.

As can be seen, the two double arrows can now span out a triangular field between three angles. These three angles depict three spheres or dimen-

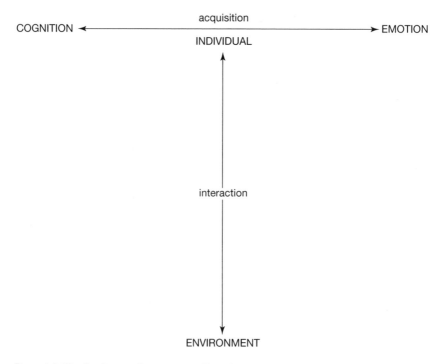

Figure 6.1 The fundamental processes of learning.

sions, and it is the core claim of the understanding that all learning will always involve these three dimensions.

The cognitive dimension is the dimension of the learning content, which may be described as knowledge or skills and which builds up the understanding and the ability of the learner. The endeavour of the learner is to construct *meaning* and *ability* to deal with the challenges of practical life and thereby develop an overall personal *functionality*.

The emotional or psychodynamic dimension is the dimension encompassing mental energy, feelings and motivations. Its ultimate function is to secure the continuous *mental balance* of the learner and thereby it simultaneously develops a personal *sensibility*.

These two dimensions are always initiated by impulses from the interaction processes and integrated in the internal process of acquisition and elaboration. Therefore all cognitive learning is, so to speak, 'obsessed' by the

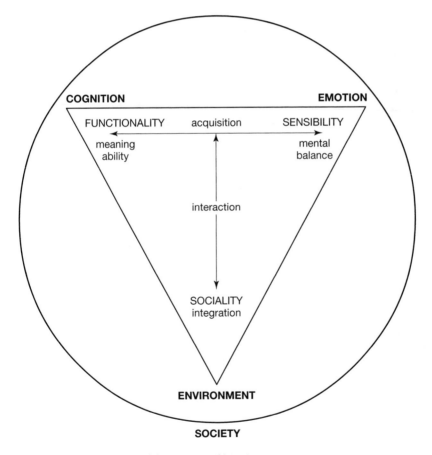

Figure 6.2 The processes and dimensions of learning.

emotions at stake – e.g. whether the learning is driven by desire, interest, necessity or compulsion. Correspondingly, emotional learning is always influenced by the cognition or understanding, e.g. new information can change the emotional condition. (Many psychologists have been aware of this close connection (e.g. Vygotsky 1978; Furth 1987). It has also recently been thoroughly investigated in neurology (Damasio 1994).)

The social dimension is the dimension of external interaction such as participation, communication and cooperation. It serves the personal *integration* in communities and society and thereby also builds up the *sociality* of the learner. However, this building up necessarily takes place through the two other dimensions.

Thus the triangle depicts what I see as the tension field of learning in general and of any specific learning event or learning process as stretched out between the development of functionality, sensibility and sociality (or, to express it in popular terms as in the original Danish version of the model: between the realms of Piaget, Freud and Marx).

As learning, furthermore, always takes place in the context of a specific society which sets the basic conditions for the learning possibilities, finally I place the triangle inside a circle indicating this basic situation (Figure 6.2).

It is also important to mention that each dimension includes a mental as well as a bodily side. Actually learning begins with the body and takes place through the brain, which is also part of the body, and only gradually the mental side is separated out as a specific but never independent area or function.

An example from everyday school life

In order to illustrate how the model may be understood and used, I shall take an everyday example from ordinary school life (which does not mean that the model only deals with learning in school).

During a chemistry lesson in the classroom, a teacher is explaining a chemical process. The pupils are supposed to be listening and perhaps asking questions to be sure that they have understood the explanation correctly. The pupils are thus involved in an interaction process. But at the same time they are supposed to take in or to learn what the teacher is teaching, i.e. psychologically to relate what is taught to what they should already have learned. The result should be that they are able to remember what they have been taught, and under certain conditions to reproduce it, apply it and involve it in further learning.

But sometimes, or for some pupils, the learning process does not take place as intended, and mistakes or derailing may occur in many different ways. Perhaps the interaction does not function because the teacher's explanation is not good enough or even incoherent, or there may be disturbances in the situation. If so, the explanation will only be picked up partially or incorrectly, and the learning result will be insufficient. But the pupils' acquisition process may also be inadequate, for instance because of a lack of concentration, and this will also lead to deterioration in the learning result. Or there may be errors or insufficiencies in the prior learning of some pupils, making them unable to understand the teacher's explanation and thereby also to learn what is being taught. Much of this indicates that acquisition is not only a cognitive matter. There is also another area or function involved concerning the pupils' attitudes to the intended learning: their interests and mobilisation of mental energy, i.e. an emotional or psychodynamic function.

In a school situation focus is usually on the learning content; in the case chosen it is on the pupils' understanding of the nature of the chemical process concerned. However, the emotional function is still also crucial, i.e. how the situation is experienced, what sort of feelings and motivations are involved, and thus the nature and the strength of the mental energy involved. The value and durability of the learning result is closely related to the emotional dimension of the learning process.

Further, both the cognitive and the emotional functions and their interplay are crucially dependent on the interaction process between the learner and the social, cultural and material environment. If the interaction in the chemistry lesson is not adequate and acceptable to the pupils, the learning will suffer or something quite different may be learned, for instance a negative impression of the teacher, of some other pupils, of the subject, or of the school situation in general.

The four types of learning

What has been outlined in the triangle model and the example above is a concept of learning which is basically constructivist in nature, i.e. it is assumed that the learner him or herself actively builds up or construes his/her learning as mental structures. These structures exist in the brain as dispositions that can be described as *schemes* or *mental patterns*.

With respect to the cognitive dimension, one typically speaks of schemes or, more popularly, of memory. In the emotional and the social-societal dimensions, one would employ terms such as patterns or, more popularly, inclinations. Under all circumstances, it is decisive that the results of learning are structured before they can be retained. This structuring can be established in various ways, and on this basis it is possible to distinguish between four different types of learning which are activated in different contexts, imply different kinds of learning results, and require more or less energy. (This is an elaboration of the concept of learning originally developed by Jean Piaget (e.g. Piaget 1952; Flavell 1963).)

When a scheme or pattern is established, it is a case of *cumulative* or mechanical learning. This type of learning is characterised by being an isolated formation, something new that is not a part of anything else.

Therefore, cumulative learning is most frequent during the first years of life, but later occurs only in special situations where one must learn something with no context of meaning or personal significance, for example a telephone number or pin code or a long string of words. The learning result is characterised by a type of automation that means that it can only be recalled and applied in situations mentally similar to the learning context. It is mainly this type of learning which is involved in the training of animals and which is therefore also referred to in the concept of conditioning in behaviourist psychology. (The concept of cumulative learning was developed by the Danish psychologist and Piaget specialist, Thomas Nissen (Nissen 1970).)

By far the most common type of learning is termed *assimilative* or learning by addition, meaning that the new element is linked as an addition to a scheme or pattern that is already established. One typical example could be learning in school subjects that are usually built up by means of constant additions to what has already been learned, but assimilative learning also takes place in all contexts where one gradually develops one's capacities of a cognitive, emotional or social-societal nature. The results of learning are characterised by being linked to the scheme or pattern in question in such a manner that it is relatively easy to recall and apply them when one is mentally oriented towards the field in question, for example a school subject, while they may be hard to access in other contexts. This is why problems are frequently experienced in applying knowledge from a school subject in other subjects or in contexts outside school.

However, in some cases, situations occur where something takes place that is difficult to immediately relate to any existing scheme or pattern. This is experienced as something one cannot really understand or relate to. But if it seems important or interesting, if it is something one is determined to acquire, this can take place by means of *accommodative* or transcendent learning. This type of learning implies that one breaks down (parts of) an existing scheme and transforms it so that the new situation can be linked in. Thus one both relinquishes and reconstructs something and this can be experienced as something painful, requiring mental energy. One must cross existing limitations and understand or accept something that is significantly new or different. The result of the learning is characterised by the fact that it can be recalled and applied in many different, relevant contexts. It is typically experienced as having understood or got hold of something which one really has internalised.

Finally, over the last decades it has been pointed out that in special situations there is also a far-reaching type of learning that has been variously described as significant (Rogers 1951), expansive (Engeström 1987) or *transformative* learning (Mezirow 1991). This learning implies what could be termed personality changes or changes in the self and is characterised by simultaneous restructuring in the cognitive, the emotional and the social-societal dimensions, a break of orientation that typically occurs as the result of a crisis-like situation caused by challenges experienced as urgent and unavoidable, making it necessary to change oneself in order to get any further. Transformative learning is thus both profound and extensive and can often be experienced physically, typically as a feeling of relief or relaxation.

As has been demonstrated, the four types of learning are widely different in scope and nature, and they also occur – or are activated by learners – in very different situations and connections. Whereas cumulative learning is most important in early childhood and transformative learning is a very demanding process that changes the very personality or identity and occurs only in very special situations of profound significance for the learner, assimilation and accommodation are, as described by Piaget, the two types of learning that characterise general, sound and normal everyday learning. Many other learning theorists also point to two such types of learning, for example Chris Argyris and Donald Schön have coined the well-known concepts of single and double loop learning (Argyris and Schön 1996), and also Lev Vygotsky's idea of transition to the 'zone of proximal development' may be seen as a parallel to accommodative learning (Vygotsky 1978).

However, ordinary discussions of learning and the design of many educational and school activities, are concentrated on and often only aimed at assimilative learning, as this is the sort of learning that the usual understanding of the concept of learning is about. But, as stated at the beginning of this chapter, today this understanding is obviously insufficient.

Another problem is that much intended learning does not take place. In schools, in education, at workplaces and in many other situations, very often people do not learn what they could learn or what they are supposed to learn. Therefore I find it important also to discuss briefly what happens in such cases.

Non-learning, defence, everyday consciousness and resistance to learning

Of course, it cannot be avoided that we all sometimes learn something that is wrong (cf. Mager 1961) and something that is inadequate for us in some way or other. In the first instance, this concerns matters such as mislearning and distortion of learning, which can be due to misunderstandings, miscommunication and the like. This may be annoying and in some cases unlucky, but simple mislearning due to 'technical' reasons is not a matter of great interest to learning theory.

However, today much non-learning and mislearning is not so simple, but has a background in some general conditions that modern society creates, and in some respects the investigation and understanding of such processes are definitely as important as more traditional learning theory to understand what is happening and to cope with it in practice.

The central point is that in our complex late modern society what Freud called *defence mechanisms* – which are active in specific personal connections (cf. Anna Freud 1942) – must necessarily be generalised and take more systematised forms because nobody can manage to remain open to the gigantic volumes of influences we are all constantly faced with.

This is why today people develop a kind of automatic sorting mechanism vis-à-vis the many influences, or what the German social psychologist Thomas Leithäuser has analysed and described as an *everyday consciousness* (Leithäuser 1976, cf. Illeris 2002). This functions in the way that one develops some general pre-understandings within certain thematic areas, and when one meets with influences within such an area these pre-understandings are activated so that if elements in the influences do not correspond to the pre-understandings, they are either rejected or distorted to make them agree. In both cases, this results in no new learning but, on the contrary, often the cementing of the already existing understanding.

Thus, through everyday consciousness we control our own learning and non-learning in a manner that seldom involves any direct positioning while simultaneously involving a massive defence of the already acquired understandings and, in the final analysis, our very identity. (There are, of course, also areas and situations where our positioning takes place in a more target-oriented manner, consciously and flexibly.)

Therefore, in practice the issue of learning very often becomes a question of what can penetrate the individual, semi-automatic defence mechanisms and under what conditions. These defence mechanisms are the most common reason for the gulf between the impulses being communicated, for example in an everyday situation, a work situation or a teaching situation, and what is actually learned.

In some important cases, for instance when a change to a basically new situation in a certain life area must be overcome, most people react by mobilising a genuine *identity defence* which demands very hard work of a more or less therapeutic character to break through. This happens typically in relation to a sudden situation of unemployment, divorce, death of closely related persons, or the like, and it is worth realising that such situations happen much more frequently today than just a generation ago.

Another psychological mechanism which may block or distort relevant learning is mental *resistance*. This is not, in itself, so very time-specific, as all human beings in any society will experience situations where what they try to accomplish cannot be carried through, and if they cannot understand or accept the barriers they will naturally react with some sort of resistance.

In practice it is sometimes quite difficult to distinguish between non-learning caused by defence and non-learning caused by resistance. However, psychologically there is a great and important difference. Whereas the defence mechanisms exist prior to the learning situation and function reactively, resistance is caused by the learning situation itself as an active response. Thus, resistance contains a very strong learning potential, especially for accommodative and even transformative learning. Often when one does not just accept something, the possibility of learning something significantly new emerges. And most great steps forward in the development of humankind and society have taken place when someone did not accept a given truth or way of doing or understanding things.

In everyday life, resistance is also a most important source of transcendent learning although it may be both inconvenient and annoying, not least for teachers. In any event, today it should be a central qualification of teachers to be able to cope with and even inspire mental resistance, as precisely such personal competencies which are so much in demand – for example, independence, responsibility and creativity – are likely to be developed in this way. This is why conflict or dilemma raising may be taken in as effective but demanding techniques in some particularly challenging educational situations.

Theoretical positions in the framework

In the above I have only very briefly referred to some of the many learning theoretical contributions which have been involved in the construction of the framework that I have sketched. It will not be possible in this chapter to go deeper into this but I can just outline how the learning triangle can function to indicate the various positions of some main approaches to learning.

The upper line of the triangle connects the cognitive and the emotional poles. Along this line most of what is usually labelled *developmental psychology* is situated, as such approaches tend to include both cognitive and psychodynamic dimensions of individual development, whereas societal conditions are usually only briefly considered. Important theorists in this area are, for instance, Piaget (Flavell 1963) and Kolb (1984) close to the cognitive pole, and Freud and Rogers close to the emotional pole. In between I can point to a contribution by Hans Furth (1987) that explicitly undertakes to investigate the basic connections between the developmental psychologies of Piaget and Freud.

The left side of the triangle goes from the cognitive pole down towards the social and societal pole. Along this line I primarily place the so-called activity theoretical approaches of the Russian cultural historical school, mainly Vygotsky (1978) and Leontyev (1981), and its successors such as Finnish Yrjö Engeström (1987) and German Klaus Holzkamp (1995). But also, for instance, Argyris and Schön (1996) must be placed close to this line as contributions here are characterised by connecting cognitive and environmental or societal conditions but paying little attention to emotional and psychodynamic impact. Special attention can here be given to American Jerome Bruner who started his work many years ago right up in the cognitive corner, but through a remarkable development gradually moved downwards along the line and with his last contribution on 'the culture of education' (Bruner 1996) came quite close to the societal pole.

Along the right sideline of the triangle, going from the emotional to the social-societal pole, the main contributions come, as I see it, from the so-called 'Critical Theory' of the German Frankfurt School and its extension in the internationally lesser-known Hanover School, including among others Oskar Negt (1971), Alfred Lorenzer (1972), Thomas Leithäuser (1976), Thomas Ziehe (Ziehe and Stubenrauch 1982) and Regina Becker-Schmidt (1987). These authors, thoroughly dealt with in my previously mentioned book (Illeris 2002), are characterised by their connection of the psychodynamic and societal sides of learning in the concept of socialisation, just as the internationally better-known members of the Frankfurt School such as

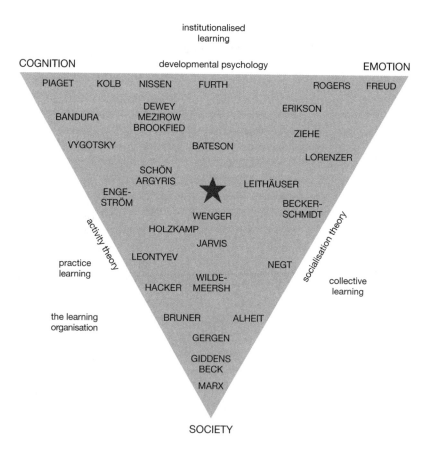

Figure 6.3 Positions in the learning triangle.

Adorno, Horkheimer, Marcuse and Habermas take their point of departure by connecting the theories of Marxism and Psychoanalysis.

In the bottom of the triangle, close to the social-societal pole, some distinctly sociological positions are situated, such as those of Anthony Giddens (1990, 1991) and Ulrich Beck (1992), who do not deal explicitly with learning theory but nevertheless, at least in my opinion, have created important contributions to the understanding of contemporary learning conditions. Also some social psychological positions, such as the before-mentioned social constructionism as signified by Kenneth Gergen, must be placed in this area.

Finally, there are some contributions which must be placed close to the centre of the triangle as they more or less directly attempt to address all the three dimensions of learning in a balanced way. I see British Peter Jarvis (1992) and American Etienne Wenger (1998) as the most prominent of such contributors – and hope that my own approach will also deserve a placement here.

In Figure 6.3 I conclude this chapter by showing how in my book I have placed the theorists who have been my main sources in relation to the learning triangle, and thereby also how I see their mutual relations. This figure also includes other names than those I have mentioned here, as the purpose of showing it is mainly to illustrate how it can be used for the positioning of authors and approaches.

Similarly, the triangle has proved to be a good reference for structuring discussions and attempts to plan or analyse learning and educational practices, as it inspires to take the whole relevant field of conditions into consideration.

References

Argyris, Chris and Schön, Donald A. (1996) *Organizational Learning II – Theory, Method, and Practice*, Reading, MA: Addison-Wesley.

Beck, Ulrich (1992) *Risk Society: Towards a New Modernity*, London: Sage.

Becker-Schmidt, Regina (1987) 'Dynamik sozialen Lernens' [Dynamics of Social Learning], in Regina Becker-Schmidt and Gudrun-Axeli Knapp, *Geschlechtertrennung – Geschlechterdifferenz* [Gender Separation – Gender Difference], Bonn: J. H. W. Dietz Nachf.

Bruner, Jerome (1996) *The Culture of Education*, Cambridge, MA: Harvard University Press.

Damasio, Antonio R. (1994) *Descartes' Error: Emotion, Reason and the Human Brain*, New York: Grosset/Putnam.

Engeström, Yrjö (1987) *Learning by Expanding: An Activity–Theoretical Approach to Developmental Research*, Helsinki: Orienta-Kunsultit.

Flavell, John H. (1963) *The Developmental Psychology of Jean Piaget*, New York: Van Nostrand.

Freud, Anna (1942) *The Ego and the Mechanisms of Defence*, London: Hogarth Press.

Furth, Hans G. (1987) *Knowledge as Desire*, New York: Columbia University Press.

Gergen, Kenneth J. (1991) *The Saturated Self: Dilemmas of Identity in Contemporary Life*, New York: Basic Books.

—— (1994) *Realities and Relationships*, Cambridge, MA: Harvard University Press.

Giddens, Anthony (1990) *The Consequences of Modernity*, Stanford: Stanford University Press.

—— (1991) *Modernity and Self-Identity*, Cambridge: Polity Press.

Holzkamp, Klaus (1995) *Lernen – Subjektwissenschaftliche Grundlegung* [Learning – the Basics of a Science of the Subject], Frankfurt a.M.: Campus.

Illeris, Knud (2002) *The Three Dimensions of Learning: Contemporary Learning Theory in the Tension Field between the Cognitive, the Emotional and the Social*, UK: NIACE.

—— (2003) 'Towards a Contemporary and Comprehensive Theory of Learning', *International Journal of Lifelong Education* 22 (4): 296–406.

Jarvis, Peter (1992) *Paradoxes of Learning: On Becoming an Individual in Society*, San Francisco: Jossey-Bass.

Kolb, David A. (1984) *Experiential Learning*, Englewood Cliffs, NJ: Prentice-Hall.

Lave, Jean and Wenger, Etienne (1991) *Situated Learning: Legitimate Peripheral Participation*, New York: Cambridge University Press.

Leithäuser, Thomas (1976) *Formen des Alltagsbewusstseins* [The Forms of Everyday Consciousness], Frankfurt a.M.: Campus.

Leontyev, Aleksei N. (1981 [1959]) *Problems of the Development of the Mind*, Moscow: Progress (collected manuscripts from the 1930s).

Lorenzer, Alfred (1972) *Zur Begründung einer materialistichen Sozialisationstheorie* [To the Basics of a Materialist Theory of Socialisation], Frankfurt a.M.: Suhrkamp.

Mager, Robert F. (1961) 'On the Sequencing of Instructional Content', *Psychological Reports* 9: 405–13.

Mezirow, Jack (1991) *Transformative Dimensions of Adult Learning*, San Francisco: Jossey-Bass.

Negt, Oskar (1971) *Soziologische Phantasie und exemplarisches Lernen* [Sociological Imagination and Exemplary Learning], Frankfurt a.M.: Europäische Verlagsanstalt.

Nissen, Thomas (1970) *Indlæring og pædagogik* [Learning and Pedagogics], Copenhagen: Munksgaard.

Piaget, Jean (1952) *The Origins of Intelligence in Children*, New York: International Universities Press.

Rogers, Carl R. (1951) *Client-Centered Therapy*, Boston: Houghton-Mifflin.

Vygotsky, Lev S. (1978) *Mind in Society: The Development of Higher Psychological Processes*, Cambridge, MA: Harvard University Press.

Wenger, Etienne (1998) *Communities of Practice: Learning, Meaning, and Identity*, Cambridge, MA: Cambridge University Press.

Ziehe, Thomas and Stubenrauch, Herbert (1982) *Plädoyer für ungewöhnlisches Lernen* [Pleading for Unusual Learning], Reinbek: Rowohlt.

Chapter 7

Cognition

Mark Tennant

One aim of this volume is to encourage a wider understanding of human learning. Ironically, the application of the study of cognition to understanding human learning has long been criticised by learning theorists and practitioners as being too narrow and compartmentalised, and as having a too restricted view of the person. However, a casual glance at any introductory text on human cognition reveals quite disparate theoretical approaches (such as functionalism, structuralism, connectionism, gestalt psychology, and so on) and widely different phenomena being studied (such as attention, pattern recognition, memory and forgetting, perception, concept development, information processing, thinking and problem solving). It appears that the study of cognition is as disparate as the field of psychology itself. However, what is common to these disparate theoretical positions and interests is 'the belief that elements inside the head are causal in directing human behaviour' (Howes 1990: 25). This seems an unremarkable statement, but the advent of behaviourism in the middle part of the twentieth century provided a strong challenge to such a belief. The re-emergence of cognitive psychology in the 1960s was made possible by the failure of behaviourism to translate mental constructs into behaviourist terms and, perhaps more importantly, the success of the challenges to behaviourism posed by structuralist theories and by a new interest in information processing models of human cognition associated with computerisation. This chapter takes up contemporary exemplars of these two apparently opposing traditions in cognitive psychology, cognitive structuralism and information processing, and looks at how they shape contemporary understandings and issues in learning. At the outset, however, I should point out a common concern in the development of both of the above traditions: the growing awareness of the need to take into account the complexities of context in order to understand the functioning of mind in situ. Thus there has been a general move away from identifying abstract, decontexualised cognitive attributes separated from meaningful action in the world towards a more inclusive understanding of cognition as it operates through engagement in everyday life. In many ways this common concern unites these traditions. In this chapter two specific exemplars (or rather legacies) of these traditions are explored: the design of computer-based expert systems, and theoretical and empirical work on situated cognition.

The design of computer-based expert systems

The literature on expertise and practical intelligence (see Chi *et al.* 1988; Tennant and Pogson 1995; Sternberg and Grigorenko 2003) illustrates quite nicely the attempt of cognitive psychology to come to grips with the complexities of context. Indeed, the interest in practical intelligence can be seen as a reaction to the abstract and decontextualised nature of traditional tests of intelligence. In the literature on practical intelligence and expertise there is a shared presupposition that expertise is built upon the knowledge and skill gained through sustained practice and experience. This presupposition is shared with a very different attempt to understand expertise: using the knowledge and experience of experts to construct computer-based expert systems.

Gordon (1992), for example, poses two questions: what is the nature of knowledge and/or skills used by an expert? And what are the implications of the nature of expertise for methods of transferring knowledge and skill? With respect to the first question, she proposes a particular viewpoint whereby the development of expertise revolves around changes in declarative and procedural knowledge. Using Anderson's distinction between declarative and procedural knowledge (the former is knowledge 'that' and the latter, knowledge 'how'), Gordon proposes a three-stage model in the development of expertise:

Cognitive stage characterised by an accumulation of declarative knowledge.
Associative stage characterised by the development of domain-specific procedures resulting from the repeated use of declarative knowledge in given situations.
Autonomous stage characterised by the procedures becoming more automatised with procedural knowledge operating quickly and automatically.

This model proposes that expertise develops through an initial use of declarative knowledge that, through experience, is gradually transformed into procedural knowledge. While the distinction between declarative knowledge and procedural knowledge is well supported by empirical work in cognitive psychology (see Gordon 1992: 102), the implications for methods of knowledge acquisition for the design of expert systems are less clear. Assuming that experts use both declarative and procedural knowledge, and that it is desirable to elicit both types of knowledge from experts, then the problem becomes how to elicit procedural (or tacit) knowledge. Declarative knowledge is fairly straightforward – any method requiring the expert to verbalise his or her knowledge would be appropriate, such as structured interviews, think-aloud verbal protocols and retrospective verbal protocols. With respect to procedural knowledge, Gordon argues: 'by definition, procedural knowledge cannot be directly verbalised. It is therefore counterproductive to ask an expert how he or she made a decision or solved a problem' (1992: 110).

So what can be done to tap into expert procedural knowledge? Gordon (1992) argues that the best way is to infer rules from the observation of expert problem solving and decision making. This requires the experts to be solving a variety of 'real world' problems from very familiar to very novel, with naturally occurring verbalisations being spoken aloud.

> To infer procedural rule, the system developer and expert 'observe' the relationship between three types of information: the situational characteristics, the intermediate knowledge states verbalised during problem solving and the final answer. This input/output information is then used to infer rules that could feasibly underlie the behavior.
>
> (p. 113)

Another approach to eliciting the experience and knowledge of experts is provided by Prerau *et al.* (1992). They distinguish between three levels of knowledge:

Experiential knowledge which refers to the heuristic rules domain experts develop through extensive experience in the field.

> Through their familiarity with the domain, their training, and their experiences in solving problems within that domain, the experts develop heuristics, or rules of thumb. We call this knowledge based on extensive field applications experiential knowledge. Such associational, experiential knowledge has been referred to as shallow knowledge.
>
> (pp. 137–8)

Deep knowledge which is knowledge of the fundamental principles of a domain, typically used by novices who, lacking enough experience to develop heuristics, use fundamental theorems or formulae to solve a problem.
Expertise knowledge which is an intermediate level between direct experience and deep knowledge.

> This level is characterised by knowledge that is shallow – however this shallow knowledge is based on some combination of the deep knowledge of the experts and their related experiential heuristics, and not directly on their practical experience
>
> (p. 138)

The authors claim to have used both the 'expertise' and 'experiential knowledge' of domain in the development of a large telecommunications expert system known as COMPASS (Central Office Maintenance Printout Analysis and Suggestion System). The knowledge elicitation process involved working with a designated maintenance expert for one week per month over a two-year period. The aim was to capture as much expert domain knowledge as possible. Prerau *et al.* (1992) describe three phases of interactions with the domain expert:

Acquaintance phase which involved the knowledge engineers becoming familiar with the problem domain and its terminology and mapping out the areas of knowledge mainly using structured and unstructured interviews. The knowledge engineers immersed themselves in the domain and the expert learnt a great deal about the expert system technology being used.
Encoding expert domain information which involves capturing the knowledge using structured interviews and real test case analysis primarily applying English 'if–then' rules to record the knowledge. The rules were then reviewed with the expert, tested on new data and modified accordingly.
Verifying and validating the program which involved comparing the expert analysis of real and hypothetical data with the expert system program analysis.

Ford and Adams-Webber (1992) argue that the above approaches to knowledge acquisition are laborious and that there are often communication difficulties between the domain expert and the knowledge engineer. They advocate more automated systems for knowledge acquisition and, in this context, propose the use of personal construct theory as a theoretical basis for the design and construction of automated knowledge acquisition tools (i.e. tools used by knowledge engineers to elicit domain expert knowledge). Personal construct theory postulates that each person constructs a model of the world and, much like a scientist, attempts to predict and control the world, forming hypotheses and testing them against experience. In this account, cognitive development entails the transformation of the structure and content of personal construct systems. As the name suggests, personal construct theory adopts a constructivist epistemology (where events can be construed in multiple ways) as opposed to a realist epistemology (where objects of our knowledge are seen as independent of our construal of them). Ford and Adams-Webber identify the implications of adopting a constructivist approach:

- Expertise cannot be 'mined' like a natural resource that is harvested, captured, transferred – rather, it is constructed by the expert and reconstructed by the knowledge engineer.
- Experts construct a repertory of working hypotheses based on experience and book knowledge – and the more expert the more the

importance of personally constructed knowledge. The aim then is to get experts to bring their personal knowledge to the surface.

- Using a group of experts to elicit expert knowledge does not produce the best outcome, largely because of differences in their personally constructed expertise. The best approach is to build different knowledge bases for each expert rather than try to identify a singular 'correct' knowledge base.

(Ford and Adams-Webber 1993, pp. 130–3)

The above approaches to designing computer-based expert systems are interesting from an educator's point of view because the various ways in which knowledge is 'elicited' from experts overlap significantly with a range of well-documented experiential learning strategies and/or research approaches to experiential learning such as brainstorming, group work, scenario analysis, laddering, repertory grids, protocol analysis, ethnography, observation, and so on. But educators are not simply concerned with how to elicit expertise, they are interested in how such expertise develops. We know that experience is important, but how is experience utilised to gain expertise and what is the role of the teacher or trainer? In this regard it is crucial to distinguish between expertise as an outcome and the acquisition of expertise as a process. For example, in Chi *et al.*'s (1988) summary of the generic qualities of expertise they note that experts are faster and more economical, partly because they do not conduct an extensive search of the data or information available. This does not imply that novices should be warned against conducting extensive searches of the data or urged to take short cuts. Quite the contrary: extensive searches of the data (using standard, abstract algorithms, perhaps learnt 'out of context') are presumably important at the novice stage, and in this sense expertise is built upon the experience of being a novice. But it may be that the generic qualities of expertise are actually developed from experience and not from the application of 'fundamental' principles to experience. Alignment on this issue demarcates different approaches to education and to the study of expertise.

The practical intelligence/expertise literature and the expert systems literature have a remarkably similar agenda in that they are both concerned with mapping the qualities of experts. In the former case the purpose is to problematise traditional conceptions of what we mean by 'intelligence', and to highlight the nature of knowledge and skill forged from experience. In the latter case the purpose is to replicate the skills of known experts in computer-based expert systems. In both cases the common problem is to identify and elicit the qualities of experts. But these qualities do not reveal themselves without effort, largely because it is acknowledged by all concerned that expertise involves a great deal of 'tacit' knowledge – knowledge which is not readily verbalised. For this reason researchers and 'knowledge engineers' respectively have developed strategies for identifying expert knowledge. But this quest immediately raised theoretical issues about precisely what it is that is being identified or elicited. Illustrative of these theoretical issues are the distinctions made between 'declarative' and 'procedural' knowledge, between 'domain specific' as opposed to 'generic' expertise, between 'shallow' and 'deep' knowledge, and between 'realist' and 'constructivist' views of knowledge. Furthermore, different models are proposed depicting the transition from novice to expert. Typically, while both strands of the expertise literature foreground the importance of context in understanding expertise, there is a pervasive view that expertise is not solely the result of accumulated experience. The literature draws attention to the importance of a more principled or higher-order representation of problems among experts. While knowledge is seen as domain specific, there is at least considerable transferability within each domain, and it is clear that expertise is built on a number of generic capacities that can be utilised in different contexts: such as problem formation, self-monitoring skills, higher-order principled thinking, and flexibility and adaptability to the environment in problem solving.

Ironically, while both generic and domain specific expertise is acknowledged, generic expertise seems to be more highly valued. Symptomatic of this is Prerau et al.'s (1992) labelling of experience-based knowledge as 'shallow' and knowledge of the fundamental principles of a domain as 'deep'. Why are these metaphors applied in this way? I suggest it is because the fundamental project of the strand of cognitive psychology, which informs much of the expertise literature, is to identify generic models of cognitive functioning, and this depends crucially on some level of expertise which is fundamental and cuts across different contexts. In relation to this point, it is instructive to note that many of the various models of the development of expertise typically have foundational 'generic' knowledge as the starting point for development. Thus, while cognitive psychology attempts to come to terms with the 'problem' of context, its traditional focus on the individual as the site of cognitive activity and the repository of knowledge precludes it from adequately addressing the 'social' dimensions of expertise.

Cognitive structuralism and the social – situated cognition

Another strand of cognitive theory, cognitive structuralism, also has a history of attempting to account for context, largely as a result of early critiques which focused on its disregard for context. For example, Piaget's emphasis on an invariant (and universal) sequence of stages leading to mature formal operational thought and his apparent disregard for psychological phenomena which defy structural analysis (feelings, beliefs, values, imagination, desire) attracted at the time a flood of what may be called 'ideology' critiques (Broughton 1981). The claim being made was that his developmental theory needed to be understood in its social and historical context, and therefore the stages he describes should be seen as an outgrowth of this context.

Piagetian developmental theory is criticised as a form of ideological legitimisation which supports the current organisation and political stratification of society and rationalises the extant socialisation processes reproducing the present social order, by showing them to be accurate reflections of 'natural', quasi-biological sequences of individual growth. From this critical perspective, both the sequence of structures and the theory of it represent purely conventional meaning systems, with no clear objectivity. The very concept of 'development' can even be construed as a reification of history deriving from the nineteenth-century ideology of progress (1981: 387).

But, as Biddell points out, it is important to distinguish between Piaget's stage theory and his constructivist theory of knowledge and not to portray him solely as presenting an asocial view of development. Biddell concedes that Piaget's 'stage theory is based on an interactionist metaphor in which the relation between the person and the social world is conceived as an individual standing apart from and interacting with a social environment' (1992: 307). In contrast, 'Piaget's constructivism implicitly supports a contextualist approach to knowledge development and stands in contradiction to the individualism of this stage theory' (ibid.). It is Piaget's constructivism (especially through the twin concepts of assimilation and accommodation) that links him to Vygotsky and ultimately to contemporary post-Vygotskian theories of situated and/or distributed cognition.

It is of course Vygotsky (1978) who is seen from a contemporary standpoint as providing a more complete account of the role of historical, social and cultural forces in development. Daniels (2001) provides a detailed account of how Vygotsky emphasises the sociocultural nature of human activity and development. The concept of mediation is central to an understanding of how culture enters into psychological processes. Basically, Vygotsky's thesis is that relations between subjects and objects are mediated by both signs and tools.

> A most essential difference between sign and tool … is the different ways they orient behavior. The tool's function is to serve as the conductor of human influence on the object of activity; it is externally oriented; it must lead to changes in objects. It is a means by which human external activity is aimed at mastering, and triumphing over, nature. The sign, on the other hand, changes nothing in the object of a psychological operation. It is a means of internal activity aimed at mastering oneself; the sign is internally oriented … The mastering of nature and the mastering of behavior are mutually linked, just as man's alteration of nature alters man's own nature … One thing is already certain. Just as the first use of tools refutes the notion that development represents the mere unfolding of the child's organically predetermined system of activity, so the first use of signs demonstrates that there cannot be a single organically predetermined internal system of activity that exists for each psychological function.
>
> (1978: 55)

He goes on to explain how the interpersonal becomes intrapersonal in the child's development:

> Every function in the child's development appears twice: first, on the social level, and later, on the individual level; first between people (interpsychological), and then inside the child (intrapsychological). This applies equally to voluntary attention, to logical memory, and to the formation of concepts. All the higher functions originate as actual relations between human individuals ... The internalisation of socially rooted and historically developed activities is the distinguishing feature of human psychology.
>
> (1978: 57)

The apparently intractable problem of how the 'interpersonal' becomes 'intrapersonal', or how the 'outside' comes to be 'inside', has been played out in a number of ways in sociology and psychology. Following Vygotskian roots, Matusov (1998) distinguishes between internalisation and participation models. He presents them as two different worldviews, in true dialectical style presenting the internalisation 'thesis' and the participation 'antithesis' as outlined below. In so doing, Matusov argues for the adoption of the participation model: 'in the participation model, sociocultural activity unites external and internal, individual and social, cultural and biological' (1998: 335). The problem with the internalisation model is that it relies on the dualism of 'individual' and 'society' and privileges the individual in this relationship in the sense that it is the individual as a psychological entity that is emphasised, as illustrated.

Daniels (2001) outlines the various 'versions' of internalisation and participation models (see Valsiner 1997; Ratner 1999). The basic tension has to do with the nature or existence of boundaries separating 'inner' and 'outer' worlds and the posited level of individual agency and autonomy for the developing human. One's alignment on these tensions clearly has an impact on pedagogical practices, especially concerning the nature of the learning activity being undertaken (e.g. the role of internal cognitive processes as opposed to collaborative activities) and how learning resources are incorporated into pedagogical practices – as Daniels remarks, 'The critical issue is with respect to whether the resources that a collective culture embodies are regarded as fixed offerings from which the individual selects or they constitute the starting points for negotiation' (2001: 42).

Ratner is highly critical of the 'individualistic' approach to cultural psychology:

> Divorcing personal interactions from social activities and conditions, the individualistic approach to cultural psychology acts as a deculturizing agent just as psychoanalysis, behaviourism, phenomenology, and

other traditional psychological approaches do. Exaggerating individual agency, autonomy, and diversity also denigrates the reality of culture altogether. Shared, organized culture becomes devalued.

(1999: 19)

Table 7.1 Contrasting internalisation and participation models

Internalisation thesis	Participation antithesis
Social and psychological planes are separate, with the social plane preceding the psychological plane in ontogenesis (e.g. development of a child).	Social and psychological planes mutually constitute each other and are inseparable.
Note: dualism of social and individual	Note: the social and the individual are inseparable.
Joint and solo activities are separate, with solo activity being psychologically and developmentally more advanced than the corresponding joint activity.	Joint and solo activities mutually constitute each other and are inseparable aspects of sociocultural activity. Sociocultural activities cannot be reduced to mental functions that can, in principle, be performed by one individual.
Note: focus on individual (solo) activity	Note: mental functions are embedded in sociocultural activity.
An individual can take skills and functions from one activity and bring them to another activity.	Skills and functions are embedded in sociocultural activity (Lave 1988).
Note: skills and attributes are features of the individual and can be applied across contexts.	Note: the individual cannot transcend sociocultural activity.
The course of development (i.e. its teleology) is objectively defined by human sociocultural nature.	The notion of development, like the notions of activity and learning, is grounded in meaning and thus is distributed, interpreted, and renegotiated.
Note: individual development is an unfolding of our true 'nature'.	Note: development is relative and contested.
Development should be studied as a comparison of individual skills and functions before, during and after a specially designed social intervention aiming to promote 'the zone of proximal development' (Vygotsky 1978) and internalisation.	Development can be observed and studied as the processes of changes of participation validated by the changing community (Lave and Wenger 1991).
Note: the focus of study is the individual.	Note: the focus of study is the community of practice.

Source: Tabled extracts from Matusov (1998: 326–49) after Daniels (2001: 40)

This is certainly not a charge which can be directed towards Lave and Wenger (1991) and Greeno (1997). These authors, who are firmly located within a 'participation' model in their conception of situated learning, provide a radical departure from traditional ways of conceiving learning and the development of knowledge. For Lave and Wenger, the essential thing about learning is that it involves participation in a community of practice, which is essentially a community engaged in a common set of tasks, with its associated stories, traditions and ways of working. At first this participation is peripheral (hence the term 'legitimate peripheral participation'), but it increases gradually in engagement and complexity until the learner becomes a full participant in the sociocultural practices of the community (an 'old timer' rather than a 'newcomer'). They cite studies of communities of practice and comment on the way in which participation in the activities of these communities mediates learning. The interest is in how learners in quite divergent communities move from peripheral to full participation. Their examples range from the quite informal and family-oriented apprenticeship of Yucatec midwives, where the learning is almost invisible, to the high technology and formal recruitment and training of quartermasters, and to the more recognisable master–apprentice relationship in the training of butchers. They point out the importance of having effective access to what is to be learned, and how the physical layout and the culture of work enhance or constrain participation by opening or closing opportunities for observation, mentoring, guidance and collaborative work. They emphasise access to practice as a resource for learning rather than instruction, and the value of relevant settings and strong goals for learning.

Their conception of learning entails quite a different mindset: away from the individual and towards the community. They are keen to distance themselves from the individualised psychological tradition which emphasises learning by doing, reflection on experience, and a decentring from the teacher to the learner, emphasising the view that learning is an 'integral and inseparable aspect of social practice' (Lave and Wenger 1991: 31).

Learning is not so much a matter of individuals acquiring mastery over knowledge and processes of reasoning, it is a matter of co-participants engaging in a community of practice. The focus is thus on the community rather than the individual. Allied to this view of the learner is a rejection of the idea that learners acquire structures or schemata through which they understand the world. It is participation frameworks which have structure, not the mental representations of individuals.

It is not surprising to find that Lave and Wenger reject the idea that knowledge can in any way be general, abstract or decontextualised. From this perspective, phenomena of interest to both psychologists and educators, such as the transfer of learning, are conceived quite differently, as illustrated by Greeno et al. (1993).

Knowing is the ability to interact with things and other people in a situation, and learning is improvement in that ability – that is getting better at participating in a situated activity. The question of transfer, then, is to understand how learning to participate in an activity in one situation can influence one's ability to participate in another activity in a different situation.

(1993: 100)

Transfer is not a matter of learners acquiring abstract knowledge and procedures which are applied to many situations; rather, it is a matter of 'learning to participate in interactions in ways that succeed over a broad range of situations' (Greeno 1997: 7). Thus 'teaching for transfer' is not enhanced through teaching abstract decontextualised concepts, or by building simple component skills in isolation until the learner is prepared for the complexities and 'wholeness' of practice: it is enhanced by taking into account the 'kinds of activities in which we want students to learn to be successful, and develop learning environments in which they can develop their abilities to participate in the general kinds of practices that are important to them' (Greeno 1997: 13). It is therefore possible to arrange learning situations that support more general learning – but the emphasis is on the 'situation' in which the learner participates, not on the knowledge and skill 'acquired' by the learner.

The value of the work of Lave and others on situated learning is that they draw attention to the need to understand knowledge and learning in context, how new knowledge comes to be invented in practice, and how learning occurs through participation in a community of practice. In pursuing their project they make a number of claims which can certainly be contested. For example, the claim that in traditional cognitive theory there is a division between learning and everyday activity certainly cannot be sustained, at least with respect to cognitive structuralism which also claims that activity is the source of knowledge. Similarly, to portray cognitive structuralism as being only concerned with the transfer of knowledge ignores its strong dialectical base, and to argue that internalisation assumes a kind of homogeneous world without conflict ignores the way in which the concept of internalisation specifically addresses the problem of conflict. But these criticisms do not necessarily detract from the main thrust of the situated learning project, which nevertheless does depend on at least two claims: first, that it makes no sense to talk of knowledge that is decontextualised, abstract or general; and second, that new knowledge and learning are properly conceived as being located in communities of practice.

The situated learning approach of Billett (1996) offers the best attempt to date at reconciling the traditional cognitive and sociocultural perspectives, thereby overcoming some of the shortcomings and limitations of the research and theory hitherto discussed. For Billett it is goal-directed problem solving in particular situations which provides the means for constructing knowledge: 'as individuals engage in goal directed activities, they access, manipulate, and transform cognitive structures' (1996: 271).

Billett departs from the cognitive tradition in his acknowledgment that different forms of social practices lead to different ways of appropriating and structuring knowledge. His working out of this idea is quite elaborate, but basically he is saying that there are a variety of knowledge sources in a community of practice (such as other workers, hints, reminders, explanations, observations, listening, dealing with authentic problems, one's personal history), and that these have an impact on the way knowledge is appropriated and structured. Billett (1994) investigated workplace learning in a mining and secondary processing plant. He interviewed fifteen shift-workers and gathered data about how participants interacted with both the structured learning arrangements at the plant and the unstructured learning resulting from daily work practice. He documented the perceived utility of different learning resources: learning guides, computer-based learning, video, mentors, direct instruction, observing and listening, other workers, everyday activities and the work environment. He found that the informal elements of the learning system were the most valued by operators in assisting with workplace tasks and the resolution of problems encountered. An interesting aspect of this study is the rating of the utility of different learning resources for the development of different types of knowledge (propositional knowledge, procedural knowledge and dispositional knowledge). The data obtained supports the perceived potency of 'everyday activities', 'observing and listening' and 'other workers' as sources of all three types of knowledge. Billett, however, warns that, while informal learning clearly supports the development of higher-order procedural knowledge, workers express concern about the possibility of developing conceptual (propositional) knowledge through informal means only. There is therefore scope for making the tacit understandings of skilled workers more explicit, which may mean periods of formal instruction.

More recently Billett (2003) warns against an 'oversocialised' conception of learning. He draws attention to the unique life histories individuals bring to their participation in social practices:

> Understanding the interdependence between individuals' learning and the social and cultural contributions to that learning is a contested project within psychological thought, as it is within sociology and philosophy. My interest in this interdependence has its origins in the representations of knowledge of hairdressers which yielded a legacy of workplace norms, practices and values that were identified as shaping the conduct of their work. However, contributions beyond the particular workplace were also identified as shaping these individuals'

vocational practice, thereby also influencing how they worked and learnt through their current work. More than being merely idiosyncratic, these contributions had their genesis in the events in the hairdressers' life histories. So, beyond the immediate social experience, premediate experiences – those occurring earlier – that, in turn, shape their postmediate experiences – those occurring later – need to be accounted for in considering the social geneses of individuals' cognition. This suggests a more comprehensive account of the social basis of learning than one privileging situational contributions, such as in communities of practice, activity systems and distributed cognition.

(2003: 2)

Billett's approach exemplifies the kind of research needed to flesh out the processes underlying the development of expertise, because it documents how workers utilise their experiences (and resources available to them) for learning of a kind which has some general applicability. His approach adds a much needed learning dimension to the quest of cognitive psychology to incorporate context.

Concluding remarks

I have argued that a key characteristic of the development of cognitive psychology is its attempt to take account of context, including the broader social and cultural context. This has led to a number of theoretical tensions, especially on the issue of the role of individual knowledge within a community of practice, the degree to which knowledge can be said to be generic and context independent, the way in which knowledge can be utilised in new situations, and the processes through which knowledge is incorporated or disbursed among individuals in a community. How are educators to make use of these tensions? A good starting point would be for educators to note Daniels' (2001) intention:

My purpose here is not to 'decide' which of these positions is 'correct'; rather I am concerned to identify the possible theoretical positions that may come to influence pedagogic practice. These theoretical debates may be seen as sites for the generation of tools which may inform pedagogic innovation.

(2001: 41)

In particular, educators need to understand how their practices invariably assume certain things about learners and knowledge and about their roles and responsibilities. Take, for example, the proposition that knowledge is generated in situ (such as a workplace). If this is accepted, are learners seen as producers of knowledge, as consumers of learning, or as performers of skills and attitudes? Or is there a shifting interplay between these conceptions of learners? Also, the 'teacher' in these circumstances can take up a number of positions: an arbiter of what constitutes worthy knowledge, a guide who assists learners to 'learn from experience', a measurement specialist who monitors performance, a facilitator who 'processes' the concerns and interests of learners, or a commentator or decoder who addresses issues of power and authority. The teacher–learner relationship in 'situational' learning is thus one which is shifting and constantly open to negotiation.

The task for teachers is not to align themselves with a theoretical orientation and adjust their practices accordingly. Rather, it is to interrogate their practice in the context of ongoing theoretical debate.

References

Biddell, T. (1992) 'Beyond Interactionism in Contextualist Models of Development', *Human Development* 35 (5): 306–15.

Billett, S. (1994) 'Situated Learning – a Workplace Experience', *Australian Journal of Adult and Community Education* 34 (2): 112–31.

—— (1996) 'Situated Learning: Bridging Sociocultural and Cognitive Theorising', *Learning and Instruction* 6: 263–80.

—— (2003) 'Individualising the Social – Socialising the Individual: Interdependence between Social and Individual Agency in Vocational Learning', Keynote Address, 11th Annual International Conference on Post-Compulsory Education and Training, 'Enriching Learning Cultures', 1–3 December, Gold Coast, Australia.

Broughton, J. M. (1981) 'Piaget's Structural Developmental Psychology: Ideology-critique and the Possibility of a Critical Developmental Theory', *Human Development* 24: 382–411.

Chi, M. T. H., Glaser, R. and Farr, M. J. (eds) (1988) *The Nature of Expertise*, Hillsdale, NJ: Lawrence Erlbaum Associates.

Daniels, H. (2001) *Vygotsky and Pedagogy*, London: RoutledgeFalmer.

Ford, K. and Adams-Webber, J. (1992) 'Knowledge Acquisition and Constructivist Epistemology', in R. Hoffmann (ed.) *The Psychology of Expertise: Cognitive Research and Empirical Artificial Intelligence*, London: Lawrence Erlbaum, pp. 121–36.

Gordon, S. (1992) 'Implications of Cognitive Theory for Knowledge Acquisition', in R. Hoffmann (ed.) *The Psychology of Expertise: Cognitive Research and Empirical Artificial Intelligence*, London: Lawrence Erlbaum, pp. 99–120.

Greeno, J. (1997) 'On Claims that Answer the Wrong Questions', *Educational Researcher* 26 (1): 5–17.

Greeno, J., Moore, J. and Smith, D. (1993) 'Transfer of Situated Learning', in M. B. Howes (1993) *The Psychology of Human Cognition: Mainstream and Genevan Traditions*, New York: Pergamon.

Howes, M. B. (1990) *The Psychology of Human Cognition: Mainstream and Genevan Traditions*, New York: Pergamon.

Lave, J. (1988) *Cognition in Practice: Mind, Mathematics and Culture in Everyday Life*, Cambridge: Cambridge University Press.

Lave, J. and Wenger, E. (1991) *Situated Learning: Legitimate Peripheral Participation*, Cambridge: Cambridge University Press.

Matusov, E. (1998) 'When Solo Activity is Not Privileged: Participation and Internalisation Models of Development', *Human Development* 41: 326–49.

Prerau, D., Adler, M. and Gunderson, A. (1992) 'Eliciting and Using Experiential Knowledge and General Expertise', in R. Hoffmann (ed.) *The Psychology of Expertise: Cognitive Research and Empirical Artificial Intelligence*, London: Lawrence Erlbaum, pp. 99–120.

Ratner, C. (1999) 'Three Approaches to Cultural Psychology: A Critique', *Cultural Dynamics* 11: 7–31.

Sternberg, R. and Grigorenko, E. (eds) (2003) *The Psychology of Abilities, Competencies, and Expertise*, New York: Cambridge University Press.

Tennant, M. and Pogson, P. (1995) *Learning and Change in the Adult Years: A Developmental Perspective*, San Francisco: Jossey-Bass.

Valsiner, J. (1997) *Culture and the Development of Children's Action: A Theory of Human Development* (second edition), New York: John Wiley.

Vygotsky, L. S. (1978) *Mind in Society: The Development of Higher Psychological Processes*, Cambridge, MA: Harvard University Press.

Chapter 8

Human learning

The interrelationship of the individual and the social structures

Peter Jarvis

Everybody is born into a social environment and so, in one sense, we are never free from our life-world. Perhaps, more significantly, even in the womb we are exposed to outside pressures that are not only of a biological nature. I well remember teaching a class on human learning at the University of Alaska when a young lady from the First Nation people exclaimed, 'My people teach us to talk to the baby in the womb.' We are exposed to our significant others before birth. Total individuality may be a myth of our own making. From our birth, we are socialised (learn to adopt) into the culture of our life-world and learn to live in harmony with it, learning the language, symbols and behaviour patterns appropriate to our position in it. Indeed, we can often reach a state within our life-world where we are so much in harmony with the culture of our life-world that we take it for granted.

> I trust the world that has been known by me up until now will continue further and that consequently the stock of knowledge obtained from my fellow men and formed from my own experiences will continue to preserve its fundamental validity … From this assumption follows the further and fundamental one: that I can repeat my past successful acts. So long as the structure of the world can be taken as constant, as long as my previous experience is valid, my ability to operate on the world in this and that manner remains in principle preserved.
>
> (Schutz and Luckmann 1974: 7)

In other words, when we are in harmony with our environment, there is little or nothing to learn in that situation and we can presume upon our world. But there are at least two major provisos in this quotation – that 'the structure of the world can be taken as constant' and 'my previous experience is valid'. However, as we age, or change our rank or social status and so on, our changed position in the society means that our previous experiences may not always be valid and, also, we are aware that the structures of society change. Consequently, the situation described here may reflect a time when society changed less rapidly than it does today, but it also reflects specific periods in most of our lives, even in contemporary society, when we can presume upon our situation and repeat our past successful acts. Two things, at least, follow from this: that society is premised on stable social structures in which socialised individuals have no need to learn – although much of the time they do learn something as we shall illustrate below – and, second, that learning occurs when we can no longer presume on our social structures. In other words, when there is no harmony between our experiences and our expectations of how we behave, then we need to learn. Elsewhere in my writings (Jarvis 1987, 1992, 2004 *inter alia*) I have referred to this state as *disjuncture*. Disjuncture can occur when individuals change, either in their social position or in their aspirations, or when society itself changes. In other words, it can be self-induced or other-induced.

However, socialised individuals also continue to learn, albeit within a more restricted framework. The Club of Rome Report *No Limits to Learning* (Botkin *et al.* 1979) illustrates this by dividing learning into two types: maintenance learning, which is 'the acquisition of fixed outlooks, methods and rules for dealing with known and recurring situations ... and is indispensable for the functioning and stability of every society', and innovative learning, which is 'the type of learning that can bring change, renewal, restructuring, and problem reformulation' (Botkin *et al.* 1979: 10). In other words, innovative learning results in changes in the way individuals act.

In the above quotation, Schutz and Luckmann refer to 'experiences', and we use the concept of experience in at least three different ways – our total life, a prolonged period of awareness, or a specific episodic experience. There are significant differences in these concepts of experience: the total life is that which is internalised within our biography whereas the other two occur at the intersection of the inner person and the outer social world. It is here that learning begins. We define learning here (see my discussion in the opening chapter of this book) as *the combination of processes whereby the whole person – body (genetic, physical and biological) and mind (knowledge, skills, attitudes, values, emotions, beliefs and senses) – is in a social situation and constructs an experience which is then transformed cognitively, emotively or practically (or through any combination) and integrated into the individual's own biography.*

With their use of the plural, Schutz and Luckmann are referring to our total life experience, or at least that part of it which is in our consciousness; disjuncture occurs initially in an episodic situation but it may persist. This episodic situation may be immediate, that is we have to decide immediately on how to behave – so that we actually learn from our immediate experience; or it may persist – so that we decide that we have to learn in order to restore that harmony, e.g. by enrolling on a course of study or through a self-directed project of learning, and it is in this latter situation that we see the relationship between disjuncture and motivation.

Since individuals age and change their social status and society changes, we can see that disjunctural states are not a rare occurrence, especially as the speed of change has increased. There have certainly been times in the past (primitive societies) when society and its structures have appeared to be relatively permanent, whereas in contemporary society, which is tremendously complex, both appear to be in a constant flux. Change, both social and personal, then, is a critical factor in our understanding of the sociology of learning, since learning is actually about processes of change. Max Scheler (1926 [1980: 76]) suggested that there are seven forms of knowledge and his categorisation is based on their speed of change. These are:

1   myth and legend – undifferentiated, primitive forms of knowledge based in religion, nature, and so on;
2   knowledge based in natural language – everyday knowledge;
3   religious knowledge – more formulated dogma, and so on;
4   mystical knowledge;
5   philosophical–metaphysical knowledge;
6   mathematical knowledge – mathematics and the natural sciences;
7   technological knowledge.

This is not the place to debate the validity of the classification – although we do need to recall that this was formulated in the 1920s so that it now needs further refinement – but his understanding of the speed of change of knowledge and culture is crucial to this argument. For him, world-view forms of knowledge range from the relatively artificial to the most artificial – the first five forms change very slowly whereas the last changed very rapidly, hour by hour, even then! For him, we may say that the first five are cultural forms of knowledge, whereas the last two are artificial because they change too rapidly to become embedded in the culture of a society. However, our social situation is wider than these types of knowledge and we respond to it in emotive and practical ways, as well as cognitive ones.

Consequently, we can postulate three broad, ideal-type forms of society that, for the sake of convenience only, we can call primitive, modern and late modern. In primitive society, the structures change more slowly and the social actors change their position within it more rapidly, due to the ageing process, and the cultural forms of knowledge predominate; in modern society, that is society that emerged after the Reformation and the Industrial Revolution, both forms of knowledge occurred and were treated as almost equally valid, so that individuals had to learn the more formal and artificial forms of knowledge through education early in their lives, but the way individuals changed their position in society was still celebrated; in late modern society, where the more artificial forms of knowledge predominate, formal school education is insufficient and society changes very rapidly. Each of these three types will now be discussed individually.

Primitive society

Primitive society is local, tribal and pre-industrial. Its forms of knowledge are cultural and they are legitimated either by claims of revelation, or by the priestly, or priest-kingly, social hierarchy. Since the knowledge is cultural and changes slowly, it can be regarded as truth. Moreover, this cultural knowledge also legitimated the authority of the social and religious hierarchy, and hence the 'god-king' type of concept emerged. This is a cyclical position, ultimately, where the cultural knowledge legitimates the social structures that, in turn, legitimate the knowledge! The social structures are fixed by decree and children are initially socialised into their position within them, but all the society's members continue to learn – maintenance learning – as Botkin *et al.* (1979) would assert. But as individuals age they change and their position within the static social structures also has to change. Most primitive societies recognise this transition and have 'rites de passage' (van Gennep 1908 [1960]) which have three stages: a leaving of the initial social status, a period of liminality (betwixt and between) in which innovative learning occurs, and a ritual of re-incorporation into the new status. These times of transition, for instance, are birth, from child to adult, single to married, married to widowhood, and death. During the period of liminality the tribe is able to prepare itself for the change, but more significantly, it prepares those who were changing their status for their new role – in other words it is a time of learning. Liminality is a time when the participants have no fixed social status: it is a time of innovative learning – a new status, new role, new identity, and so on, which become integrated into their biography, or total life experience. During liminality those being initiated into their new position are excluded from the everyday life of the people and undergo a period of learning.

Turner (1969: 81) described this period for puberty thus:

> Liminal entities, such as initiation or puberty rites, may be represented as possessing nothing. They may be disguised as monsters, wear only a strip of clothing, or even go naked, to demonstrate that, as liminal beings, they have no status, property or insignia, secular clothing representing rank or role, position in the kinship system – in short, nothing that may distinguish them from their fellow neophytes or initiands. Their behaviour is normally passive or humble; they must obey their instructors implicitly, and accept arbitrary punishment without complaint. It is as though they are reduced or ground down to a uniform condition to be fashioned anew and endowed with additional powers to enable them to cope with their new station in life.

In other words, the liminal period is one of being prepared for the new status and role in society, which in its turn reinforces the social structures themselves and, as Turner (1969: 89–90) points out:

> The wisdom (*mana*) that is imparted in sacred liminality is not just an aggregate of words and sentences; it has ontological value, it refashions the very being of the neophyte ...
>
> The neophyte in liminality must be *tabula rasa*, a blank sheet, on which is inscribed the knowledge and wisdom of the group, in those respects that pertain to the new status.

The humiliation that the neophytes undergo is a symbolic destruction of the previous status and a preparation for their new position. Innovative learning is socially structured but offered within a 'safe' situation beyond the structures of society. It might be regarded as a sacred act that has its own specific set of pedagogics. This social exclusion is necessary because the structures of society are clearly defined and legitimated and are at risk as individuals pass through them, but all the knowledge learned during this period might still be regarded as cultural since it remains the same for succeeding generations. Once re-incorporated into the new status, the transformed individual conforms to the new role and society and its structures are re-established and reinforced, and then maintenance learning is re-established.

Modern society

With the Reformation in Western Europe came an emphasis on literacy, so that people could read the Bible; this created an opportunity for innovative learning since it offered an opportunity to learn about things beyond the sacred – that is, other than that provided by the Church. It was followed almost inevitably by the Industrial Revolution – when literate people, inspired by their reading of the Bible, wanted to explore and understand the cosmos and master and control the creation. In a sense all research is innovative learning because it moves beyond the known and experienced social structures. Modern society is the one in which the nation state emerged: one that sought to centralise and control both structure and culture; one in which maintenance learning was initially central to the learning processes. Gradually, however, first for theological reasons and thereafter for secular ones, scientific research began: research was, in those early days, a form of self-directed innovative learning. As the Industrial Revolution proceeded, the more artificial forms of knowledge emerged, ones that were not considered essential for the smooth functioning of society. Mathematical and technological knowledge, not embedded in culture nor learned through the sacred rituals of a people, grew in significance. While these new forms of knowledge were seen as threatening to the more traditional ones, the two existed side by side – even though there was the occasional skirmish between religion and science in the new academic circles. Slowly the need grew for more people to learn these new and more artificial forms of knowledge, and there was a gradual movement towards universal education for children. Schools were established and young people were prepared for their life in a more industrial society – initial education was born – but the learning still occurred beyond the social structures since children were being exposed to learning that was unnecessary for the maintenance. Theoretically school children were free to gain sufficient knowledge to enter social structures other than the ones occupied by their parents.

In a sense, however, children in school were rather like the neophytes in liminality – they were supposed to be equal and free to learn and their learning was regarded as a preparation for adulthood. It was a form of innovative learning conducted under much more formalised structures, although often in conditions nearly as callous as those described above. Education served the same function as liminal learning – reproducing society's structures and culture, so that individuals learned to conform to the social patterns of behaviour and thought. Indeed, John Stuart Mill actually claimed that the content of education was to be found in 'the culture which each generation purposely gives to those who are to be their successors' (cited from Lester-Smith 1966: 9). In other words, the knowledge being transmitted was cultural. However, as time passed and the content of the learning changed, more scientific and technological (artificial) knowledge was included in the curriculum. Schooling theoretically did allow for children to achieve a different status and occupy a different place within society from that of their parents. While this has frequently been one of the claims of modern education, the fact that most school education was not totally removed from the structures of society – was not actually liminal – meant that the learning it offers tends to be reproductive of the wider cultural and social structures. Moreover, the shape of society and its workforce changed little, so that there were not the structural opportunities for a great deal of social mobility.

But the nature of the learning ritual was also changed; no longer was it threefold (exit from one social status, liminality, enter a new social status). It was attenuated – only the stage from liminality to the new status. It became either an exit from one social status, or an induction ceremony into a new one – often as a result of the education received at school or the apprenticeship undertaken with a master craftsman. One element or another was emphasised – graduation rituals emphasise the exit from one social status of being a student, while new job rituals emphasise the entry into a new social status. Initially, the learning prepared young people to take their place in a still rather slowly changing society, although the signs of change were there.

In precisely the same way, organisations grew up which had their own distinct ethos that was quite foreign to the traditional ones of primitive tribes – bureaucracies, with a form of rational-legal authority (Weber 1947) legitimating their social structures. Indeed, this was also an organisational society. Office-holders in the organisation were no longer there by sacred legitimation but because they had specified spheres of competence, and 'candidates were selected on the basis of technical qualifications. In the most rational case, this is tested by examination and guaranteed by diplomas certifying technical competence, or both. They are *appointed*, not elected' (Weber 1947: 333). Neither did they occupy their position as a result of their birth. The new artificial knowledge formed the basis of the position in the organisational hierarchy, and individuals joining the organisation had to learn its rules and regulations as part of the process of becoming a member. This was innovative learning, which occurred during a probationary period at the start of employment. Once learned, however, those who achieved membership adhered to the rules and regulations and there was little change in its structures, only changes in personnel. The ongoing learning assumed a maintenance form.

The two forms of learning are quite distinct, and throughout most of the period of modern society this pattern persisted, although there was a gradual change as the cultural forms of knowledge became less significant and the artificial ones grew in importance, so that gradually innovative learning became more common.

In the modern society, adult membership initially demanded an institutionalised innovative learning process before becoming a member, but society changed very slowly because of the predominance of the cultural forms of knowledge and demanded only maintenance learning. This was also true of bureaucracies. In a sense both the organisation and the society demanded rituals of incorporation into adult membership, but they were becoming more symbolic and less ontological and sacred. Liminality had lost its significance in an organised world – but learning was still institutionalised in society in order to protect society's structures although these were becoming more open and more easily permeated.

As industrial society developed, so the significance of artificial knowledge grew. The front-end model of initial education expanded and young people were taking longer and longer to learn the knowledge necessary for them to play their adult roles in a modern world: further education, professional education, higher education and continuing education all emerged in rapid succession. And as society became more orientated to these scientific forms of knowledge, their artificiality became more evident as they began to change rapidly with new discoveries and new research. Society itself was forced to become more flexible to cope with these changes and the structures were loosened – society was becoming open and it became easier for persons to pass through the barriers without ritual. Learning new knowledge enabled individuals to transcend their position in society and to achieve another one, but that learning was innovative and not all of it institutionalised.

Late modern society

This form of society has emerged as a result of globalisation and is driven by the demands of advanced capitalism and information technology. Immediately, then, we see that these demands derive from those artificial forms of knowledge that change 'hour by hour'. No longer does this knowledge legitimate the structures of society and no longer is it cultural. Indeed, this is global society where the boundaries of nationhood and statehood have been transcended. Cultural knowledge has declined in significance as the discourse of late modern society has emerged. Kerr *et al.* (1973) captured this when they suggested that education is 'the handmaiden of industrialism'. Basically they argued that the 'higher education system of industrial society stresses the natural sciences, engineering, medicine, managerial training ... [and t]here is a relatively smaller place for the humanities and the arts' (Kerr *et al.* 1973: 47). They were emphasising that now the knowledge base of such a society is artificial and the necessary learning innovative. With the rapidly changing forms of knowledge, education was forced to change; first it lengthened its provision to cover almost the whole of childhood and young adulthood, and then it has been forced to offer learning opportunities to individuals on a recurrent basis throughout their lifespan. And other institutions, such as work, also offered opportunities for learning. The cultural forms of knowledge, and even maintenance learning, have become less significant – although not redundant!

Consequently, a more open society emerged, and the social situations within which people's experiences are constructed are changing rapidly, so that situations rarely repeat themselves. Consequently, new experiences are constantly being constructed and new learning – throughout the whole of life – takes place. This society with its rapidly changing knowledge was soon to be called the knowledge society, one that, as Stehr (1994) points out, is based on scientific knowledge. Now the knowledge that changes 'hour by hour' forms the basis of society and the life-world. The very openness of society allows for changes in action, or innovative learning, and this can only occur with the decline in the significance of those cultural forms of knowledge that legitimate a slowly changing culture and social structure, and maintenance learning – while still very much part of every day – appears to occupy little place in the social or even educational discourse. But once this happened, it was no longer possible to confine innovative learning to institutionalised periods of separation or within an educational framework – it has become lifelong. Now we have the learning society in which innovative learning has become de-institutionalised and has been incorporated into the ordinary processes of everyday life in precisely the same manner as maintenance learning has always been an everyday occurrence. The functions of maintenance learning have declined and the structures of society are now legitimated by their functionality. In other words, the learning society is a pragmatic one. No longer are social structures, nor contemporary knowledge, legitimated by religion or inspiration, and this is a point to which we will return below.

The same process is occurring within bureaucracies – the barriers and hierarchies of the organisation are very slowly being broken down as it is recognised that organisations are more efficient if they are led rather than managed, and managers have to release some of the reins of power in order to allow this to happen. Where this happens, then innovative learning can occur beyond the employees' probationary period and these organisations are becoming known as learning organisations. Senge (1990: 14) captures this situation when he suggests that the learning organisation is:

> an organization that is continually expanding its capacity to create its future. For such an organization, it is not enough merely to survive. 'Survival learning' or what is more often termed 'adaptive learning' is important – indeed it is necessary. But for a learning organization, 'adaptive learning' must be joined by 'generative learning', learning that enhances our capacity to create.

His terms 'survival learning' and 'generative learning' have precisely the same meaning as 'maintenance learning' and 'innovative learning'. And so we can see that as society has changed two distinct forms of learning have been brought together, with innovative learning that formerly occurred beyond the structures of society now dominating everyday learning, and change has become endemic. It might be claimed that this process has occurred as those artificial forms of knowledge – scientific and technological – have formed the dominant discourse about society but also because globalisation is providing the driving forces for change. Yet not every society in the world underwent the Reformation or the Industrial Revolution, and they too are being affected by globalisation. Indeed, the spread of globalisation has been rather like the ripples on a pond when a stone has been thrown in – spreading out from a nodal point. There have been three nodal points from which globalisation has spread – the United States of America, Western Europe and the Pacific Rim countries – but those societies at the edge of the 'ripples' may be barely touched by globalisation and they still exhibit some of the characteristics of primitive society. In this sense 'primitive' bears no relation to time since primitive societies are contemporary, co-existing with those that might be described as late modern. But some other countries closer to the centre, such as some Islamic countries, may oppose some, or all, of the forces of globalisation.

Within both types of society there are also those who have adopted some of the types of knowledge and learning of the other, but not the beliefs or lifestyles. This has become more possible because societies have become much more open and the different elements of their culture have no need to be in complete harmony with each other – American Protestant fundamentalism and Islamic fundamentalism, for instance, may to different degrees both espouse cultural knowledge and maintenance learning, but their lifestyles and beliefs are totally different. Indeed, many American fundamentalists maintain a separation between the different forms of knowledge, accepting both the artificial knowledge of modern society and the cultural knowledge of fundamentalism. Individuals are now able to choose the social situation within which they construct their experiences. These differences between societies, and within them, demand either tolerance or some other form of reaction or opposition.

Barber (1995 [2003: xii]) calls societies that have adopted the knowledge and beliefs of late modern society 'McWorld' – 'integrative modernism and aggressive economic and cultural globalization' – whereas those societies that still espouse the characteristics of primitive societies he calls 'Jihadic', which he defines as 'disintegral tribalism and reactionary fundamentalism' (p. xii). Consequently, it is possible to describe all forms of religious fundamentalism as Jihadic, and therefore American fundamentalists, for instance, might be a combination of both McWorld and Jihadic at the same time, since individuals act in different sectors of the same society. Hence they learn from different social situations and have different experiences, and people are free to choose from which social situation they learn at any time, but with those who espouse fundamentalist religion, the religious setting may take precedence. In McWorld, innovative types of learning framed within the terms of artificial knowledge dominate, while in the Jihadic, maintenance learning and cultural forms of knowledge legitimated by religion and revelation are the more significant.

Clearly the Jihadic movements in Jihadic societies have opposed both the spread of globalisation and McWorld, with all its artificial forms of knowledge and innovative learning and all the economic exploitation and social inequalities that have accompanied the neglect of cultural forms of knowledge. While some of these countries tolerate the situation because they are powerless to do anything about it – or even because some countries, like India for instance, are benefiting from it – others have declared war on McWorld, and we see the growth of what we, in the West, define to be terrorist activities.

However, late modern society is now a segmented society and some people may have both McWorld and Jihadic responses to it. When the late modern societies respond in a tolerant manner it may lead to innovative learning and responses to the situation, but when they respond in a Jihadic fashion, because those in power choose this response, whatever the excuse they give for it, we have a holy war, or a 'war on terror'.

Conclusion

In primitive society maintenance and innovative learning were, and still are, kept apart and the latter occurred in liminality in order to safeguard the structures of society. In addition, the knowledge learned was cultural and tribal. Different tribes had their own cultural knowledge, and while there were battles between them there were also clear territorial boundaries, which enabled them to co-exist despite their differences. To a certain extent this condition still existed within modern society, even though we were beginning to see innovative learning break free of the confines of education and artificial knowledge become more significant than cultural knowledge, and the skirmishes between those who espoused both forms occurred within societies. But late modern contemporary society is segmented and global. Both innovative learning and artificial knowledge and maintenance learning and cultural knowledge are to be found throughout the various countries of the world in differing degrees. Consequently, the cultural forms of knowledge in primitive society, and the maintenance learning that has always accompanied them, have been threatened. In the West, there was a relatively peaceful and slow transition from placing greater emphasis on cultural knowledge and maintenance learning to the time when innovative learning and artificial knowledge assumed a more dominant place, but it has also tolerated those groups (usually religious, but also political) who also emphasised the importance of cultural knowledge and maintenance learning. In societies where the transition to the global world has been sudden, there has been insufficient time for toleration of difference to emerge, so that McWorld threatens their cultural knowledge and its maintenance learning, and the stability of their society is threatened if the two forms of learning are not kept apart. Ultimately, then, we enter the realm of politics.

References

Barber, B. (1995 [2003]) *Jihad versus McWorld*, London: Corgi Books.

Botkin, J., Elmandjra, M. and Malitza, M. (1979) *No Limits to Learning*, Oxford: Pergamon.

Gennep, A. van (1908 [1960]) *The Rites of Passage*, London: Routledge and Kegan Paul.

Jarvis, P. (1987) *Adult Learning in the Social Context*, London: Croom Helm.

—— (1992) *Paradoxes of Learning*, San Francisco: Jossey-Bass.

—— (2004) *Adult Education and Lifelong Learning: Theory and Practice* (third edition), London: Routledge.

Kerr, C., Dunlop, J., Harbison, F. and Myers, C. (1973) *Industrialism and Industrial Man* (second edition), Harmondsworth: Penguin.

Lester-Smith, W. (1966) *Education – An Introductory Survey*, Harmondsworth: Penguin.

Scheler, M. (1926 [1980]) *Problems of a Sociology of Knowledge*, London: Routledge and Kegan Paul.

Schutz, A. and Luckmann, T. (1974) *The Structures of the Life-World*, London: Heinemann.

Senge, P. (1990) *The Fifth Discipline*, New York: Doubleday.

Stehr, N. (1994) *Knowledge Societies*, London: Sage.

Turner, V. (1969) *The Ritual Process*, London: Routledge and Kegan Paul,

Weber, M. (1947) *The Social and Economic Organization*, New York: Free Press.

Chapter 9

Morality and human learning

Mal Leicester and Roger Twelvetrees

Introduction

> But now we are poised for the greatest revolution of all – understanding the human brain. This will surely be a turning point in the history of the human species for, unlike those earlier revolutions in science, this one is not about the outside world, not about cosmology or biology or physics, but about ourselves, about the very organ that made those earlier revolutions possible. And I want to emphasise that these insights into the human brain will have a profound impact not just on us scientists but also on the humanities, and indeed they may even help us bridge what C. P. Snow called the two cultures – science on the one hand and arts, philosophy and humanities on the other.
>
> (Reith Lecture no. 1, Ramachandran 2003)

An important principle for the papers in this collection is that contributors should take a multi-disciplinary approach to human learning, while seeking to understand both its cognitive (rational) and affective (emotional) dimensions. This is appropriate to our focus on moral learning. We believe that a multi-disciplinary approach to understanding the sheer complexity of the moral domain is likely to be fruitful. Moreover, not only do we recognise that both reason and emotion are important in learning to make moral judgements, the main argument of this chapter is that emotion has a necessary and central role in all our cognitive functioning.

We have chosen to draw on philosophy and natural science by undertaking a philosophical exploration of issues arising from new empirical discoveries about the brain, selecting some developments in neuroscience which have educational implications. We have used the recent Reith Lectures 2003 on 'The Emerging Brain' (Ramachandran 2003) as a useful repository of some of these new insights.

Since brain functions and learning are inextricably connected, new ideas in neuroscience are likely to be relevant to the educator's task of facilitating learning. Moreover, it is timely to consider new developments in neuroscience since new technology (e.g. Magnetic Resonance Imaging [MRI]) has yielded previously unattainable access to brain functions. In addition, Consciousness Studies has itself emerged as a multi-disciplinary study. Philosophers have gained new ways of thinking about the mind/brain duality, neuroscientists are, as indicated, making important empirical discoveries and computer scientists, in investigating artificial intelligence, throw light, too, on the human/evolved natural brain. In short, we agree with neurologist/philosopher Antonio Damasio who argues that neurobiology will play an important role in future explanations of 'ethical behaviours' provided we 'factor in ideas from anthropology, sociology, psychoanalysis and evolutionary psychology, as well as findings from studies in the fields of ethics, law and religion' (Damasio 2003). Our mental life, including our moral judgements, is the interacting product of biological and social forces. Thus, to focus on biology or on culture alone will produce an understanding of our learning which can only be partial (in both senses of the term).

Ironically, however, the neuroscience which is likely to add to our understanding of the complexities of moral learning is itself revealing an enormously complex picture of brain functions. In the midst of this complexity, we have merely tried to undertake some modest reflection on the following questions:

- What is the relationship between 'learning' and 'education'?
- What implications might studies of 'neural networks' have for moral learning?
- What are the moral educational implications of the current prevailing neuroscientists' model of the brain as 'interactive' and adapted?
- After considering emerging insights about the 'normal' brain (generated by looking at the behaviour of those with brain lesions) what further lessons can we learn as (moral) educators?

The concept of learning: science and social science

Philosophers used to distinguish between 'learning' and 'education'. The latter was a subset of the former, since not all learning was deemed to meet such educational criteria as: being worthwhile; having a 'wide cognitive perspective' (Peters 1966); being intentionally facilitated; being consciously apprehended, etc. Because of the criterion of worthwhileness, 'education' was described as a normative concept (ibid.). 'Learning', by contrast, was thought to include both worthwhile and negative learning, and therefore was not taken to be necessarily used with a normative implication. With the recent global movement to lifelong learning (Field and Leicester 2003) the two concepts 'education' and 'learning' have blurred. 'Lifelong learning' is used to imply worthwhile learning across the lifespan, whether formally or informally acquired. It is used more or less interchangeably with 'lifelong education'. Thus 'learning' has also become a normative concept. We suggest that the use of 'learning' in the context of neuroscience is similar, in having this normative implication, to the use of 'learning' in the context of lifelong learning. The brain, being subject to evolution, adapts to learn that which is useful for survival, i.e. worthwhile learning. (Though unlike educative learning, survival learning is not necessarily 'conscious', 'cognitively wide' or 'intentionally acquired'.) Since learning is central to human being, it is not surprising to find that it is a central concept in a range of discourses, including daily life, neuroscience and education, and that there are differing nuances and assumptions in these different contexts. In this chapter, therefore, we use 'learning', as in neuroscience, to refer to all adaptive changes in behaviour, and 'education' only for such changes as are deliberately facilitated by an 'educator'. Thus, a medical intervention which is undertaken to restore a damaged capacity to learn may be helpful (even a necessary prerequisite) for education to proceed efficiently, but it does not count as education per se.

Neural networks

Neuroscientists have discovered that neural networks are the building blocks of the brain. Engineers have shown how it occurs that when a number are linked together and then trained with reference data, they can then perform functions such as recognition of subsequent instances of the same class of data with great speed and efficiency (Beale and Jackson 1990). It is believed that when we learn some new task such as driving a car we create new pathways in the network linking the new experiences of the world together in new ways. These new pathways extend the pattern recognition database so that new situations and outcomes can be stored away. When we have learnt to drive, we have the necessary minimum of new actions and outcomes stored away so that we can recognise the new world of the new task and react successfully. How can these processes possibly happen fast enough to enable us to react in an emergency situation where speed is essential, such as when a rabbit runs out in front of the car while it is travelling at speed? Are our brains really fast enough to weigh up all the pros and cons of each action before it is too late? In our evolution the speed at which such decisions could be made must have been a powerful force for survival and hence natural selection. Rudimentary analysis of the amount of data to access and the number of decisions to be made in the time available shows that a conventional data processing task could not achieve the required speed to avoid sudden danger.

Damasio has proposed that the process of reacting to changes in the world is based on our emotional reaction to situations. We recognise a dangerous situation and the emotion of fear is generated. If something can be done to escape from that situation, there will probably be several options, and the brain must choose the option with the best outcome in a fraction of a second. The method used to assess which outcome is the best is to examine the emotions associated with these outcomes and pick the most agreeable. The sequence is therefore:

- recognise the pattern;
- look at the last few times this pattern was experienced and take on the associated emotion;
- look at the actions taken in the past when this emotion was experienced;
- choose the action with the best emotional outcome.

In our driving situation, the driver first sees a shape that he recognises as a rabbit. His driving database tells him that the rabbit is in his path, and he feels remorse from the past outcomes of similar situations (first or second hand). At the same time his driving database tells him that if he tries to swerve at this speed he will experience fear. The strong desire to avoid fear guides him in his choice of actions, and so he does not swerve. A second or so later (when it would probably have been too late to take any action), the reasoning functions of the brain produce the same answer. Many of Damasio's conclusions came from his work with patients with an injury that had impaired their capability to experience emotions. His discovery was that if a person cannot experience an emotion he cannot interpret a situation that would normally give rise to that emotion, or understand the emotion in others. In its simplest terms, if the patient cannot feel fear, then he cannot deal with a dangerous situation successfully. This applies even if he has been instructed many times how to deal with that exact situation and can repeat the instructions back to the teacher. Without feeling the emotion of fear he cannot recognise the situation as the one he has been taught to deal with. That condition is permanent unless some medical procedure can restore the capability to feel the emotion. However, provided that an individual is capable of a full range of emotions, then it is within the scope of education to extend and refine his emotional experiences so that he is fully competent at dealing with life situations.

To simplify Damasio's findings a little for the sake of brevity, we view the world through the window of our emotions. Those emotions are associated with patterns in the world as observed by the body's senses. As we live our life, we see more of the world, and we extend and refine our database of patterns. Each pattern of the perceived world has its associated emotion, and each action arising out of that, an 'emotional outcome'. There is experimental evidence that primates and lower order creatures' brains work in the same way. However, there is a vital difference between the human and the primate when it comes to how each refines and extends their database of experiences. Humans have become able to communicate experiences to others, which has led to a radical extension of learning capability. When we have someone else's experience communicated to us, then the brain processes it as if we had experienced it ourselves and attaches an emotion to it for future reference. In our sophisticated world, the communication is often delivered in such a way as to pre-select the emotion that the communicator wishes to have associated. Of course, this pre-selection is less easily implanted if it is not consonant with prior experiences, whether experienced at first or second hand. Clearly then, one of the functions of moral educa-tion is to extend and refine the student's experience of the moral patterns in the world, and to cause her to consider the moral outcomes of various actions. This allows the student to analyse subsequent communicated experi-ences from a moral basis, but it is interesting to note that the database from which the analysis is drawn has been assembled through the medium of feeling the emotions attached to problems of morality and moral behaviour.

The interactive and adapted brain

As Cohen and Leicester have argued, it has been accepted by neuroscien-tists that for any specific task undertaken by an individual, several regions of the brain are working simultaneously.

> Scientists have discovered that there is not just one brain area for one function, and are developing a much more complex model of an interac-tive brain. The brain uses a different complex set of 'organs' for each of its functions and, just as with body organs like the liver, each brain organ may play a part in more than one function. In order for an individual to live in the world successfully several brain areas tend to act in parallel, in complex ways, constantly shifting with our ongoing tasks in the world. Instead of control centres or tiers, Greenfield's metaphor is 'a cocktail of brain soup and spark' (1997). This captures the fluidity, the diversity and the recursive interactions of brain functioning. However, our own unease with this metaphoric mixture of fluids and electrics suggested to us an alternative metaphor – permeable, branching and flexible moving pathways criss-crossing and recursively interacting with each other and with incoming information from the external world (imagine Spaghetti Junction 'reeling and writhing' and repeatedly re-assembling)
>
> (Cohen and Leicester 2003).

Thus individual brains interact with the world and develop recursively, and somewhat individually. When a particular bit of the brain is damaged, other areas of the brain sometimes develop to replace the lost function. Collectively, these interactive brains have developed cultural practices/ interpersonal knowledge, which continues to recursively interact with our environment-adapted individual brains.

Thus for us, our common environment ... provides a kind of changing common framework within which our individual experience person-alises our individual – but nevertheless very similar – brains.

(Cohen and Leicester 2000: 68)

The educational implications drawn from this were that education should not emphasise universal competencies (e.g. a national curriculum at school with a remedial 'filling of gaps post-school') but, rather, should emphasise the promotion of individual strengths (e.g. the differentiated curriculum and individual learning plans – in school and across the lifespan). The educator will be guided less by common or general goals and be more facilitative of the student's self-directed goals.

What, though, could we say about the interactive and adapted brain in the specific context of moral learning? We have a model of individual brains interacting with a common interpersonally constructed framework. In moral terms, then, we can recognise individual characters with unique combina-tions of personality traits, our individual profiles of moral strengths and weaknesses (understood in terms of survival as a social creature), together with recognition that an interpersonal ethical framework has been collec-tively constructed in an evolutionary process concerned with maximising species (and thus individual) survival. Species survival connects with the notion of a common good. The moral educator, therefore, will seek to develop the individual so as to maximise moral strengths – those character traits, dispositions and behaviours, those perspectives and understandings which are connected with flourishing as a social being but which are also required for the maintenance of the common ethical framework.

All this is not contrary to but, rather, supportive of the literature on moral education and development. Character education is about the devel-opment of individual moral strengths, traits, dispositions and behaviour. Understanding universal principles of morality, such as the principle of justice, is consonant with coming to understand the collectively constructed common framework.

It is interesting, too, that consonant with Gilligan's emphasis on 'care' (1982) to the enrichment of Kohlberg's work on stages of rational under-standing of moral principles (Kohlberg 1984), the functioning of neural networks, as discussed above, could be seen to support the thesis that there is an integral emotional dimension to our rational judgements about moral aspects of our experience of the world.

The emerging brain

As study of the brain has progressed, partly through medical investiga-tions with brain-damaged individuals, a map, much more complex than the old phrenology picture, is beginning to emerge. Such studies show the importance of the frontal lobes and have implications for (at least) three issues in the moral domain: the place of emotion in moral judgement, the ontological status of free will, and the nature of the self.

Emotion

The frontal lobes seem to be the emotional areas of our brain, and though there is no moral centre as such, an emotional dimension accompanies all cognitive functioning, including functioning in social situations. Indeed, as Damasio points out, some of our emotions, such as sympathy, embarrassment, shame, guilt, pride, jealousy, envy, gratitude, admiration, indignation and contempt, are 'social' emotions. The primary (or basic) emotions (fear, anger, disgust, surprise, sadness, happiness) which are readily identified in human beings across cultures and in non-human species too, can be identified as sub-components of social emotions in varied combinations. The primary emotions 'nest' in these social ones.

Think of how the social emotion 'contempt' borrows the facial expressions of 'disgust', a primary emotion that evolved in association with automatic and beneficial rejection of potentially toxic foods. Even the words we use to describe situations of contempt or moral outrage – we profess to be disgusted – revolve around the nesting.

Damasio goes on to argue that work with individuals who have frontal lobe brain damage is showing us that inability to feel social emotions impairs cognitive judgements and decisions in social situations. For example, the relatives of such brain-damaged individuals have noticed a lack of empathy in individuals who were caring and affectionate before suffering impairment. These individuals soon become unable to function as independent human beings. In other words, claims that emotions are an integral part of our moral judgements and behaviours is supported by the judgements and behaviours of brain-damaged individuals, in whom the link between that part of the brain that deals with emotion and other areas has been severed. In the Reith Lectures, for example, Ramachandran tells us about Cotord's syndrome, where an individual sees his mother as an impostor, because, though he is able to 'recognise' her, having no associated emotional response he assumes her to be an impostor. In this context, the medical practitioner would be required to mend damaged neural pathways while the moral educator would be required to recognise the importance of children's emotional education in their development as functioning moral agents.

Though Damasio is primarily seeking to persuade us that, in the light of evolutionary principles, emotions are a necessary part of our survival and flourishing, what he shows about the importance of social emotions in our cognitive judgements and decisions seems to us to be consonant with the work of thinkers such as Hoffman and Gilligan. Hoffman conducted extensive research on empathy and its role in moral action and his work tends to correct a research bias focused on cognitive development in separation from the affective domain (Hoffman 1991). Gilligan also emphasises the importance of care/compassion in our 'rational' moral judgements (Gilligan 1982). The ability to understand and apply abstract universal moral principles, such as the principle of justice (Kohlberg 1984) should (logically and ethically) be integrated with our capacity to care for others.

Free will

The question of whether human beings have free will and can choose to 'act' as they do, or are in some manner caused/predetermined/constrained to this 'behaviour', is a longstanding philosophical problem. It has been pointed out that only if we can freely act can we be held responsible for what we do. Thus, only if free will exists can we be considered to be moral agents. Much complex discussion of the issue has taken place. Ramachandran suggests, in his final Reith Lecture, a lecture entitled 'Neuroscience – the New Philosophy', that the study of hysteria can contribute to this discussion. Study of a patient with hysterical paralysis of the arm, using a PET scan, revealed something very interesting. When he is asked to move his arm, the patient's pre-motor area of the brain lights up, indicating that he intends to move it. However, in addition, parts of the frontal context light up too, indicating a veto on the movement. These frontal lobe areas are 'intimately linked to the limbic emotional centres in the brain. And we know that hysteria originates from some emotional trauma that's somehow preventing him from moving his arm.'

With a 'normal patient', the pre-readiness area lights up before the patient experiences a conscious intention to move the finger and almost immediately does so. Ramachandran draws this conclusion:

> So you see the amazing paradox is that on the one hand the experiment shows that free will is illusory, right? It can't be causing the brain events because the events kick in a second earlier. But on the other hand it has to have some function because if it didn't have a function, why would evolution bother delaying it? But if it does have a function, what could it be other than moving the finger? So maybe our very notion of causation requires a radical revision here as happened in quantum physics.

Thus, one could argue from Ramachandran's PET scan data that the notion of free will is illusory unless we construct a radical new view of causation, a suggestion that has also been made by philosophers concerned with free will. We suggest, however, that it can be argued from Damasio's work that the thesis that emotional experiences (stored in our memory) play some part in our actions is entirely compatible with the notion of free will. We surely understand by 'acting freely' that our actions are understandable in terms of our emotions – compatible, in some sense, with what we want to do. It may be that the pre-readiness area referred to above had in fact been triggered by an emotionally routed response before the conscious mind has had time to respond. Nevertheless this means that we are acting on the basis of our own emotions. What else would we mean by acting freely than acting according to our own feelings? What is fascinating, though, is this glimpse into how empirical data about the brain is likely to have a huge impact on our philosophical ideas.

The self

Central to the notion of 'being a moral agent' is the notion of the 'self'. As with free will, the nature of the self is an issue of key philosophical and ethical importance. Ramachandran, at the finale of the final and most philosophical of his Reith Lectures, addresses this question. He points out that the self and qualia (the experienced contents of consciousness) are two sides of the same coin. You can't have free-floating sensations or qualia with no one to experience it. And you can't have a self devoid of sensory experience, memories or emotions. He points out, as we saw in his patients with Cotard's syndrome, that when sensations and perceptions are disconnected from the emotional centres this leads to a dissolution of self.

He goes on to define 'self' in terms of four defining characteristics:

- continuity (a sense of time past and of future);
- unity (you experience yourself as one person);
- embodiment (your sense of being anchored to your body);
- agency (your sense of free will, of being in charge of your own destiny).

He argues that the studies (his and others) of patients with brain disease show that these different aspects of our experience of self can be differentially disturbed. He suggests that when we can fully explain continuity, unity, embodiment and agency in terms of what is going on in the brain, then the problem of 'what is the self' will 'vanish or recede into the background'.

Alternatively, he suggests a radical shift in perspective may teach us that there is no essential difference between self and others or that the self is an illusion.

Of course, if the 'self' is an illusion, then morality and moral education become impossible. If, however, we accept his plausible 'defining' characteristics, it is interesting that we can immediately recognise that the 'moral self' does indeed presuppose their reality. For it is an individual embodied agent who owns past deeds and who feels guilty or virtuous, for example, and who makes ongoing moral decisions for which that individual self is accountable (responsible). Moral discourse and this kind of view of the self are inseparably interrelated. Significantly, the breakdown of any one of these four characteristics rendered Ramachandran's patients cognitively and morally severely functionally impaired.

Conclusions: empathy, education and moral learning

There are many theories of moral development, both secular and religious. They have, in the main, been developed by psychologists. Over nearly four decades, as R. Murray Thomas has pointed out, Kohlberg's theory has consistently been the most discussed. 'The standard psychological journal literature over the 1970–95 era reports more than 770 investigations are based on Kohlberg's work' (Murray Thomas 1997: 65). In response to Gilligan's charge that Kohlberg erred in defining moral development solely in terms of levels of rational understanding of justice, Kohlberg 'willingly admitted that compassionate caring was an important aspect of moral thought and action (Kohlberg 1984)' (ibid.). What we have argued, consonant with our reflections about neural networks and the interactive brain, is that what needs to be constructed is a comprehensive theory of moral development which interrelates emerging neurological knowledge about emotional development and psychologically gained understanding of moral reasoning. We need a kind of synthesis of the insights of Kohlberg and of Gilligan, together with the emerging neurological insight about the central role in human learning of the development of the social emotions. We would also suggest a useful distinction in considering emotional development: a distinction between medical intervention and general education and specifically moral learning.

A medical intervention might restore an individual's damaged capacity to experience emotions, including empathy. Given a (restored) capacity for empathy, empathetic insight into the emotions of others can be used to facilitate a wider general education. The individual learner can store both directly experienced (first-hand) emotional data and indirectly experienced (second-hand) emotional data of others, communicated by others through narrative, story, research findings, etc. It is interesting that David Lodge, in discussing consciousness and the novel (Lodge 2002), makes reference to the work of Damasio. Damasio recognised the narrative nature of consciousness and also the parallel emergence of the concept of consciousness and the rise of the novel. Lodge points out that novelists seek to render visible (public) the interior (private) world of qualia – the inner consciousness of their characters. 'Truth', in fiction, is partly about the possibility of our gaining understanding of other people, from the novelist's insights into human emotions. This adds to our database of patterns in the 'real' world. The emotional data of others is assimilated by the learner through comparison with his or her own first-hand data (using, for example, analysis and discussion). The wider general education from this assimilation, in turn, enriches moral learning, because to learn with increasing competence about how to function in positive relationship with others relies, very substantially, on the learner's widening neural database about the emotions of others. This database of experience has, as we have discussed, its associated emotions. Thus, moral learning presupposes emotional development; and enriched moral learning, it may be plausibly assumed, will flow from a more discriminating repertoire of emotional response.

References

Beale, R. and Jackson, T. (1990) *Neural Computing: An Introduction*, London: Institute of Physics.

Cohen, J. and Leicester, M. (2000) 'The Evolution of the Learning Society, Brain Science, Social Science and Life Long Learning', in J. Field and M. Leicester (eds) *Lifelong Learning: Education Across the Lifespan*, London: RoutledgeFalmer.

Damasio, A. (2000) *The Feeling of What Happens: Body, Emotion, and the Feeling of Consciousness*, New York: First Harvest Edition, Harcourt.

—— (2003) *Looking for Spinoza: Joy, Sorrow and the Feeling Brain*, London: Heinemann.

Field, J. and Leicester, M. (eds.) (2003) *Lifelong Learning: Education Across the Lifespan*, London: RoutledgeFalmer.

Field, J. and Leicester, M. (2000) 'Lifelong Learning or Permanent Schooling?' in J. Field and M. Leicester (eds) *Lifelong Learning. Education Across the Lifespan*, London: RoutledgeFalmer.

Gilligan, C. (1982) *In a Different Voice*, Cambridge, MA: Harvard University Press.

Greenfield, S. (1997) *The Human Brain – A Guided Tour*, New York: Basic Books.

Hoffman, M. L. (1991) 'Empathy, Social Cognition and Moral Action', in W. H. Kurtines and J. I. Gewirtz (eds) *Handbook of Moral Behaviour and Development: Vol. 1 Theory*, Hillsdale NJ: Erlbaum, pp. 275–301.

Kohlberg, L. (1984) *The Psychology of Moral Development*, San Francisco: Harper and Row.

Lodge, D. (2002) *Consciousness and the Novel*, Sydney: Random House, pp. 1–91.

Murray Thomas, R. (1997) *Moral Development Theories – Secular and Religious. A Comparative Study*, Westport, CT: Greenwood Press.

Peters, R. S. (1966) *Ethics and Education*, London: Allen and Unwin.

Ramachandran, V. S. (2003) *The Emerging Brain*, London: BBC. Available at http:/www.bbc.co.uk/radio4/reith2003/

Chapter 10

Emotional intelligence and experiential learning

Carol Hall

> On a personal level emotional intelligence can help learners to access and surface unconscious feelings, to control negative thoughts and anger, and to reduce conflict. This will enable learners to take greater control of their feelings and emotions so as to progress towards more productive behaviours that they wish to develop, such as increased calm, the ability to challenge a belief set, or the development of increased sensitivity to self and others.
>
> (Beard and Wilson 2002: 118)

The term 'emotional intelligence' (Mayer and Salovey 1993; Goleman 1996) is relatively new, but the appreciation of the part that emotions play in shaping human learning and behaviour is an ancient one (Aristotle, 384–322 BC). This chapter focuses on emotions and the part they play in human learning. The term 'emotional intelligence' is used as a catch-all to encapsulate the concept of an active human intelligence which both drives and shapes our perception of lived experience, our 'inner world' and our behaviour in social interaction, the world 'out there'. The discussion of the ways in which our early emotional experiences shape our construction of 'perceived realities' (Mahoney 1991) is informed by self-concept and self-esteem theory. The popularised notion of 'emotional intelligence' is defined and its usefulness as a concept in developing humanistic approaches to holistic learning argued. The chapter concludes with a discussion of experiential ways to 'educate the emotions' (Macmurray 1972) for both teachers and students, with a learning curriculum designed to enhance emotional intelligence itself.

Emotional intelligence

Emotional intelligence and the popular imagination

Mayer, DiPaolo and Salovey coined the term 'emotional intelligence' in an academic paper authored in 1990, 'Perceiving Affective Content in Ambiguous Visual Stimuli: A Component of Emotional Intelligence' (Mayer *et al.* 2001: 9).

However it took the work of a scientific journalist, Daniel Goleman in 1995, *Emotional Intelligence: Why It Can Matter More Than IQ*, to unwittingly ignite a spark in the academic and public imagination which burns to this day. The extent to which the phrase captured the zeitgeist can be gauged from the fact that although the work was written in a somewhat journalistic style, it was soundly based in academic research, and still became a number one bestseller, a feat many academics would be delighted to emulate. So successfully did the term appeal to the public that in 1995 the American Dialect Society selected 'emotional intelligence' as the most popular and useful phrase of the year. Goleman (1998) himself reports that after the publication of *Emotional Intelligence* in 1995, he was inundated by 'a tidal wave of letters and faxes, e-mails and phone calls, requests to speak and consult, I found myself on a global odyssey, talking to thousands of people' (Goleman 1998: 4).

The widespread appeal of the concept has continued unabated and spawned a plethora of publications in its wake. However it is tempting to forget that academics, researchers and educators have been writing about the links between emotion, cognition, learning and pedagogy for more than a century and much of this earlier, seminal work remains unacknowledged by current writers. It appears that the public was ready to embrace a concept which offered a fresh insight and a more hopeful way of describing human intelligence and potential than anything which had gone before.

Perhaps part of its appeal may have had its seeds in the widespread disillusion with the promise that central government reform would improve schools, and that curriculum change, and increasing numbers of paper-based tests, would somehow produce a more motivated, successful and skilful learner. However, at the heart of central government reforms still lay an unchanging belief in the primacy of the intellect as the key determinant of a learner's ultimate worth. Throughout the twentieth century, education systems all over the world have been dominated by the legacy of IQ and the cognitive competencies that it purported to measure. The test itself, devised in 1911 by Alfred Binet and Theodore Simon, allowed psychologists and teachers to measure intellectual ability on a scale stretching from 'genius' to 'feeble-minded'. As a consequence, schooling and the training of teachers has been geared to the improvement of students' intellectual rather than emotional or relational competence and to see examination success as the 'gold standard' by which we judge each other and educational institutions themselves. We have been conditioned to think of human intelligence as a unidimensional concept and the yardstick by which our worth as human beings in and to the world is ultimately judged.

Jersild (1952) argued that the myth is self-perpetuating, as the educational establishment by its very nature comprises those individuals who have excelled academically, and therefore may be consciously or unconsciously promulgating the concept of the supremacy of the intellect.

The more people with a pronounced intellectual approach to life control the academic requirements imposed upon the population at large and the more they dictate the kind of intellectual nourishment which the population is to receive, the more they will tend to set up a curriculum designed to build all creatures in their image.

(Jersild 1952: 56–7)

Howard Gardiner of Harvard University agrees, and in conversation with Daniel Goleman described the 'IQ way of thinking' which has led us to believe that

people are either smart or not, are born that way, that there's nothing much you can do about it, and that tests can tell you if you are one of the smart ones or not. The SAT test for college admissions is based on the same notion of a single kind of aptitude that determines your future. This way of thinking permeates society.

(Goleman 1996: 38)

Many apparently successful and confident men and women in the public, business and artistic worlds still feel the need to apologise if they failed the 11+ or haven't had a university education. Even those lucky enough to go to universities may be reluctant to disclose the classification of their degree if they didn't get a 2.1 or a first, so powerful is the grip of the myth that academic success is the measure of personal worth.

However, we know that IQ alone, measuring as it does cognitive intelligence related to verbal and mathematical reasoning, denies any possibility that there might be a symbiotic relationship between thought and feeling, of a relationship between our intellectual and emotional selves. At an intuitive level we know this to be nonsense, and that the learner's ability to reason and problem-solve is intimately bound up with how they *feel* about these competencies. For this reason alone, learners need to explore the constructions of their self-esteem if they are to set themselves realistic learning goals.

Where a relationship between cognition and affect has been acknowledged, it has been conceptualised as potentially problematic. This quasi Freudian view positions feelings and emotions as somehow mischievous and unpredictable, id-like, needing to be held in check and contained by the rational, restraining force of the superego. Thus the development of the learner's emotional life has been relegated to the educational sidelines, confined to the pastoral dimension. Tutors are taught 'counselling skills' (Hornby *et al.* 2003) in order to contain and control the distress caused by feelings of learner alienation to the dominance of the intellectual in the curriculum. Nevertheless, scholars have continued to remind us that the process of education must aspire to be more than a servant of the intellect:

Though there *is* a higher and a wider significance to life, of what value is our education if we never discover it? We may be highly educated, but if we are without deep integration of thought and feeling, our lives are incomplete, contradictory and torn with many fears; and as long as education does not cultivate an integrated outlook on life, it has very little significance.

(Krishnamurti 1968: 11)

The notion of EQ as an active partner of IQ which has the power to drive, shape and determine human potential means that educationalists must take the development of EQ in the learner more seriously. Goleman's (1996) work describes how in schools in the USA this is already being done, and Hall (2003) provides examples from both secondary and higher education in the UK. Not only are researchers (Mayer *et al.* 2000) refining our understanding of the term 'emotional intelligence' but others are working on ways to measure it (Sirin *et al.* 1995; Bar-On 1997; Cooper and Sawaf 1998). This allows for the possibility of assessing current levels of emotional functioning in the individual and devising appropriate learning strategies to increase competence.

Not only young learners would benefit. In the world of work, where it is clear that relationships between colleagues can make or break businesses (Argyris 1989), all could benefit from increasing their emotional intelligence. If we incorporated our understanding of EQ into positive parenting programmes, parents and carers also might be encouraged to be more self-consciously strategic in their child-rearing practices.

Being able to define and measure what we mean by emotional intelligence offers the promise that we might also formally 'credit' intra and interpersonal skills (Gardiner 1983) with the same degree of academic respectability as that which we currently afford, say, mathematics or languages. Those individuals who then 'score highly' on emotional intelligence may ultimately find themselves as valued and rewarded for their competence as those with high IQs.

However, it is foolhardy to attempt to divorce emotional intelligence from intellectual intelligence, and while teachers may wish to debate appropriate pedagogical and curricula approaches to the development of a particular skill set, it is important to recognise the influence of emotion on all learning. Emotionally intelligent people are intelligent learners.

The emotional life is not simply a part or an aspect of human life. It is not, as we so often think, subordinate, or subsidiary to the mind. It is the core and essence of human life. The intellect arises out of it and is rooted in it, draws its nourishment and sustenance from it, and is the subordinate partner in the human economy.

(Macmurray 1972: 75)

Emotional intelligence defined

When my father died some years ago, I was dreading going back to work and facing the sympathetic glances and murmured condolences from colleagues. As I walked nervously into the staff common room, the first person I met was my then boss. At a glance he took in both my discomfort and distress and without words or embarrassment gave me a reassuring hug. His non-verbal gesture showed both understanding and compassion. In that moment I felt fully understood and accepted as a person, and my feelings of grief, loss and confusion acknowledged and respected. He made it OK for me to cry and talk about my father's death through this simple, tender gesture of emotional kinship. This for me was an example of EQ in action.

Using Mayer *et al.*'s description of the four components of emotional intelligence:

1   reflectively regulating emotions;
2   understanding emotions;
3   assimilating emotion in thought;
4   perceiving and expressing emotion.

(Mayer *et al.* 2000: 269)

It is possible to examine the process which lay behind that profoundly empathic gesture. First, he was able to accurately perceive how I was feeling and to respond in tune with my emotional state (1). He was able to understand his own emotional reaction to my grief (2) and make an intelligent decision about how to behave in relation to my need (3). He was also able to hold back his own feelings of loss and grief from similar life events in order to attend to my emotional state (4).

It is interesting to note that an unlooked-for outcome of this short episode for me was that a simple, generous gesture of acceptance, at a time of tremendous emotional shock, created a bond of loyalty and friendship which continues to this day. He also provided me with a role model of how to behave appropriately when I met similar circumstances in my own life, so unwittingly facilitated my emotional learning. Subsequently I felt much more ready and able to return to teaching and handle my feelings with greater confidence in front of classes. So my boss's empathy also led to the maintenance of organisational efficiency.

Cooper and Sawaf (1998) discuss the application of emotional intelligence to leadership in the workplace and argue that each of us in our own way is required to demonstrate leadership and that success in the role is as dependent upon EQ as IQ. Thus we need to be colleagues capable of persuading and influencing, motivating and energising as well as task leaders, problem-solvers and decision-makers. Cooper and Sawaf also provide an important caveat about the moral and ethical purpose that underpins such behaviour, which Zohar and Marshall (2000) might call 'spiritual intelligence'. They remind us that emotionally intelligent behaviour springs from integrity of heart and spirit:

> Emotional intelligence emerges not from the musings of rarefied intellect but from the workings of the human heart. EQ isn't about sales tricks or how to work a room. And it is not about putting a good face on things or the psychology of control, exploitation, or manipulation.
>
> (Cooper and Sawaf 1998: xii)

They go on to define it: 'Emotional intelligence is the ability to sense, understand, and effectively apply the power and acumen of emotions as a source of human energy, information, connection, and influence' (Cooper and Sawaf 1998: xiii).

However emotional intelligence is defined (and the term is a notoriously slippery one), most theorists would agree that it encompasses three broad dimensions (Goleman 1996; Bar-On 1997; Steiner and Perry 1999; Bagshaw 2000; Boyatzis *et al.* 2000), but would undoubtedly argue emphasis or hierarchy of influence:

Intrapersonal: self-knowledge and self-awareness which gives rise to a willingness to be in touch with inner feelings and thereby have greater control over their effects and verbal and non-verbal expression;
Interpersonal: relational competence which includes the ability to read others' feelings and choose appropriate pro-social micro behaviours in relation to those readings;
Organismic authenticity: the choice of courses of action or assertive behaviours which may be deemed socially unpopular in order to preserve personal integrity and authenticity and which provide emotional resilience to stressful life events.

In the next section, the effects of self-concept and self-esteem on emotional functioning will be discussed, and learned emotional and behavioural strategies which inhibit the development of emotional intelligence outlined.

Self-concept and self-esteem

Self-concept, self-image and self-esteem are often terms which are used interchangeably. However, there are important discriminations between these hypothetical constructions in relation to the development of emotional intelligence. Self-concept is the term psychologists use to refer to the individual's global construction of the self. This self is acquired, not ready-made, and the ways that it is constructed subject to an emotional evaluation, which we call self-esteem (sometimes called self-worth or self-love).

The picture that we paint of ourselves is called the self-image and is subject to constant emotional evaluation by the self-esteem. Thus it would be impossible for me to describe myself (self-image) as a woman, white, mother, friend, middle-class, short-haired, daughter, academic, friendly, energetic, and so on, without have feelings attached to these characteristics. These feelings will in turn help to determine my beliefs about myself (Lawrence 1998). These self-evaluations emerge from a dynamic interplay of formative influences: familial, social, racial, cultural, biological, educational, and so on. As a white girl growing up in a working-class family with two parents and two brothers and attending a middle-class grammar school, it is clear to me today how these formative experiences still shape my reality, even though the external circumstances of my life have changed beyond all recognition.

The self-esteem is based on attitudes, feelings and beliefs which we hold about ourselves and are therefore not in themselves necessarily 'rational' or subject to change via logical argument. If my experience of maths at school led me to believe I was hopeless, no amount of rational argument or cajoling will convince me otherwise. An even more extreme example is provided by people who suffer from eating disorders: an anorexic who believes him or herself to be grossly overweight will persist with the delusion, even when there is irrefutable medical evidence to the contrary.

If the self-concept can be understood as a map of our own individual psychological territory, then self-esteem provides the contours. These contours are shaped via interactions with significant figures in our lives: parents, siblings, relatives, peers, teachers, and so on. Clearly, in the early years parents are the most significant influence in helping to create and maintain self-esteem in their children (Mruk 1999). However, parental influence can be, as Carkhuff (1969) terms it, either 'facilitating' or 'retarding' of their children's self-esteem and most of us will have experienced a mixture of both during our formative years. The perfect parent, after all, does not exist.

So-called facilitating parents have the capacity to help a child develop a deep inner belief in their own personal value and the value of others. This child will experience unconditional acceptance and love and come to understand that they are both worthy of being loved and capable of love in return. The child will develop an optimistic outlook, predict success and not be bowed by experiences of failure. He/she will believe in their own potential to succeed and have the determination to stick at it. Characteristically, such children believe in their own ability to shape their destiny and that they can influence and control events.

Conversely, 'retarding' parents will repeatedly send the message, both verbally and non-verbally, that the child is inadequate, a failure, no good and subject them to repeated criticism or blame – for example, 'You've always been a good-for-nothing', or 'You'll never amount to much', and so on. Such children internalise the messages and come to believe themselves deeply unworthy of love or approval. Love becomes a reward, conditional upon 'approved' feelings and behaviours, but to the child the list is both infinite and unpredictable. In this way it is possible to understand how a parent can unwittingly condition the emotional responses of a child, in the manner of a Pavlovian dog. A small child who is treated badly every time they are in the presence of one parent will quickly experience a drench of fear every time that parent is present. This reaction may continue into adult life, even long after the death of the parent, and the conditioned response may even generalise to people who look like the parent or to members of the same sex. Similar conditioned learning can, of course, work in the opposite direction. Some of these conditioned behaviours, which are forms of emotional learning, can be extremely debilitating. A phobic reaction that prevents a person from leaving their home leads to a restricted life, and yet the fear reaction can be unlearned. A drug addict is controlled by the pleasure of the short-term reward. These are extreme examples, but if asked to consciously reflect most of us could find examples of the way our lives are shaped by the emotional rewards and punishments we have received in the past. In order to gain control over these learned patterns and moderate their influence, it is necessary to engage in learning where the focus is to actively encourage self-examination. In such an experiential learning context the learner is supported in bringing the subjective narratives of their life into awareness, which is why emotional education is central to the process of all learning.

Both the inner, subjective world and the outer, perceived reality of the child pose threats to the self-esteem, such as shame and humiliation, anger and disapproval, even ultimately withdrawal of love. Such a risky emotional environment can lead to potentially dysfunctional learned patterns of behaviour such as passivity, manipulation or overt aggression, as well as a catalogue of defensive routines which are well documented in the psychological literature (O'Connell and O'Connell 1980). These patterns of dysfunctional intra and interpersonal emotional responses directly influence the learner's capacity to learn and grow in a positive direction. Children with low self-esteem are the learners who characteristically avoid taking risks, easily give up trying and believe that events are largely out of their influence or control. For teachers they can be recognised as the 'heartsink' learners, the student who, no matter how hard the teacher encourages, never fully believes they are capable of change or success.

As we grow, the influences on our self-esteem change. By adolescence, parental influence has waned and the influence of peers takes over. Later in life we come to evaluate ourselves increasingly by our own lights. It is at this point as adult learners that those who wish to develop their emotional intelligence need to work at understanding the antecedents of their self-esteem.

The importance of being able to take control of and responsibility for our lives, including taking control of emotional conditioning, has been around for some time and discussed in areas such as 'locus of control' (Lefcourt 1976) and more recently 'self-efficacy' (Bandura 1997).

Educating the emotions experientially

The influence of humanistic psychology on affective education

Third Force, existential or humanistic psychology (O'Connell and O'Connell 1980) developed out of a reaction against the essentially mechanistic theories of human behaviour as proposed by psychoanalysts, behaviourists and cognitive scientists. Third Force psychology insisted that there is more to human behaviour than blind reactions to rewards and punishments and the effect of events in the first five years of life which the scientific, experimental research paradigms focused upon. Instead, psychology should shift to understanding the first-person perspective and develop appropriate qualitative research methods to study experiential, subjective accounts of the self in order to generate learning about how best to direct 'the growth of the individual towards his or her highest creative potential' (O'Connell and O'Connell 1980: 10). For this reason it was often termed 'growth psychology' and thus found a ready audience in teachers, counsellors and those professionals whose roles involved developing the human potential of their client groups. Influential writers in the field are Rogers (1961), Maslow (1962) and Kelly (1955). Rogers' work in particular influenced the development of psychotherapeutic research and practice in the second half of the twentieth century. He insisted that the counselling relationship must be 'person-centred' if the client was to be supported towards achieving their life or relationship goals. Moreover, he spelled out the 'core conditions' of empathy, positive regard and counsellor authenticity or genuineness which must be present if the therapeutic relationship was to be successful (Rogers 1962). Rogers subsequently developed similar notions for education, and 'student-centred' teaching was born (Rogers and Freiberg 1994). Again, the emphasis was on the emotional intelligence of the teacher as a prerequisite for a successful teacher–learner relationship.

Above all others, it is Rogers who offers the greatest insight into the effects of emotionally intelligent behaviour on the relationship between teacher and learner. Rogers (1961) describes those with high emotional intelligence as 'persons in process' or 'fully functioning' people.

Rogers' ideas were readily taken up by educationalists. 'Affective education' was the term used to describe the application of these psychological theories to education and learning (Brown 1971; Lipka and Beane 1984). This movement generated a plethora of practical materials for learners of any age. They were designed to change the ways that teachers organised and thought about the learning experience. Instead of traditional lectures, whole-class instruction or seminars, teachers were encouraged to use experiential workshops, multi-sensory and imaginal approaches, outdoor pursuits – in fact any activity which brought the learner emotionally closer to the source of learning and moved away from an emphasis on theory and abstraction. After all, the map, they argued, is not the territory. These experiential exercises were designed to encourage the learner to develop a greater awareness of both their cognitive and their affective selves, and to reflect upon and examine the relationship between the two in order to inform future goal-setting and action-planning. As a result of this emphasis on the emotional life of the learner, students invariably reported that they developed a better understanding of their own inner feelings, gained more control over their emotions and learned how to express them more appropriately in social situations. While some of the work was designed for what might be called 'emotion across the curriculum', harnessing feelings to support cognitive development, there were also learning opportunities being created at the other end of the spectrum – to focus entirely on intra and interpersonal relationships from an experiential perspective. These workshops were described variously as encounter groups, sensitivity groups, awareness-raising groups, process groups, and so on (Hall *et al.* 1999) and are discussed in a later section of the chapter. Two writers who stand out in the descriptions of these groups are Schutz (1971) and Stevens (1971).

The role of the teacher in developing emotional intelligence

No doubt all of us have memories from our schooldays of teachers whose emotional intelligence, or lack it, made a lifelong impact on our self-esteem and confidence as learners. As an enthusiastic pupil in my early days at grammar school, I was eager to make a positive impression on my teachers. I energetically put up my hand to answer questions in class and take part in discussion and debate. This confidence and enthusiasm took a knock one day when, out of the blue, my Latin teacher (who also happened to be the headmistress, which made the judgement doubly authoritative) announced to the class that it was no coincidence that 'Carol and Careless begin with the same letter'. I was covered with embarrassment and shame. My enthusiasm evaporated from that moment on and I was beset with an anxiety that if I got things wrong in public, humiliation would swiftly follow. It is interesting for me to notice that some forty years later I still have a residual fear of saying the wrong thing or 'getting it wrong' in public. Such a lack of empathy and sensitivity to the emotional needs of young learners led the philosopher John Macmurray as long ago as 1935 to declare emphatically,

> we should recognize that it is as ridiculous to put the emotional training of children in the hands of teachers whose emotional life is of a low grade or poorly developed, as it is to commit their intellectual education to teachers who are intellectually unintelligent and stupid.
>
> (Macmurray 1972: 70)

The psychologist Gordon Allport (1938) was no less unequivocal in arguing that the characteristics of the 'emotionally mature' teacher are threefold. First, they are likely to possess a developed sense of humour with the capacity to laugh at themselves and their own foibles as well as appreciate humour in others and life events. Second, they would be capable of deriving a profound sense of personal fulfilment and satisfaction from supporting and caring for others. Finally, they would possess a values system or philosophy consistent with the notion that education is more than the inculcation of subject-based knowledge but a broader encompassing of the social, moral and ethical questions which we might now describe as citizenship education.

Rogers and Freiberg (1994) similarly recognised that the emotional intelligence of the teacher was central to the process of education and that all student learning was related to the role of teacher or, as they preferred to term the role, facilitator of learning. Aspy and Roebuck's famously titled *Kids Don't Learn From People They Don't Like* (1977) provides research evidence that teachers who scored highly on Rogers' core conditions of genuineness, positive regard and empathic understanding (1962) created a learning environment in which students developed more positive attitudes to self, school and others, met fewer discipline problems, achieved improved school attendance, and increased IQ scores and cognitive growth.

The Emotional Development Curriculum

What would a curriculum specifically designed to enhance the characteristics of emotional intelligence look like? Goleman describes what he claims might be a 'model course in emotional intelligence' (1996: 261) being held at the Nueva Learning Center, San Francisco, USA. The students take a course in 'Self Science' and he quotes the developer of the curriculum, teacher Karen Stone McCown, as saying, 'Learning doesn't take place in isolation from kids' feelings. Being emotionally literate is as important for learning as instruction in math and reading' (Goleman 1996: 262).

Goleman acknowledges the debt to the work of the affective education movement of the 1960s, but claims that the Self Science Curriculum goes one step further because instead of 'using affect to educate, it educates affect itself' (1996: 262). This is a claim too far, and even a cursory glance at the relevant literature reveals that the affective education movement set out to do both. Closer to home, Hall (in Hornby *et al.* 2003: 55) has developed an 'Emotional Development Curriculum' which is specifically 'designed for teachers as well as students'. It is meant to be followed first by teachers on in-service training courses who wish to develop their own emotional intelligence as a precursor to working with their students. The curriculum covers the following:

Learning to relax: developing awareness and the ability to stay in control.
Learning to listen: to myself and others.
Learning to talk: so others can hear.
Learning to feel: so that I can understand myself.
Learning to express feelings: so that others can understand me.
Learning to love, care and support: myself and others.
Learning to lose: grieving and letting go.
Learning to live: being fully alive to experience.
Learning to think: reflecting on behaviour and developing skills and strategies for change.
Learning to handle challenging moments: being skilful in crisis.

The development of the curriculum was informed by research into the outcomes of experiential learning on teachers from all sectors who attended in-service training courses designed to increase their emotional intelligence. This research goes back over a period of some thirty years (Hall and Hall 1988; Hall *et al*. 1996; Hall *et al*. 1997; See *et al*. 1999). The Emotional Development Curriculum has been extensively trialled with clusters of inner-city primary and secondary schools in Nottingham, UK. One interesting outcome reported in the evaluation of the project has been the significant increase in the reported confidence and competence of teachers to 'deliver' a curriculum such as this, alongside the benefits to students.

It can be mapped on to Mayer *et al.*'s (2000) four-level hierarchy of emotional competencies: perceiving and expressing feelings, assimilating emotion into cognitive activity, understanding emotions, and reflecting upon and regulating emotional responses; and Goleman's (1998) five elements of emotional intelligence: self-awareness, motivation, self-regulation, empathy and adeptness in relationships.

Hall (2003) argues, like Macmurray, that it is a *sine qua non* that teachers who are unable to understand and regulate their own patterns of emotional responses, both internal and external, will be unable or inadequate to the task of facilitating this process for students. Along with Jersild (1952), Hall further suggests that an essential part of initial teacher education and continuing professional development should be the provision of experiential courses which focus explicitly on aspects of developing emotional intelligence.

Educating the emotions: experiential learning

There is a cartoon of an overweight woman stretched out comfortably on a sofa surrounded by the detritus of binge eating – crisp wrappers, chocolate boxes, bottles of diet Coke, and so on – with her eyes firmly fixed on the video being played on the TV in front of her. The caption reads, 'As part of her new fitness programme Penelope watched her step aerobics video every day without fail.' It would be tempting – but inevitably futile – to believe, like Penelope, that personal growth and development programmes could be successful merely by vicarious observation of others, or passively listening without any active, personal engagement with the process itself. Achieving long-lasting and positive changes to our emotional repertoire is only achieved through an active engagement with a structured experiential learning process.

However, the term 'experiential learning' has a range of technical meanings for educators as discussed by Warner Weil and McGill (1989), and can therefore be misleading. In the context of educating the emotions, experiential learning can be defined by the following characteristics:

- The tutor's role is one of 'facilitator of learning' (Rogers and Freiberg 1994) and a role model for appropriately mature emotional behaviour. There is a close match between the espoused values and theories of the facilitator and their behaviour in the learning group: espoused theory and theory in use (Bulut 2003).
- Learners are encouraged to develop and articulate self-theories through personal and group interaction and test them out with the group, which can provide a feedback mechanism to inform theory refinement.
- The facilitator strives to create a feeling of 'relaxed alertness' in the learners; at the outset of the session the facilitator uses their theoretical, practical and emotional expertise to design learning structures which create a state of dynamic disequilibrium (Joyce 1984) in the learners.
- The facilitator designs the learning structures or exercises so that the learner is able to draw on past life experience as well as here-and-now feelings, and consciously reflect on resistance to change or future goals.
- The facilitator is able to 'hold' or 'contain' whatever feelings emerge in the group and enable learners to use the experience constructively.
- Learners are given permission to opt in or out of structured exercises, in relation to personal evaluations of their emotional readiness/preparedness to engage with the process.
- Learners are encouraged to use their own experience, imagination and life stories as material for learning interactions in pairs and small groups.
- Learners are encouraged to consciously hone their self-awareness as an aspect of understanding themselves and others more profoundly.
- Learners are offered opportunities to explore and express emotional reactions to sense data – sight, sound, smell, touch, movement, fantasy and through guided imagery.
- Learners are offered opportunities to both give and receive feedback from other group members. The group itself is a source of learning because it provides a source of exploration and learning in relation to group dynamics.

- Learners are encouraged to keep personal learning journals as a basis for both recording and reflecting upon learning.
- Learners are encouraged to use an appropriate vocabulary in order to 'own' personal thoughts and feelings ('I' rather than 'we', 'one', and so on).
- The learning environment is appropriately boundaried in terms of time and the physical organisation of space.

Some exponents of experiential learning claim that there are two forms of learning, the use of guided imagery and the process group or encounter group, which are particularly potent for accessing subjective, inner emotional states. Not only are they considered to be powerful tools for accessing personal feelings which may be just out of the conscious awareness of the learner, but also the experiential method itself, because of its focus on intra and interpersonal process and active reflection (Kolb 1984) is capable of generating fresh insights into attitudes and behaviours. These insights can lead to greater understanding of and control over thoughts, feelings and behaviours, self-regulation.

There is evidence that accessing forms of imagery in experiential learning contexts can produce highly relaxed states in the learner. This is conducive to the generation of learning about not only subjectively experienced emotional states but also complex processes or abstract concepts which may not be visible to the naked eye (Hall et al. 1991). An example of the approach is Accelerated Learning, where imagery and relaxation are used in the learning of languages and the anxiety often accompanying the learning appears to diminish. A further example is from nurse education, where trainee nurses were taught to understand non-observable physiological processes through the use of imagery and relaxation (Gascoigne 2004). One example was of a boat floating through the bloodstream with different characters jumping on board, to illustrate the absorption of oxygen into the blood. The nurse educator found that using a series of imaginal stories of this nature with the nurse trainees resulted in a dramatic improvement in both their examination results and the application of the learning to clinical practice. Imagery and fantasy have been used widely in personal and social education in schools and less often for understanding concepts in academic subjects (Hall et al. 1991): what is common to both is that students report high memorability, enjoyment and relaxation.

Guided imagery is also used in psychotherapeutic contexts where the process of guiding the client through an imagery journey appears to permit the direct experience of emotions in a relaxed state, any possible feelings of fear and anxiety surrounding the accessing of these emotions being diminished. Once accessed, the client can then begin the journey to understanding, expressing and having a greater control over feelings – in other words, increasing their emotional intelligence (Jones 1994).

Small group work is a very pure form of experiential learning that focuses directly on intra and interpersonal process and is used routinely as part of counselling and psychotherapy training, where the emotional intelligence of the counsellor is of paramount importance to the success of the therapeutic relationship (Hall *et al.* 1999). It is also used in more general educational contexts, for example the training of teachers, social workers and pastoral counsellors, where the aim is to increase the emotional and social competence of the adult professional (Hall *et al.* 1999).

Small group training is an umbrella term for a range of activities with a variety of names, such as t-groups, sensitivity training, process groups or encounter groups. There are, however, discernible features that such groups hold in common. They usually consist of around twelve members, plus or minus four. There is a group leader, usually called a facilitator, whose task is to focus the group's attention on the 'here and now' of the immediate experience of interpersonal or group process.

In a long-term follow-up of the small group training experience (Hall *et al.* 1999), the learners ascribed a range of feelings and experiences to the small group which they found revealing, including being disturbed (positively) and being confused (positively), as well as reporting feelings such as being challenged and enlightened. This pattern of being at once stimulated, (both thoughts and feelings) and disturbed, may be regarded as the optimal conditions for personal learning to take place and what Joyce (1984) has described as 'dynamic disequilibrium'.

Conclusion

The term 'emotional intelligence' has caught the public imagination. It is a shorthand term which foregrounds the part that our emotions play in the learning process. Theoretically impoverished and morally fragile conceptions of human intelligence, as measured by traditional IQ tests, have dominated educational discourse for over a century. This privileging of the part that cognition plays in learning has effectively obscured what many psychologists and educators have been arguing: the need for a more balanced theory of how learners learn and the place of affect in the process. This more holistic view rightly acknowledges and respects the part that our emotional selves play in the learning process.

> We have paid a drastic price – not only in our organizations, but in our lives – for trying to disconnect emotions from intellect. It can't be done. Not only do we know intuitively that it can't be done, modern science is proving every day that it is emotional intelligence, not IQ, or raw brain power alone, that underpins many of the best decisions, the most dynamic organizations, and the most satisfying and successful lives.
>
> (Cooper and Sawaf 1998: xi–xii)

This chapter has argued that emotion is not subservient to mind but, like a two-headed coin, an indivisible part of an integrated whole. The development of emotional intelligence in learners is the fourth 'R' – *relationship* – of the curriculum. Relationship to the self, to others and to a broader, more holistic view of what it means to be human; what Zohar and Marshall (2000) have called 'spiritual intelligence'.

However, to educate the emotions means ultimately to educate the mind, and in order to develop holistic learning experiences for students of all ages, we need teachers who are sufficiently fit for the purpose. Teachers who have sufficient self-knowledge that they can understand what moves others, teachers who are vital and spontaneous enough to see potential for joy and laughter in each moment. Teachers who have the flexibility of mind and resilience of heart to weather the storms of despair and failure with their learners. Teachers who are thoughtful enough to help us work through our puzzles, dilemmas and knots and who are wise enough to let us think that we unravelled them alone. Compassionate guides and wise companions on the learning journey that is our lives.

References

Allport, G. W. (1938) *Personality: A Psychological Interpretation*, London: Constable.

Argyris, C. (1989) 'Strategy Implementation: An Experience in Learning', *Organizational Dynamics* 18 (2): 5–15.

Aspy, D. N and Roebuck, F. N. (1977) *Kids Don't Learn From People They Don't Like*, Amherst, MA: Human Resource Development Press.

Bagshaw, M. (2000) *Using Emotional Intelligence at Work: 17 Tried and Tested Activities for Understanding the Practice and Applications of Emotional Intelligence*, Cambridgeshire: Fenman.

Bandura, A. (1997) *Self-Efficacy: The Exercise of Control*, New York: W. H. Freeman.

Bar-On, R. (1997) *The Emotional Quotient Inventory (EQ-i): Technical Manual*, Toronto: Multi-Health Systems.

Beard, C. and Wilson, J. P. (2002) *The Power of Experiential Learning*, London: Kogan Page.

Boyatzis, R. E., Goleman, D. and Rhee, K. S. (2000) 'Clustering Competence in Emotional Intelligence: Insights from the Emotional Competence Inventory', in R. Bar-On and J. D. R. Parker (eds) *The Handbook of Emotional Intelligence: Theory, Development, Assessment and Application at Home, School and in the Workplace*, San Francisco: Jossey-Bass, pp. 343–62.

Brown, G. I. (1971) *Human Teaching for Human Learning*, New York: Viking Press.

Bulut, S. (2003) *A Study of Espoused-Theory and Theory-in-Use in a Group of Human Relations Facilitators in a Higher Education Institute*, unpublished Ed.D. thesis. School of Education, University of Nottingham.

Carkhuff, R. R. (1969) *Helping and Human Relations*, New York: Holt.

Cooper, R. and Sawaf, A. (1998) *Executive EQ*, London: Orion Business Books.

Gardiner, H. (1983) *Frames of Mind: The Theory of Multiple Intelligences*, London: Fontana.

Gascoigne, F. (2004) Personal communication, University of Nottingham.

Goleman, D. (1996 [1995]) *Emotional Intelligence: Why It Can Matter More Than IQ*, London: Bloomsbury.

—— (1998) *Working with Emotional Intelligence*, London: Bloomsbury.

Hall, C. (2003) 'The Emotional Development Curriculum', in G. Hornby, C. Hall and E. Hall (eds) *Counselling Pupils in Schools*, London: RoutledgeFalmer, pp. 55–68.

Hall, E. and Hall, C. (1988) *Human Relations in Education*, London: Routledge.

Hall, E., Hall, C. and Leech, A. (1990) *Scripted Fantasy in the Classroom*, London: Routledge.

Hall, E., Hall, C. and Sirin, A. (1996) 'Personal and Professional Development for Teachers: The Application of Learning Following a Counselling Course', *British Journal of Educational Psychology* 66: 383–98.

Hall, E., Hall, C. and Abaci, R. (1997) 'The Effects of Human Relations Training on Reported Teacher Stress, Pupil Control Ideology and Locus of Control', *British Journal of Educational Psychology* 67: 483–96.

Hall, E., Hall, C., Harris, B., Hay, D., Biddulph, M. and Duffy, T. (1999) 'An Evaluation of the Long-term Outcomes of Small-group Work for Counsellor Development', *Counselling Psychology Review* 27 (1): 99–112.

Hornby, G., Hall, C. and Hall, E. (eds) (2003) *Counselling Pupils in Schools*, London: RoutledgeFalmer.

Jersild, A. T. (1952) *In Search of Self*, New York: Teachers College, Columbia University.

Jones, D. (ed.) (1994) *Innovative Therapy: A Handbook*, Buckingham: Open University Press.

Joyce, B. R. (1984) 'Dynamic Disequilibrium: The Intelligence of Growth', *Theory into Practice* 23 (1): 26–34.

Kelly, G. A. (1955) *The Psychology of Personal Constructs, Vols 1 and 2*, New York: Norton.

Kolb, D. A. (1984) *Experiential Learning*, Englewood Cliffs, NJ: Prentice Hall.

Krishnamurti, J. (1968) *Education and the Significance of Life*, London: Victor Gollancz.

Lawrence, D. (1998) *Enhancing Self-esteem in the Classroom*, London: Paul Chapman.

Lefcourt, H. M. (1976) *Locus of Control: Current Trends in Theory and Research*, Hillsdale, NJ: Erlbaum.

Lipka, J. A. and Beane, R. P. (1984) *Self-Concept, Self-Esteem and the Curriculum*, Newton, MA: Allyn and Bacon.

Macmurray, J. (1972) *Reason and Emotion*, Whitstable: Faber and Faber.

Mahoney, M. (1991) *Human Change Processes*, New York: Basic Books.

Maslow, A. T. (1962) *Towards a Psychology of Being*, Princeton, NJ: Van Nostrand.

Mayer, J. D. (2001) 'A Field Guide to Emotional Intelligence', in J. Ciarrochi, J. P. Forgas and J. D. Mayer (eds), *Emotional Intelligence in Everyday Life: A Scientific Inquiry*, Philadelphia: Taylor and Francis, pp. 3–24.

Mayer, J. D. and Salovey, P. (1993) 'The Intelligence of Emotional Intelligence', *Intelligence* 17: 433–42.

Mayer, J. D., Salovey, P. and Caruso, D. R. (2000) 'Emotional Intelligence as Zeitgeist, as Personality, and as Mental Ability', in R. Bar-On and J. D. A. Parker (eds) *The Handbook of Emotional Intelligence: Theory, Development, Assessment, and Application at Home, School, and in the Workplace*, San Francisco: Jossey Bass, pp. 118–35.

Mruk, C. (1999) *Self-Esteem*, London: Free Association Books.

O'Connell, A. and O'Connell, V. (1980) *Choice and Change*, Englewood Cliffs, NJ: Prentice Hall.

Rogers, C. R. (1961) *On Becoming a Person: A Therapist's View of Psychotherapy*, Boston: Houghton Mifflin.

—— (1962) 'The Interpersonal Relationship: The Core of Guidance', *Harvard Educational Review* 32 (4): 416–29.

Rogers, C. R. and Freiberg, H. J. (1994) *Freedom to Learn*, New York: Merrill.

Schutz, W. C. (1971) *Joy: Expanding Human Awareness*, London: Souvenir Press.

See, H. K. P., Hall, C. and Hall, E. (1999) 'Changes in the Attitudes of Hong Kong Teachers and Their Students Following an Experiential Counselling Skills Training Course', *Asian Journal of Counselling* 5 (1): 1–11.

Sirin, A., Hall, E., Hall, C. and Restorick, J. (1995) 'Item Analysis of the "My Use of Interpersonal Skills Inventory" ', *British Journal of Guidance and Counselling* 23 (3): 409–18.

Steiner, C. and Perry, P. (1999*)* *Achieving Emotional Literacy*, London: Bloomsbury.

Stevens, J. O. (1971) *Awareness*, Moab, UT: Real People Press.

Warner Weil, S. and McGill, I. (1989) *Making Sense of Experiential Learning: Diversity in Theory and Practice*, Buckingham: SHRE and Open University Press.

Zohar, D. and Marshall, I. (2000) *SQ – Spiritual Intelligence: The Ultimate Intelligence*, London: Bloomsbury.

Chapter 11

The spiritual and human learning

R. E. Y. Wickett

For those who believe that there is a spiritual dimension to human nature, a holistic sense of learning must incorporate this spiritual dimension. For those who believe that there is a greater spiritual power in the universe, the spiritual must be considered as we review any aspect of human experience of the world, including learning.

Leona English (1999) suggests that there is a craving for the spiritual in the world, although she indicates that there is a 'general distrust' of organized religious institutions. The search for the spiritual often occurs outside the realms of existing churches, synagogues and temples. Dent Davis (2003) suggests that it is in the realm of informal learning where we often find learners experiencing the spiritual. If the assessment by these authors of this situation is correct, our religious communities need to consider its implications. It also means that some adults will search elsewhere in order to learn about the spiritual. Our work in many adult education agencies or in other settings may be influenced by this search. Recent research indicates that existing institutions may need to change in certain ways in order to accommodate the new learners. English believes that the changes needed to enhance spiritual learning will involve attempts at greater inclusiveness and at engagement and dialogue versus simply preaching or lecturing. This means that adult education activities need to be open and involve all relevant parties to the discussion. It means that we cannot simply tell people what to believe about the spiritual. We have to participate with them in a mutual learning process of exploration and growth.

Davis (2003) wants us to open our thinking in existing institutions, including churches, in order to be inclusive of people's experience. The need for a holistic approach with respect to human experience becomes clearer as we learn more about the learners.

Adult education can engage the learner in a process that will achieve a holistic approach to learning and an investigation of content that is meaningful to the learner. As a result of this, I believe that the spiritual dimension can be addressed in our work. The questions to be asked should reflect not if but how we are able to do so.

This chapter will review adult learning theories of relevance to the process of religious learning. It will consider the connections that we need to make when we engage with adult learners, with particular reference to the issues of spirituality. Reference will be made to such aspects of spirituality as the nature of human spirituality, spiritual intelligence, spiritual audits, spiritual journeys, and alternate approaches to spirituality.

Adult learning theories

Adult learning theories can assist us to understand an important aspect of the process of spiritual growth. The three theories that have gained prominence in recent decades with respect to the learning of adults are referred to as experiential learning, self-directed learning, and transformative learning. This section will consider each of these theories and their possible connections with spiritual learning.

Experiential learning has been an important part of the literature of adult education and learning for many years in the works of authors from Kolb (1984), whose early major writings defined the area, to the recent writings of adult educators such as Merriam and Caffarella (1999) and other authors. People who have a sense of the spiritual often believe that they have experienced the spiritual in some way or another. It may be possible to provide new learning experiences for people that allow for the examination of this aspect of their lives. It may also be possible for them to learn through a review of prior experience with a spiritual perspective.

One example of spiritual experience and learning is seen in Canada's first nations or Indian peoples. Children often learn in the context of creation. They do not enter a classroom, but walk in the environment as the nature of creation is explained by an elder. There is a connection between theory and practice that is most effective for the learning process. If part of our experience is spiritual, we need to consider how this integrates with other aspects of our being and our learning experiences.

The second major area of adult learning theory comes from the research and writing about self-directed learning. This area began with the research of Allen Tough (1979) but has broadened out in many ways since the 1970s. It refers to the learner's attempts to determine the nature of learning in which they are involved. The literature that followed the findings of Tough and others in this area of learning theory describes the development of both learning contracts and learning covenants to enable students to have greater control over their learning experiences. Malcolm Knowles (1975, 1986) began the work on learning contracts, while Wickett (1999) developed the concept of learning covenants to include a religious dimension to the activity of learning. The ability to plan one's own learning enables the incorporation of dimensions that other planners might not consider. Of course, this includes the possibility of including the spiritual dimension.

Leona English (2000), who works extensively with learners in the area of self-directed learning, suggests that the ability to organize learning plans for individualized activities allows the potential for a higher level of person involvement and growth. The denial of self and one's own attributes may occur when others plan the learning. Learner participation in these activities can be valuable in all areas, including the spiritual.

The third major area of theory in adult learning in the latter part of the previous century is known as transformative learning. It was influenced by the work of Paolo Freire in addition to the critical perspectives of other North American groups. Its major proponents include Jack Mezirow (1991) and Edmund O' Sullivan (1999). According to Edmund O'Sullivan (1999), transformative learning has important spiritual implications. He describes this as a dimension of learning that must be considered at the most fundamental level. I agree with his suggestion that contemporary education suffers because it lacks the depth that only comes with an examination of the spiritual aspects of life.

Working with adult learners

There continues to be the issue of our connection with the learners with whom we work. Where does all this fit for us as educators with respect to them? I suggest that the spiritual dimension is relevant to us as educators when we can discover the spiritual dimension in ourselves and in others. This will assist us to understand ourselves and them and to relate to them in the learning process. It will mean that we can support their growth holistically and, in particular, as spiritual beings. A recognition of the existence of a greater spiritual dimension in the universe can enable us to grow in relation to that aspect of our work. We can learn and develop in the context of a relationship to that greater spiritual dimension, as can the learners with whom we work.

Spirituality

Henri Nouwen (1966), a writer whose work examines human spirituality, has suggested that we need to consider the spiritual in three specific dimensions. The first is the individual, or one's own, spiritual dimension. The second is the spiritual dimension that is found in others. The third is the spiritual dimension that is represented by what we understand as God, the spiritual force that is in the universe. This understanding of the spiritual can be found in the world's great religions as well as among those who do not subscribe to a particular, institutional set of religious beliefs about God.

As educators, we are required first to consider the spiritual dimension that is within ourselves. If we believe that such a spiritual dimension exists, what are the implications of this dimension in all aspects of our lives, including our work as educators? How does it shape who we are and what we are? Self-understanding is the beginning of a true openness to the spiritual dimension of others. I believe that Nouwen is correct in this suggestion. We must begin with ourselves.

If we believe that we have a spiritual dimension within ourselves, most of us do not believe that we are the only person to experience or possess this. A similar spiritual dimension will be found in others. Our ability to recognize and accept this dimension of others will help us to connect and work with them. If the spiritual dimension is part of the human experience, is it connected with a greater spiritual dimension in the universe that surrounds us? Do we recognize this dimension of all that makes up our experience, either directly or indirectly? If the answer to this question is yes, the implications for our work are considerable. In order to understand these aspects of human experience we need to consider the various ways in which spirituality is being examined in our world. We must then connect them with concepts of education and learning that will allow us to incorporate them into our work.

Spiritual intelligence

Howard Gardner (1993) has opened the door to a variety of ways of considering human intelligence. Subsequent authors such as Robert Emmons (2000) have asked the question about the ways in which spirituality can be examined as a form of intelligence. This theory enables the possibility of the consideration of a connection between the psychology of religion and spirituality.

Gardner (1993) was explicit in his view that spirituality was not one of the multiple intelligences, but Emmons (2000) suggest that there are five ways in which spirituality may connect with the theory of intelligence. These ways are:

1   the capacity to transcend the physical and material;
2   the ability to experience heightened states of consciousness;
3   the ability to sanctify everyday experience;
4   the ability to utilize spiritual resources to solve problems;
5   the capacity to be virtuous.

To what extent these ways can be connected with the concept of abstract reasoning with a coherent symbolic system is the key to our acceptance of the concept of spiritual. Emmons (2000) suggests that the capacity to use the abilities connected with spirituality to help us to solve problems is consistent with traditional concepts of intelligence. One of the dangers inherent in this approach is that the connection with intelligence suggests a connection with an ability to measure. We need to consider how we could measure spiritual intelligence if we are to consider it in the same way as we do other forms of intelligence.

We must begin by asking certain questions. How can we measure the capacity to transcend the physical and material? Is it possible to measure people's ability to experience heightened states of consciousness? We may find ourselves moving into a form of analysis of spirituality that causes discomfort for us and for those with whom we work. Spiritual intelligence has the capacity to enable us to see connections. After all, we are advocating a holistic approach to learning and learners that suggests that there is a connectedness for the person's seemingly disparate dimensions. But we must be careful about the application of such connections. There is a considerable distance to go with these ideas before they will be truly useful to us as educators concerned with the spiritual dimension of human learning.

Spiritual audit

A new term, the spiritual audit, has come into recent use. This term has both individual and collective dimensions. Fred Smith (1998) examines the personal dimension of this by suggesting the ways in which one can conduct an examination of one's spiritual dimension. Ian Mitroff and Elizabeth Denton (1999) extend this concept to the workplace. Smith's approach is very pastoral and clearly connected with enabling others to examine their spiritual situation. His questions are simple and straightforward with respect to the spiritual nature of people. They include such basic issues as having a quiet centre to one's life and a genuine awe of God. They ask us to consider our prayer life and its effectiveness and whether or not we have a sense of our own ministry.

Each person needs to consider the nature of their spiritual condition. Smith's audit provides a simple way to do that. But it is limited in nature and focused on the individual. Perhaps this is an area where input from others can help us to be more informed. We may need to have the feedback that comes from a spiritual advisor or director to enable us to do this sort of thing more effectively. Moreover, I am suspicious about doing this in a manner that is 'measurable' or quantifiable in any way.

In the preface to the book by Mitroff and Denton (1999), the authors suggest that many organizations are spiritually impoverished. They have a particular concern about the workplace but what they say may be true of certain other human organizations as well. The authors suggest that the more successful organizations are those that take into account the whole person in their particular approach to organizational structure and function. Mitroff and Denton found that people defined spirituality as 'the basic desire to find ultimate meaning and purpose in one's life and to live an integrated life'. The second finding was, in my view, incredibly important. They suggest that 'people do not want to compartmentalize or fragment their lives'. These conclusions will be as true for the places where people learn as for those where they work.

If we wish to provide learning opportunities for people, we cannot ask them to 'check their spiritual side at the door'. We need to recognize the whole person. This means that we must consider their search for meaning and purpose in their lives and the need to be treated holistically as opposed to compartmentalized.

Spiritual journey

Many religious persons have used the metaphor of the spirituality journey to describe people's experiences over time as they search for a deeper relationship with the ultimate meaning of life. The implications of our interconnectedness and the progress that is made in the concept of the spiritual journey or path can be helpful for those who try to conceptualize this area.

The historical approach to spirituality has led us to see this as valuable whether it occurs in a monastic or in a societal context. I came across the work of Charles Asher recently, which makes the connection between the spiritual journey and psychological therapy. Asher (e.g. 2001) suggests that contemplation is a key part of the process of the spiritual journey and the activity of healing and growth. Asher describes contemplation as something that is process oriented versus something that is product oriented. As people who work with adult learners, we may need to ask the question about our own focus on product or results. To what extent are we content to support people on their journey without being too judgmental about their progress? If we are to consider the spiritual dimension, we need to be more open to people's determination of their own requirements and of the progress that they feel they need to make in their journey.

Alternate approaches to spirituality

As educators, it is vital that we recognize alternate approaches to spirituality among the people with whom we work. There are many who will wish to participate in learning activities in agencies outside their faith communities who bring a different understanding of the spiritual than that which may be held by the educator. Our openness to these people must be clear and respectful. As someone who lives in a community where there are peoples of many cultures in addition to a strong aboriginal group, I am well aware of the diversity that we may encounter. As the world transforms itself into the global community of the twenty-first century, we must develop policies in our institutions that include others of differing views and perspectives on spiritual issues.

Jeffrey Orr describes the implication for adult education among aboriginal peoples whose sense of spirituality is central to their very being and to all that they do in life. One aspect of this approach to spirituality, the medicine wheel or the circle, talks about the interconnectedness of the four aspects; spiritual, emotional, mental, and physical. It is also true that, when one is in a circle, all are important as part of the whole. There is no beginning or end, but all are connected.

The spirituality of certain groups within our world is one that is lived rather than one which is written or described to outsiders. In certain aboriginal communities, only the elders comment on religious or spiritual issues. It is important to respect this approach. It means that, although people do not 'check their spirituality at the door' when they enter a learning situation, they may choose to share it indirectly through who they are and what they are as persons rather than verbally or in other explicit forms. Many religions and cultural groups ascribe to an approach to life that incorporates all aspects of their being. Many learners reject an approach that causes them to disconnect from a part of their being. It is not acceptable to people to deny their spirituality when they enter certain learning situations or, indeed, other life situations.

Spiritual direction

Many religious communities have a basis for providing support to the person who engages in a spiritual journey. These people are called by many names, such as a spiritual director or a spiritual advisor. They normally work within the structure of the belief system of the faith community. Their various ways of working are too numerous to be included here.

It is my contention that a very important part of their work is the support of a learning process. The very substance of a spiritual journey involves the things that learners 'gain and retain' in their search. Knowledge and understanding are key components of the spiritual journey. Spiritual directors or advisors should begin to consider the people that they work with as learners and their role in the support of their learning.

Spiritual learning

The questions for those who believe in the spiritual revolve around the nature of the spiritual and of spiritual development as the way of learning. Leona English suggests that there are three aspects of spirituality that we need to remember when working with adult learners. The first is a 'strong sense of self'. This will enable us to reach out to others. The second involves our care and outreach to others. This is the natural extension of our spirituality. The third reflects the continuous construction of meaning and knowledge. There is a clear spiritual dimension in finding meaning in everyday life.

Relationships with learners on the journey

What types of relationships do we need to have with our learners? If we are qualified as spiritual directors, there are certain ways in which we can work effectively with learners. If not, we must consider other ways of working with learners in groups or individual situations. The focus of this chapter will continue to be for those who do not follow the ministry of spiritual direction.

The metaphor of the journey is used to describe many spiritual experiences through the life span. In this metaphor, all of us are described as being on a journey toward the central spiritual force in the universe. The nature of the ultimate goal of that journey may be described in various ways, but it is our pursuit of that journey that is important. And learning is an important part of that journey. Our own experiences of the journey may help us to support others in the process. The sharing of experience creates a context in which this can happen. The sharing of our stories may be the first stage of this process. Later stages may include sharing insights or reactions that are designed to be supportive and helpful.

Of course, we need to recognize and respect the diversity of journeys that may occur. Both the individual's and separate faith community's definitions need to be considered when we look at the learner's faith journey. As educators, we experience our own journey and we share in the journey of others. Whether or not we are spiritual advisors or directors, we can still participate in this process. We may be mentors or co-voyagers. We shall always be learners during the process, no matter what type of relationship we may have with others.

The issue of how to support others in their journey as educators is also found in Nouwen's writings. He suggests that we create an environment in which the spiritual dimension is respected and enhanced. There is the sense of comfort which people need in order to engage in spiritual development. The educator needs to find a way to provide this. Nouwen describes the sense of hospitality that is essential to the growth of others. When they are in our presence, they need to feel welcomed. He compares this to the feeling experienced by a truly welcome guest. When we are pleased to have a guest in our presence, they are able to feel the warmth and acceptance of their presence. Deirdre LaNoue (2001) suggests that the feeling of intimacy is at the heart of what Nouwen writes about the relationships between people. What underlies Nouwen's perspective is the view that 'all human beings were meant to love others and to be loved by them'. Nouwen contrasts fear and love with respect to intimacy. According to LaNoue, the former type of intimacy based on fear is manipulative and depends upon a process of taking from the other person. The latter form, love, is based on forgiveness and openness. In the book *Reaching Out* (1966), Nouwen uses the words 'hostility' and 'hospitality'. He discusses the way in which we can create a free and friendly space in order to ensure that those with whom we come into contact can feel welcome in the space that we occupy together.

As educators, it is our responsibility to convey this feeling of warmth in the places where we meet with learners. We must create the environment of acceptance when learners feel welcome to share their spiritual dimension and their journey with us. Nouwen suggests the creation of a learning environment that will consider the possibilities for comfort for the learning situation, including the physical surroundings, the process of learning, and the interaction with the educator. A comfortable location with appropriate furniture arranged in a suitable manner will assist us to create a feeling of hospitality. An interactive process that accepts the learner's experiences and thoughts will generate a positive climate for learning. Our own personal relationship should be one of acceptance and trust. When we give due thought to these factors, we will be able to make the learner's experience more positive and useful.

If the spiritual is an important dimension of our work, we must ensure that this atmosphere of hospitality is maintained in the learning environment. If we consider it to be a part of holistic learning and an element in the learning situation, we must be equally committed to hospitality in the learning situation. This atmosphere of hospitality must be created before learners begin their learning interaction with us. It should begin with our initial contact at the start and continue throughout the learning interaction. Each opportunity to reinforce their sense of welcome and acceptance must be taken. This can be done through the formation of relationships with the learners and in the activities that occur before and during the learning situation.

Perhaps the relationships which we have with learners are the most important aspect of hospitality. We know from interpersonal relationships we form with others that the sense of welcome we experience in their presence influences much that we are able to do together. When we are accepted, the possibilities for positive things to happen will increase. We are more open with those with whom we have a feeling of security and welcome. We communicate more freely with those with whom we have built a relationship of trust.

The next issue to be considered is that of the processes of learning in which we, as educators, play a part. Activities that involve positive learning processes and outcomes should be built into any learning situation. Activities that value the learner as a spiritual person are important. We need to be inclusive of people's experience and to connect this with the content that they are exploring in the learning process in order to foster hospitality.

The evaluation of any learning activities should be done in a positive manner that is designed to give support to the learning activity. Evaluation need not be a judgmental or a negative experience. We need to focus on those forms of evaluation that support the learning process. Positive feedback to the learner can be reinforcing and create the proper climate for the learning experience. Feedback that supports growth and deeper understanding can be delivered in ways that engage, not alienate, the learner. We are not critical of our guests.

As educators, we need to find ways to ensure that we are doing as much as possible to support the learning process. Programme evaluation is critical to this process. We need to receive feedback on our own work that will enable us to be more effective in future situations. We must provide learners with the opportunity to engage with us in order to develop better programmes and to enable our ability to work with future learners.

Concluding thoughts

As adult educators, we need to consider the whole person when we engage in support of their learning. We need to incorporate the individual in a learning process that is welcoming and accepting. We need to address their requirements for content based upon their shared experience of life situations. The ways in which we do these things will be based upon an understanding of the total person or persons with whom we work. It must consider the nature of learning and the essential processes for successful learning. It should reflect the things that they seek to learn in the context of their overall life situation. Our consideration of these factors is vital to our ability to work with them, but it must be done in a manner that includes a sense of the spiritual dimension that is such an important part of the human experience in general and of human learning in particular.

Recognizing our own spiritual dimension will help us to understand the spiritual dimension of others. This can occur in the context of close, personal or 'intimate' relationships. We must strive to build these close relationships in our work with the learners, in order for them to have the opportunities for deeper learning experiences and spiritual growth. Although not all of our work as adult educators falls into the realm of the spiritual, we must remember that the spiritual continues to be a part of the human condition. We may not touch upon it directly in our classes or other learning situations, but it will continue to be present in all aspects of life for the learners who share the learning situation with us. I have always considered it a privilege to be allowed into the lives of learners, to share in their pursuit of something that is important to them. Such a privilege must be recompensed with the due care and attention that recognizes the value of the learner or learners and their life experiences, including their spiritual dimension.

References

Asher, C. (2001) 'The Contemplative Self: The Spiritual Journey and Therapeutic Work', in P. Slattery and L. Corbett (eds) *Depth Psychology: Meditations in the Field*, Einseideln, Switzerland: Pacifica Graduate Institute.

Davis, D. C. (2003) 'Encounter with God: Pedagogical Implications of the Human Experience for Religious Education in the Church', paper presented at the Joint

Conference of the Religious Education Association and the Association of Professors and Researchers, Chicago, November.

Emmons, R. A. (2000) 'Is Spirituality an Intelligence? Motivation, Cognition, and the Psychology of Ultimate Concern', *International Journal for the Psychology of Religion* 10 (1): 3–26.

English, L. M. (1999) 'A Postmodern Vision of Adult Religious Education', *Didache* 4, Winter: 3–5.

—— (2000) 'Spiritual Dimensions of Informal Learning', in L. M. English and M. A. Gillen (eds) *Addressing the Spiritual Dimensions of Adult Learning: What Educators Can Do. New Directions for Adult and Continuing Education No. 85*, San Francisco: Jossey-Bass.

Gardner, H. (1993) *Frames of Mind: The Theory of Multiple Intelligences*, New York: Basic Books.

Knowles, M. S. (1975) *Self-directed Learning: A Guide for Learners and Teachers*, Englewood Cliffs, NJ: Prentice Hall.

—— (1986) *Using Learning Contracts*, San Francisco: Jossey-Bass.

Kolb, D. A. (1984) *Experiential Learning: Experience as the Source of Learning and Development*, Englewood Cliffs, NJ: Prentice Hall.

LaNoue, D. (2001) *The Spiritual Legacy of Henri Nouwen*, New York: Continuum.

Merriam, S. B. and Caffarella, R. S. (1999) *Learning in Adulthood: A Comprehensive Guide* (second edition), San Francisco: Jossey-Bass.

Mezirow, J. and Associates (1991) *Fostering Critical Reflection in Adulthood: A Guide to Transformative and Emancipatory Learning*, San Francisco: Jossey-Bass.

Mitroff, D. and Denton, E. (1999) *A Spiritual Audit of Corporate America: A Hard Look at Spirituality, Religion, and Values in the Workplace*, San Francisco: Jossey-Bass.

Nouwen, H. (1966) *Reaching Out: The Three Movements of the Spiritual Life*, New York: Doubleday.

O'Sullivan, E. (1999) *Transformative Learning: Educational Vision for the 21st Century*, London: Zed Books.

Smith, F. (1998) 'Conducting a Spiritual Audit: Twelve Questions to Keep Your Personal Accounts in Order', *Leadership* 19, Winter: 40–6.

Tough, A. (1979) *The Adult's Learning Projects: A Fresh Approach to Theory and Practice in Adult Learning* (second edition), Toronto: Ontario Institute for Studies in Education.

Wickett, R. E. Y. —— (1999) *How to Use the Learning Covenant in Religious Education: Working with Adults*, Birmingham, AL: Religious Education Press.

Chapter 12

Fabricating new directions for women's learning

Case studies in fabric crafts and fashion

Joyce Stalker

Learning is an inevitable part of life; indeed, it is essential for survival. Although we all learn through many media, some media are more the domains of women than of men. This chapter explores learning through two such areas: fabric crafts and fashion. At first glance, some might label the focus of these case studies as inconsequential, trivial, retrogressive, and frivolous or marginal to this book's focus. However, as this chapter will demonstrate, both are deeply connected to it. Indeed, throughout history and in tune with various cultural customs, men, women, boys and girls have learned their lives through fabric crafts and fashion.

The marginalisation of these areas in relationship to learning raises two issues for me. The first concerns my observations of my women colleagues, graduate and undergraduate students. I have watched them intellectually engage these topics with ease and enthusiasm while men fumble awkwardly with them. Indeed, I wonder if these areas are often dismissed precisely because in contemporary times they are more closely associated with women. I wonder if they are demeaned because they locate women as the prime knowers and experts and because they are areas of learning which can be more readily controlled by women, both in practice and in theory. They are areas in which women can have an authoritative voice, experience the power of having extensive, legitimate and valuable knowledge, (de)construct and experiment with our identities – these are rich and very powerful learning moments. It perplexes me that they have not been used more often among facilitators as a starting point to engage learners. In particular, they seem to offer an ideal starting place to engage women learners, those learners who continue to be vulnerable in our society.

Second, I am intrigued by the invisibility of these areas as worthy of research and as a suitable base from which to foster women's learning and authority. After all, the 'practices which a culture insists are meaningless or trivial, the places where ideology has succeeded in becoming invisible, are practices in need of investigation' (Evans and Thornton 1991: 50). It would seem that it is time to extend the borders of women's learning to include these areas.

In this chapter I will explore the potential of these areas with specific reference to women's learning. This is for three reasons. First, as I have hinted above, women around the world constitute the majority of the illiterates, vulnerable and violated, and the minority of decision makers. This different approach to women's learning may offer useful insights into the resolution of these persistent problems.

Second, although I am not entirely comfortable with the notion that there is a thing called 'women's learning', I believe that I share a world of experiences with other women that is different to men's world. As I will explore below, the idea of women's learning has always seemed too reductionistic, too simplistic and too dangerous to me. The blunt placement of women in opposition to men too often seems more problematic than beneficial to us. However, at the same time it has been my experience across a wide range of cultures and circumstances, that these areas elicit energetic attention and enthusiasm from many women, and certainly more interest from women than from most men. Thus, I suggest that these areas have a strong potential to foster women's learning. Equally importantly, they have the ability to be vehicles by which we *un*learn – that is, through them we can uncover the taken-for-granted understandings and unexamined assumptions through which we may unknowingly support our own oppressions. They are thus locations by which we can simultaneously learn through our oppression (Belenky *et al.* 1986) at the same time as we learn our way out of it.

Given the above, my purpose in this chapter is to explore the potential of fabric crafts and fashion to foster women's (un)learning. In order to address this purpose, I first overview some of the dilemmas which make the notion of 'women's learning' problematic. Second, I explore the key discourses in fabric craft and fashion theorisation and relate them to their relevance as learning sites for women. Third, I explore the implications of these ideas for those who work with women. Finally, I conclude with a brief summary and look to the future.

Dilemmas embedded within the notion of 'women's learning'

The idea that women's learning is distinct from men's learning came to the forefront of popular and academic attention in the 1980s. In 1982, Carol Gilligan proposed that women defined our 'self' in a particular way that included empathy, caring, intimacy and relationships. More prominence was given to this kind of idea when Belenky *et al.* (1986) undertook an all-female research project in reaction to William Perry's 1968 research. For two decades his all-male study had defined learning styles for adults. Belenky *et al.*'s study supposedly demonstrated that women have 'ways of knowing' which are different to Perry's developmental stages. These studies reflected some of the energy generated around 'women's issues' in the 1970s and 1980s, including the United Nations' International Decade of Women from 1975 to 1985 and the growth of the visibility of the women's movement in many parts of the world.

The notion that women's learning is different from men's has always had a certain appeal to me – after all, it values women and at least places female perspectives into adult learning theories. In addition, it appreciates women as unique, with distinctive learning characteristics, styles, motivations, and psychological and psychosocial drivers.

This modernist approach, however, can be easily questioned for its dichotomous positioning and its inattention to diversity and difference. Dichotomy is not, in and of itself, a negative thing. However, there are several negative implications associated with that positioning. First, it comes dangerously close to locating the discussion of women's learning in biological determinism. Fundamentally, biological determinism argues that men and women have unique 'natural' differences. As a consequence, women are deemed to be 'naturally' more nurturing, less interested in positions of authority, and so on. As well as emphasising the individualised, biological person, the approach leads to the dangerous notion that there can be a scientific, conscious manipulation of women's (mis)behaviour.

Second, a singular, biological explanation also reinforces stereotypes and locates the origins of different expectations, attitudes and values in psychological rather than political, economic, social and cultural constructs. Third, the homogenisation of the concept of 'woman' which results from a biologically determined model too easily leads to a one-model-fits-all explanation of women's learning. The implications of the intersections of gender, class, ethnicity, ability and sexual orientation are demeaned. Thus this model based in dichotomous positionings has received considerable critique (Hayes and Colin III 1994; Hayes and Flannery 2000; Sheared 1994; Tisdell 1993).

Finally, between men and women differentiation inevitably works to the disadvantage of women. History has almost always demonstrated that 'social and cultural understandings of sexual differences are related to the oppression and exploitation of women ... Masculine characteristics attitudes, beliefs and behaviours are valued as the norm, and the feminine counterparts are devalued. Men are empowered, women are disempowered' (Collard and Stalker 1991: 72).

There are, of course, some learning experiences which are unique to women, and it is ironic that they are biologically located. Among these are childbirth, menstruation, menopause and pre-menstrual tension. Although modern medicine from time to time attempts to demonstrate that some of these have male equivalents, they remain the domain of women. What is most perplexing for me is that they have not become a focus for those who work with women to find new ways of being and acting. Based in our worlds, one would think that these areas would be a natural starting point to begin a learning dialogue.

There are also other issues which are less exclusively, but still primarily, the domain of today's women. These sadly still include domestic violence, casual employment contracts, lower pay for work of equal value, overwork in the private sphere, limited career progression, and on and on. Despite male allies, some of these concerns continue to exist.

Among the dismal and grim statistics associated with these areas, there are two discourses which offer a more hopeful point of initial connection with women. I am not suggesting that women should ignore the misogyny embedded in the issues above (see Stalker 1998) or respond to them only in 'nice' ways. Newman has written eloquently of the dangers of niceness and its ability to seduce us into making naïve, individualistic, counselling solutions to social, economic, political and cultural problems (Newman 1994).

Nonetheless, it is my experience, and the literature confirms, that many women experience discomfort with direct argument, counter-argument and 'confrontational learning' (Jackson 1995: 199). Furthermore, it is clear that many mainstream learning discourses do not include women (Lewis and Simon 1991). It would appear that a key issue is how to engage women in (un)learning discussions and activities which are comfortable, familiar and yet also yield useful insights. This is an issue not only for educators in traditional institutions. It is relevant for all facilitators who work with women who are seeking new ways to understand and act.

I suggest that the subjects of fabric crafts and fashion can be useful as catalysts for women's learning. Based within discourses with which many women are already familiar, the worlds of fabric crafts and fashion can be used as vehicles to learn our realities, unlearn our oppressions, strengthen our voices and encourage our action against harsh misogynistic issues such as those noted above.

The potential of fabric crafts and fashion as sites for women's (un)learning

Although history can demonstrate that it has not always been so, the current discourses of fabric crafts and fashion are dominated by women. This makes them unique sites, particularly suited as case studies of women's learning. Few other sites offer women two media which are more ascribed to and used by women than by men, which have been a key part of our identity formation and which can be used readily for both explicit and coded protest. Before I explore these ideas, I need first to define both fabric crafts and fashion.

Fabric crafts are located in the interstices between 'high' and 'low' culture (Bourdieu and Passeron 1990). They bring together the aesthetic/practical, public/domestic and innovative/traditional. In this chapter, fabric crafts involve cloth which is constructed from non-metallic fibres and can include needlework embellishment. Examples include tapestry, rag rugs, crochet, quilts, banners, soft toys, knitting, crochet, lace and felt.

Fashion operates in many fields. There are, for example, 'fashionable' house designs, colours and theories of adult learning. For the purposes of this chapter, I have narrowed the meaning of fashion to the notions of apparel and adornment. Braham cleverly reminds us that the 'essence of fashion in clothes is that it compels us to discard a garment before it has outlived its usefulness' (1997: 121). Fashion is a complex phenomenon, however, and interacts with individuals, culture and also the economy through its processes of manufacture and retailing.

As the sections below will explore, fabric crafts and fashion have the potential to give women voice and to act against our oppressions. That is particularly so because of their special connections with women and their roles in helping women to form – that is, learn and unlearn – our identities.

Special connections which facilitate women's (un)learning

Both fabric crafts and fashion have special connections with women. Often they are identified as 'women's media'. Both, although not the exclusive domain of women, are primarily ascribed to and practised by women. They are part of a culture, learned by many women, which exists within the broader culture of society (Harding 1996). Although men may engage with both fabric and fashion, even today their involvement tends to be the exception rather than the rule.

The notion that fabric crafts are particularly suited to women reflects unique historical, theoretical and practical relationships which women have to fabrics (for a more detailed examination of this, see Stalker 2004). In terms of women's historical relationship to fabrics, first it is clear that for hundreds of generations women have learned and taught others how to spin, weave and sew. Our creation of cloth has been an integral and necessary part of our societies from ancient times to the Industrial Revolution (Barber 1994), when it was a significant economic force which belonged primarily to women.

Fabric craft work also has always played a significant social and cultural role, for through it women have learned, taught, maintained and resisted our cultures. Even today, although modern-day, 'First World' women may not create fabric crafts in the same quantity as our mothers and grandmothers, there is some discussion that women are continuing to learn fabric crafts since 'needles are the new black' (Hallinan 2003) – that is, fabric crafts have become a trendy statement. Certainly there is evidence that there is a surge in the popularity in women learning to knit (White

2003). The second historically bound relationship between women and fabric crafts concerns the gender (and class) divisions which for centuries have connected them. Art was deemed to be the arena of men and the upper class, while craft was allocated to the domain of women and the working class. Women have learned, acted out and resisted these simplistic divisions for generations.

At the theoretical level, several authors argue that fabric crafts have a particular connection to women. They suggest that there is more than a linguistic relationship between textiles which are the key element of fabric crafts, and the 'texts' or narratives which women hope to inscribe in, on and through our fabric crafts. Lippard, like others (Lakerink 1998; Lawrence 1997), views textiles as a 'prime visual metaphor for women's lives, for women's culture' (cited in Jefferies 2000: 190). Freud's dated interpretation argues that women's weaving is a symbolic invention which can 're-enact nature's art of concealing with pubic hair that which is women's great genital deficiency' (cited in Jefferies 1995: 169).

Finally, at the practical level, fabric crafts traditionally offered, and continue to offer, women an activity which is compatible with the demands of child care and child watching (Barber 1994). Archaeological evidence from 490 BC illustrates two enduring advantages of much fabric work – its mobility and its simplicity. These attributes were important to nomadic tribes in harsh circumstances, and continue to have relevance to women today. As Brown notes, fabric crafts are particularly suited to women because they

> do not require rapt concentration and are relatively dull and repetitive; they are easily interruptible and easily resumed once interrupted; they do not place the child in potential danger; and they do not require the participant to range far from home.
>
> (cited in Barber 1994: 30)

Fashion similarly has a special relationship with women. First, women link to fashion through fabric and fabric crafts which can be manipulated into costumes. This relationship to fashion has both practical and aesthetic purposes. In the domestic sphere, historically women have learned to be the sewers, knitters and weavers of essential items of clothing (Barber 1994; Nicholson 1998). Today women are more often the consumers rather than the creators of clothing and accessories for ourselves and others in our households. This leads to the second way in which women are linked to fashion, for we have learned to be keen consumers. In Canada, for example, in 2002,

> more than half of every dollar spent on clothing and accessories went toward women's clothing and accessories. Men's clothing and accessories

commanded a comparatively smaller 29 per cent, while clothing and accessories for girls, boys and infants and other apparel made up the rest.

(Lin 2003: para. 9)

As vehicles to (un)learn our identities

The unique location of both fabric crafts and fashion as primarily women's media merges with their important role in helping women to learn – that is, form – our identities. Identity formation is a complex notion and according to differing interpretations is based in psychological or sociological factors, internal or external influences, conscious or unconscious processes and early childhood or adult variables (Hayes and Flannery 2000). For the purposes of this chapter, identity formation is about how women set ourselves apart and distinguish ourselves as unique beings within our societies.

Fabric and fabric crafts offer women a way in which we can learn our identities. In general terms, they 'embody the social and economic reality of a community ... [they] form the material signature, the bodily mark of a loved one" (Jewish Museum of Australia 1997: 10). Our fabric craft work thus is an important way in which we learn about, preserve and support the dominant cultures and, indeed, colonise other cultures (Hood 2001). This role still exists, for

> even if contemporary women have, to some extent, thrown off their traditional role in the home, it seems they nevertheless take great pride in their female heritage within the family. They display with love and awe the extraordinary handwork of previous generations.
>
> (Isaacs 1987: 6)

Fabric crafts, however, can do much more than be a vehicle of learning which colonises and represents dominant cultures. Fabric crafts have provided a place within women's restricted lives where we could take space and learn to express ourselves creatively, emotionally and intellectually. They are a way in which we can create a narrative based in our lives and our experiences. Quilts, for example, have been identified as

> distinctively female patterns of thought and activity ... [with an] imaginative and emotional power ... that impels women of the past and present, of almost every race and class ... to make quilts in such abundance, out of proportion to any actual need.
>
> (Donnell 1990: ix)

Similarly, sewing has been identified as 'a solace for isolated women – solace for inactivity and powerlessness' (Hedges and Wendt 1980: 5). In terms of intellectual expression, when educational opportunities were not available to women, we were allowed to gather in sewing circles to learn a useful craft. These occasions became the places where women 'legitimately' or sometimes subversively learned to read and write. Fabric crafts offered us a place to express ourselves and also to 'read the text' of other women's lives inscribed in our handicraft. Today, these same kinds of activities still provide women with a means to attain 'personal individuation' (Bauer and Elsey 1992: 85): that is, to achieve a sense of personal achievement and identity.

Like fabric crafts, fashion is a 'cultural subject ... a badge or means of identity' (Braham 1997: 121). For centuries it has been a marker of social standing and, once learned, often was used to exclude the lower socio-economic groups. Mass production of fashion items allowed these boundaries to be blurred and people learned to use their clothes and adornment to create a public self. People were no longer so clearly allocated into a class by their clothes. Rather, fashion became a way through which everyone, women included, could express and indeed create their identity.

Fashion also is a vehicle by which women can learn and express the uniqueness of our gender and cultural identity (Crane 2000). Some argue that those identities are more prescribed for, rather than chosen by, the wearer (Lauer and Lauer 1981; Goldstein-Gidoni 1999). Some have noted that fashion is an important venue through which women learn femininity (Evans and Thornton 1991; Maynard 1999). Rolley (1990) argues that fashion and femininity are mutually reinforcing, since fashion represents society's ideals to women and women learn the necessary 'fashion sense' to perpetuate these definitions. Others suggest that particular practices like fashion parades play an important role in the construction of women and our identities. They are seen to be 'visual and behavioural training grounds for women, offering them ideal codes of conduct and techniques of self-fashioning' (Craig, in Maynard 1999: 203). Connected to these arguments is the negative presentation of women in 'the image of consumers as manipulable, passive dupes' (McRobbie 1999: 37) who supposedly follow fashion as defined and marketed to us by haute couture fashionistas.

There is another more positive interpretation of how women learn their identity through fashion. The more contemporary argument is that women today

> have reconstructed, through fashion, the feminine, not as a monolithic moment, but as a productivity of femininities. Contrary to some views it seems the splintering and creation of new femininities and images is empowering to women and proving unprofitable for both manufacturers and retailers.
>
> (Maynard 1999: 203)

This view locates women as actors and agents who learn, unlearn and then manipulate our identities to create power for ourselves.

As vehicles to express resistance and protest

My arguments above, that fabric crafts and fashion are media which have special connections to women and which are integral to women learning and maintaining our identities, converge in this section. As hinted at above, these two media can be used by women as vehicles to resist and protest against our oppressions. At first glance, one might assume that fabric crafts and fashion are merely frills added to women's lives – amusing interruptions as we continue to adapt and cope with our positions of oppression. This simplistic analysis cannot be sustained, despite its popularity.

There is little doubt that there is a strong popular discourse about fabric crafts and fashion which works to the disadvantage of women. It positions us as passive and subservient in relation to men, our culture's patriarchal demands and consumerist pressures. Too often fabric crafts are dismissed as 'ladies' work' and merely one of many women's domestic crafts and techniques which are neither worthy of note nor appropriate for feminist inquiry. This position has been queried by many craft theoreticians (e.g. Chadwick 1996; Hedges and Wendt 1980; Rowley 1997). Often, fashion has been presumed to 'belong to the irrational and abnormal' (Braham 1997: 132). Many would agree with Buzzi that the dominant view is that 'the vicissitudes of female dress ultimately undermine the woman and render her subservient to (and the victim of) the man who retains his iconographic stability' (1997: 120).

Both fabric crafts and fashion, however, have an ability to disrupt dominant discourses. Both are a means by which women, often constrained from free and open expression of our creativity and ideas, can learn to make oppositional statements. Both offer locations which allow for ambiguous messages, and that ambiguity is a key to their richness, for 'ultimately, ambiguity embodies a certain kind of social power, and makers have traditionally emphasised this characteristic in opposition to social norms' (Inglis 1996: 47).

Fabric crafts offer women a familiar space to learn to defy and resist stereotypes of women. Despite their association with the domestic, the pretty and the homey, fabric crafts are perfectly capable of presenting explicit, overt and confrontational messages of defiance. I have explored this theme in some depth elsewhere and will not repeat it here (Stalker 2003). Suffice it to say that women have learned to use fabric crafts to make visible women's lives, to undermine our oppressors, to suggest strategies to overcome injustices, to provide a rallying point and to challenge stereotypes about women. The messages in these five themes are clearly defiant and challenge views which suggest women cannot learn our way out of passivity.

It is also true that fabric crafts can present much more subtle and covertly defiant messages. First, the context in which these items are produced and 'read' can mean that they challenge the status quo. Thus, Vivienne

Mountfort's felt and embroidery piece which shows the faces of 111 New Zealand women within the windows of the building immortalised on the iconic Edmonds' Cookbook does more than memorialise those women (Fusco 1999). In today's context, it is a visual communication about the important role of women in New Zealand's formation and about the imprisonment of women within old roles. In short, it challenges us to learn about male domination. Similarly, ASTE's (Associate of Staff in Tertiary Education [in New Zealand]) frilly and colourful banner which says 'Women's unions, women's wisdom' carries a rather gentle message with which many members can associate. Yet, in the context of the peace rally in Auckland in March 2003, the banner was also a powerful tool of protest and a rallying point for activism from which are learned some of the meanings of women's unionism (see Muir 2000; Burke and Calhoun 1990).

Second, we must take care in our interpretation of the rules which govern fabric crafts. Although the strong traditional rules which surround fabric crafts can represent yet another way in which women learn to constrain our lives (Parker 1996), they can also help to create community. Precisely because fabric craft rules are extensive and detailed, they require continuous learning and teaching. For generations women have met in twos and threes or at sewing circles and quilting bees to exchange technical information. Also, because the skills and knowledge are complex, there is seldom one 'expert' teacher. Co-operative and collective learning is required and horizontal teacher/learner relationships tend to flourish. Furthermore, the special skills and knowledge often require an exclusive language which is unique to that craft community. Together, these elements offer women learners a strong sense of collective which can be extended to foster social dialogue and change.

Fashion can also provide a location for resistance to the norm. It can become a performance piece which provides the 'wherewithal for commenting upon, parodying and destabilising gender identities' (Crane 2000: 202). Although this is not the same as 'alleviating the social constraints imposed by gender' (ibid.), it allows us to learn subversive and even clearly oppositional positions in relation to social expectations for us. We can reject the stereotypical view of women as a mere 'visual commodity' (ibid.). We can play with our projected images to confuse, confound and subvert the male gaze. We can learn to project ambiguous, offbeat sexualities and gender and thus both break through our invisibility as women and reject traditional expectations for our behaviours. Our statements can range from the subtle to the powerful as seen in power-dressing, cross-dressing (Shapiro 1987), punk fashions (Richards 1998) or sexualised clothing fetishes (Steele 1996). A woman thus can learn to be the maker as well as the wearer of her identity.

Through fashion, we can also learn to challenge the idea that women are naïve consumers and defined by others. Despite hype to the contrary, there is evidence that women increasingly are openly rejecting unrealistic beauty ideals and trendy 'looks' and 'lines' (Maynard 1999: 191). The 'splintering and creation of new femininities and images' (ibid.), noted above, is 'empowering to women and proving unprofitable for both manufacturers and retailers' (ibid.). As women learn to own and control our fashion ability, we simultaneously can learn to use our power.

Finally, women can learn through fashion to create and identify with a community. Fashion is based on a shared knowledge system and can differentiate between genders, and among races, classes and ethnicities. Around the world, women have learned to use it as an effective tool to resist national, class, ethnic and gender positioning and to create new identities through both overt and covert expressions (Gill 1993; Torrens 1999).

Implications for facilitators of women's (un)learning

Above, I have highlighted the appropriateness of fabric crafts and fashion as sites of learning for women. Not only do women have a special, close relationship with them, but they play an important role in our identity formation. Without romanticising their potential to provide sites for resistance and protest, I hope that it is evident that these two areas offer cracks and spaces for women learners. For facilitators who work with women and who seek to redress gender-based inequalities through political, economic, social and cultural change, these two areas hold an important potential.

It is possible to use fabric crafts and fashion as bases for working with women learners, and to move discussions from our lived experiences to explorations of the political, economic, social and cultural drivers of our (dis)location and oppressions, towards strategies for our social agency and political activism.

For example, facilitators could explore the tensions between the potential and possibilities for these areas noted above and the negative, dismissive discourses which surround them. It would be fruitful to play with the interactions between the two. The tyranny of rule-bound fabric crafts and fashion could be cast against their ability to de- and re-construct women's identities into stronger forms. The elitism of fashion which we have learned to expect, could be contrasted to fashion's ability to break down the barriers between classes, genders and sexualities. 'Effective' opposition through dress could be explored relative to false oppositions such as 'power-dressing' (Entwistle 1997: 311).

Ultimately, by exploring the origins, drivers and consequences of women's lived experiences in these two areas, it is possible to move learners' analysis from liberal preoccupations with attitudes, motivation and socialisation to sharper explorations of economic, political, social and cultural drivers. This shift is necessary. Learners need to acquire an understanding of macro-level obstacles in order to generate action which results in structural changes – and those kinds of changes are crucial for real and permanent removal of inequalities in our societies.

Macro-level conversations could develop around 'First World' and 'Developing/majority' economic relationships based on fashion and fabric. Out-working, sociology of consumption, globalisation and colonisation – all these concepts can easily arise from the many-sided and complicated discourses which surround fabric crafts and fashion.

Similarly, questions about knowledge production and ownership, and about the creation of discourses, can develop. A beginning point could be to take a critical look at the dominant discourses which demean and dismiss and place these areas outside the borders of women's mainstream learning. Presented as sites of struggle and contestation, fabric crafts and fashion can give excellent entrée at the grassroots level to learn about, and act against, economic rationalism, patriarchy, misogyny and many other concepts and theories relevant to women's position of disadvantage. The few examples above demonstrate that fabric crafts and fashion have a huge potential to engage women learners in the study of macro-level concepts of power, authority and control, particularly in relation to our global experiences of oppression, sexism and patriarchy.

In sum, this chapter suggests a new way forward for all those who are concerned about the continuing disadvantaged positions of women. By using life experiences and discourses which are dominant in women's lives as legitimate starting points for learning with women, we can begin to theorise the development of what I want to name 'wommage'.[1] A wommage is a robust composite – a mosaic of parts which blur the borders between the feminine and the activist feminist. Together they create a coherent, joyful, whole woman learner. Wommage integrates the traditional 'feminine' concerns for collective action, nurturing and caring with feminist desires for gender-sensitive leadership, control and power over decision-making. It combines flowers, sequins, feathers and frills with decisive management and strong partnerships in both our private and public spheres. In many respects, wommage theorises that unstable, complex, multi-layered reality that many women already know as we learn new ways of living.

Conclusion

In this chapter, I illustrated, through two case studies, the richness of women's (un)learning which occurs and might occur through fabric crafts and fashion. I explored the dilemmas inherent in the notion of women's learning and then teased out the special connections between women and these two areas. I focused particularly on the roles of fabric crafts and fashion as instruments through which women can (un)learn our identities, and learn to express our resistance and protest.

For those who are concerned about women's continuing (dis)locations, it is clear that the discourses surrounding these areas can be an effective starting place to foster women's (un)learning. From these familiar bases, women's learning can move from a micro- to a macro-level analysis of, and action against, our disadvantages and oppressions. The challenge is for facilitators to push back the rigid borders which define the areas of 'legitimate' learning in order to engage with the rich and complex realities of women's day-to-day lives.

Notes

1 This word pays tribute to Miriam Schapiro, a feminist in the 1980s who created 'femmages' which deliberately blurred the boundaries between fabric quilts and high art.

References

Barber, F. (1994) *Women's Work: The First 20,000 Years. Women, Cloth and Society in Early Times*, New York: Norton.

Bauer, M. and Elsey, B. (1992) 'Smocking: Traditional Craft as the Expression of Personal Needs and Adult Community Education in Australia', *Australian Journal of Adult and Community Education* 32 (2): 84–9.

Belenky, M. F., Clinchy, B. M., Goldberger, N. R. and Tarule, J. M. (1986) *Women's Ways of Knowing: The Development of Self, Voice, and Mind*, New York: Basic Books.

Bourdieu, P. and Passeron, J. C. (1990) *Reproduction in Education, Society and Culture*, London: Sage.

Braham, P. (1997) 'Fashion: Unpacking a Cultural Production', in Paul du Gay (ed.) *Production of Culture/Cultures of Production*, London: Sage, pp. 121–69.

Burke, G. and Calhoun, A. (1990) *Art and Organised Labour*, Wellington, NZ: Wellington City Art Gallery.

Buzzi, S. (1997) 'Clothes, Power and the Modern Femme Fatale', in S. Buzzi (ed.) *Undressing Cinema: Clothing and Identity in the Movies*, London: Routledge, pp. 120–44.

Chadwick, W. (1996) *Women, Art and Society*, London: Thames and Hudson.

Collard, S. and Stalker, J. (1991) 'Women's Trouble: Gender and the Learning Environment', in R. Hiemstra (ed.) *Creating Environments for Effective Adult Learning*, San Francisco: Jossey-Bass, pp. 71–82.

Crane, D. (2000) *Fashion and its Social Agendas: Class, Gender and Identity in Clothing*, Chicago: University of Chicago Press.

Donnell, R. (1990) *Quilts as Women's Art. A Quilt Poetic*, Vancouver, BC: Gallerie Publications.

Entwistle, J. (1997) 'Power Dressing and the Construction of Career Woman', in M. Nava, A. Blake, I. MacRury and B. Richards (eds) *Buy This Book: Studies in Advertising and Consumption*, London: Routledge, pp. 311–23.

Evans, C. and Thornton, M. (1991) 'Fashion, Representation, Femininity', *Feminist Review* 38: 50–66.

Fusco, C. (1999) 'Reflections on the Fibre Art of Vivienne Mountford', *Textile Fibre Forum* 54: 28–9.

Gill, L. (1993) ' "Proper Women" and City Pleasures: Gender, Class and Contested Meaning in La Paz', *American Anthropological Association* 20 (1): 72–88.

Gilligan, C. (1982) *In a Different Voice: Psychological Theory and Women's Development*, Cambridge, MA: Harvard University Press.

Goldstein-Gidoni, I. (1999) 'Kimono and the Construction of Gendered and Cultural Identities', *Ethnology* 38 (4): 351–70.

Hallinan, L. (2003) 'Blanket Approval', *New Zealand Star-Times*, 16 February: D4.

Harding, S. (1996) *Whose Science? Whose Knowledge? Thinking from Women's Lives*, Ithaca, NY: Cornell University Press.

Hayes, E. and Colin III, S. (1994) 'Racism and Sexism in the United States: Fundamental Issues', in E. Hayes and S. Colin III (eds) *Confronting Racism and Sexism*, San Francisco: Jossey-Bass, pp. 5–16.

Hayes, E. and Flannery, D. (2000) *Women as Learners: The Significance of Gender in Adult Learning*, San Francisco: Jossey-Bass.

Hedges, E. and Wendt, I. (1980) *In Her Own Image. Women Working in the Arts*, New York: Feminist Press.

Hood, Y. (2001) 'The Culture of Resistance: African American Art Quilts and Self-defining', *Uncoverings* 22: 141–69.

Inglis, S. (1996) 'Overview: Forming Discourse', *Textile Fibre Forum* 46: 46–7.

Isaacs, J. (1987) *The Gentle Arts. 200 Years of Australian Women's Domestic and Decorative Arts*, Sydney: Lansdowne Publishing.

Jackson, K. (1995) 'Popular Education and the State: A New Look at the Community Debate', in M. Mayo and J. Thompson (eds) *Adult Learning, Critical Intelligence and Social Change*, Nottingham: NIACE, pp. 82–96.

Jefferies, J. (1995) 'Text and Textiles: Weaving Across the Borderlines', in K. Deepwell (ed.) *New Feminist Art Criticism. Critical Strategies*, New York: Manchester Press, pp. 164–73.

Jefferies, J. (2000) 'What Can She Know?', in F. Carons and C. Pajaczkowska (eds) *Feminist Visual Culture*, Edinburgh: Edinburgh University Press, pp. 189–205.

Jewish Museum of Australia (1997) *Material Treasures*, Melbourne: Jewish Museum of Australia.

Lakerink, R. (1998) 'Textiles: Positioning and Other', *Textile Fibre Forum* 53: 42.

Lauer, R. and Lauer, J. (1981) *Clothes as Masculine and Feminine*, Englewood Cliffs, NJ: Prentice-Hall.

Lawrence, K. (1997) 'Second Look', *Textile Fibre Forum* 48: 16–17, 26.

Lewis, M. and Simon, R. (1991) 'A Discourse Intended for Her: Learning and Teaching with Patriarchy', in J. Gaskell and A. McLaren (eds) *Women and Education* (second edition), Calgary: Detselig Enterprises, pp. 457–92.

Lin, J. (2003) *A New Look: Retail Clothing Sales in Canada*, Ottawa: Statistics Canada. Retrieved September 2003 http://www.statcan.ca:80/english/research/11–621-MIE/11–621-MIE2003006.htm

McRobbie, A. (1999) *In the Culture Society. Art, Fashion and Popular Music*, London: Routledge.

Maynard, M. (1999) 'Living Dolls: The Fashion Model in Australia', *Journal of Popular Culture* 33 (1): 191–205.

Muir, K. (2000) 'Feminism and Representations of Union Identity in Australian Union Banners of the 1980s and Early 1990s', *Labour History* 79: 92–112.

Newman, M. (1994) *Defining the Enemy. Adult Education in Social Action*, Sydney: Stewart Victor Publishing.

Nicholson, H. (1998) *The Loving Stitch*, Auckland: University of Auckland Press.

Parker, R. (1996) *The Subversive Stitch. Embroidery and the Making of the Feminine* (revised edition), London: Women's Press.

Perry, W. (1968/1970) *Forms of Intellectual and Ethical Development in the College Years: A Scheme*, New York: Holt, Rinehart and Winston.

Richards, M. (1998) 'Anti-fashion and Punk Culture', in N. Cawthorne (ed.) *Key Moments in Fashion. The Evolution of Style*, London: Hamlyn, pp. 144–55.

Rolley, K. (1990) 'Fashion, Femininity and the Fight for the Vote', *Art History* 13 (1): 47–71.

Rowley, S. (1997) 'Introduction', in S. Rowley (ed.) *Craft and Contemporary Theory*, St Leonards, NSW: Allen and Unwin, pp. xiv–xxvi.

Shapiro, S. (1987) 'Sex, Gender and Fashion in Medieval and Early Modern Britain', *Journal of Popular Culture* 20 (4): 113–28.

Sheared, V. (1994) 'Giving Voice: An Inclusive Model of Instruction', in E. Hayes and S. Colin III (eds) *Confronting Racism and Sexism*, San Francisco: Jossey-Bass, pp. 27–38.

Stalker, J. (1998) 'Women's Participation in Adult Education: Misogynistic Responses', in S. Scott, B. Spencer and A. Thomas (eds) *Foundations of Canadian Adult Education*, Toronto: Thompson Publishing, pp. 238–49.

—— (2003) ' "Ladies' Work" and Feminist Critical Pedagogy', in D. Flowers (ed.) *Proceedings of the Forty-fourth Adult Education Research Conference*, San Francisco: San Francisco State University, pp. 399–404.

—— (2004) ' "Ladies' Work" and Popular Education: Fabricating New Approaches', *Studies in Continuing Education* 31 (2): 21–35.

Steele, V. (1996) *Fetish: Fashion, Sex and Power*, New York: Oxford University Press.

Tisdell, E. (1993) 'Interlocking Systems of Power, Privilege and Oppression in Higher Education Classes', *Adult Education Quarterly* 3 (4): 203–26.

Torrens, K. (1999) 'Fashion as Argument: Nineteenth Century Dress Reform', *Argumentation and Advocacy* 36 (2): 77–87.

White, C. (2003) 'Knitting, like Drugs, Threatens Order, Induces Euphoria', *The Peninsula Gateway*, Gig Harbor, WA, 12 February: 4D.

Chapter 13

Life cycle development and human learning

Mary Alice Wolf

> Of magic doors there is this
> You do not see them even as you are passing through.

This chapter looks at the relationships between aging and learning, mental agility and physical well-being, survival and stagnation. It explores the life cycle development of human learning, initiates consideration of meaning-making and personal differentiation as a mode of development and gives suggestions for further reading about the potential for growth throughout the life course. The first part looks at the core of the developmental process, learning through the lens of human emotion. The second part connects the domains of cognitive and physical requirements for physical growth and development within an educational framework. It looks at the worlds of older adults who continue to expand their potential for vibrant lives. Suggestions for creating learning experiences and further resources are given.

Learning as a life course mandate

Imagine being born into the world and being one with it. That is the infant's state for the first six months of life (Greenberg and Mitchell 1983; Mahler 1968; Stern 1985). Such a simple image, really: I am integrated, I am one with Mom.[1] This is known as symbiosis (Mahler 1968). The infant, fully connected to the parent (Mom), knows of no plots, evils, Algebra, room-mate problems or arthritis. This fully attached human being knows of no boundaries between self and other. The awareness that she is separate and vulnerable at around six months requires her to learn a whole new system of interacting. She still has to have her physical needs met, but now she will have to learn to ask for what she needs and to rely on caretakers for suste-nance. She is separating from what she first knew, differentiating herself from others and always studying and learning about her changing environ-ment. New questions emerge: How can she manipulate those around her, gain attention and receive physical care? This is a lifetime task: Gaining independence and mastery requires learning how to interact with others for survival. Throughout life, well into old age, we differentiate, we make new meaning, as we perceive ourselves vulnerable. We learn because we must survive.

The core of learning is adaptation; the core of adaptation is learning. Throughout our lives, environment and circumstances direct us to organize our thoughts and behaviors toward exploration and achievement. As infants we learn to focus on number one: ourselves. As we grow through childhood and adolescence, we learn that, though number one is of prime importance, others, too, command our attention. And it is this interaction (me and "it" – or "others") that shapes our development. Our job is to adapt to each new reality, each new meaning. So, too, in adulthood, personal relationships, identity, vocation, parenting, health and other concerns require us to explore new strategies for interaction and cognition (see Merriam and Caffarella 1999; Modell 1996; Wolf and Leahy 1998).

Older adulthood is no different: while certain roles and responsibilities may slip away, others become more pressing (Wolf 2002). Indeed, the biological mandate for survival depends on our ability to connect with the world in new ways, make meaning of what is happening to us, become inter-dependent. Did you ever wonder why old people are often referred to as pioneers, explorers coming home to rest? That is the nature of life cycle development and human learning: We start and we end within a framework of integration and oneness. Aristophanes says, in Plato's *Symposium*,

> This becoming one instead of two was the very expression of his ancient need. And the reason is that human nature was originally one and we were a whole, and the desire and pursuit of the whole is called love.
>
> (Greenberg and Mitchell 1983: 270)

Each of us begins in symbiosis and ends in integrality (Erikson 1968; Mahler and Furer 1968). Ours is a lifespan process of differentiation and adaptation. Jean Piaget's description of object permanence at age eighteen months and the understanding of adaptation through assimilation and accommodation permit a glimpse into the process by which human beings detach and connect throughout the lifespan (Piaget 1968; Piaget and Inhelder 1969). When we understand a challenge (i.e. differentiate an object, see a need, a new reality) we attempt to adapt new strategies to complete the challenge. It is human nature to rise to a challenge. The cognitive and affective paths of development are fully entwined with the biological mandate to set out, explore, and return. Elders often return to their earliest memories in telling narratives of survival and evaluative life reviews, through history and autobiography (Beatty and Wolf 1996; *Generations* 2003; Johnson 1995; Jung 1933; Vaillant 2002; Webster and Haight 2002).

Autonomy or attachment

Relationship is essential to our experience throughout life. Is there no such thing as a truly separate person? Perhaps not. Emotion and connection are involved in each and every stage of the life course. Our connections and attachments take precedence over our need to separate: rather, there is an interaction between the connection and the differentiation that can be detected through our emotions (Kegan 1994, 1996). John Bowlby observed:

> Many of the most intense emotions arise during the formation, the maintenance, the disruption, and the renewal of attachment relationships. The formation of a bond is described as falling in love, maintaining a bond as loving someone, and losing a partner as grieving over someone.
>
> (Bowlby in Cassidy 1999: 7)

One of the most touching concepts of development was coined by Margaret Mahler (1968) when she defined the act of "refueling." This is the process by which the infant, now undergoing the urge to separate and explore the environment, suddenly returns to the parent's lap. She needs a hug. She clings. But, then, as seamlessly as before, she sets out again to take on the world. Erik Erikson (1968) says that she has "a love affair with the world" (p. 255). Certainly, refueling is a lifelong process yet unarticulated in life course developmental theory.[2]

The individual will return again and again with renewed vigor – even as she becomes more autonomous. Indeed, Daniel Stern's (1985) interpretation of infant interaction states that all growth is not in service of autonomy but in the domain of relatedness. He suggests that "zones of intimacy" enhance our motivation, growth and ability to learn. This view of development has been explored by feminist scholars during the past fifteen years (see Belenky *et al.* 1997; Jordan *et al.* 1991; Miller 1986; Miller and Stiver 1997; and others) and is now becoming adapted as a gender-neutral template. We know that older women survive better than men because they are in the habit of confiding and connecting in relational settings. Surely, in a life course perspective which includes infants and elders, there is a mandate for relationship and connection.

Attachment and loss are at the heart of emotional well-being, growth, differentiation, and human connection. It behooves the learning specialist to explore the broad underpinning of this phenomenon. The counselor, educator, human resource manager who seeks to provide an environment for growth and change would do well to remember that all growth is costly in that the learner must leave one known (but outgrown) meaning system for another, one comfort zone for what at first blush appears to be chaos. Robert Kegan (1994, 1996; Kegan and Lahey 2001) defines this time of transition as a deconstruction of reality. The learner's environment is essential for a successful transition (Merriam 1998). Holding on to the learner, allowing him to leave, return, refuel and leave again is the role of the helping professional. Winnicott (1965) called this the holding environment: It is a useful concept for all of the lifespan. Each developing individual must connect with supportive holding environments.

Survival vs stagnation

How do these principles of early life play out in the life course perspective? How can the gerontologist connect the literature of early development with the challenges facing an aging society? What will be the new role of learning in the second half of life? Is there potential for learning in old age?

The first new discovery will be to explore how science and gerontology are integrating the research and theory of the final years of the life course. The most important direction in the field for the past fifteen years has been to separate ordinary ("natural") aging from the view that aging is synonymous with disease. Researchers are now looking at the lives of healthy older people, examining how they adapt and adjust to changes in environment, roles, physical, social and spiritual integration (Chiva 1996; Schaie and Willis 2002). What we do know is that many mid-life people predict a dismal aging process for themselves based on past experience with cultural beliefs. And we must appreciate that there are deep connections between learning and emotions and between learning and physical well-being (Volz 2004/5: 77). Nonetheless, there is still a general repulsion about the end of the life course: the anticipation of physical and cognitive decline. This is our cultural inheritance. The following notation, for example, is displayed under the J. M. W. Turner painting *The Bay of Baiae, with Apollo and the Sibyl*:

> The Cumaen Sibyl, Deiphobe, accepts from her lover Apollo as many years of life as she holds grains of sand in her hand. However, she rejects his offer of eternal youth and wastes away through the ages until only her voice remains.

Our vision of aging has been socially constructed throughout the centuries (Berger and Luckmann 1966). Do we continue to believe that old age is the time for integration and settling for potential senility and dementia? Or do we buy the latest hype that model/actress Lauren Hutton proclaims on the recent cover of the *AARPTheMagazine* (November/December 2003) that "Sixty is the new Thirty"? The answer may be that aging can be paradoxical: Never have you experienced so many losses and never have you been so dependent on touching your own inner resources to maneuver and prosper. Indeed, starting in mid-life, the individual begins the process of learning to age.[3]

Learning to age

Rather than catalogue losses and decline, current perspectives on cognition and health focus on enhancing lifestyle. This is the new mandate in learning about the second half of life. Meaning-making of older persons is viewed as connected to their manipulation of their environments and their adaptation to the challenges inherent in growing older. Further, we know that the body/brain and mental abilities are related. Learning, then, becomes a means of providing control over one's shifting environment (Baltes 1993; Beatty and Wolf 1996; Fisher and Wolf 1998, 2000). Indeed, beginning in late middle age, there is a new consciousness of the challenge of adaptation (Chiva 1996; Vaillant and Koury 1993; Wolf 1999). Schaie and Willis have called this stage "reorganizational" (2002: 347). "What should I know?" is replaced with "How should I use what I know?" (p. 348). Much of the "What should I know?" concerns well-being and quality of life for older adults (Neugarten 1964; Vaillant 2002; Wolf 2002, among others).

It is assumed that cohorts currently coming of age (i.e. the famous Baby Boomers) will focus on dimensions of sustained identity in their older years. These aspects will include a renewal of identity, a commitment to well-being and an acceptance that physical and cognitive stimulation are necessary to maintain equilibrium. Learning will involve a quick-step course in strategies for building and sustaining healthy and positive life ways. Late mid-life and older adults will need to relearn personal caretaking and focus on what resources they still have. "The *Achieves of Internal Medicine* recently reported that older women who started a walking program showed lower levels of cognitive decline than sedentary women when tested six to eight years later" (Restak 2004/5: 37). For elders who have participated in longitudinal studies, exercise and intellectual stimulation are found to enhance flexibility (Schaie and Willis 2002). A recent Johns Hopkins Prescription for Longevity stated that the number one and "single most important anti-aging measure anyone can follow, regardless of age, disability or general level of fitness is to exercise." To be effective, exercise should include endurance training and strength training. Nursing home residents are now being encouraged to attend regular exercise training including stationary bicycles and lifting weights: these exercises are prescribed well into the ninth decade.

Recent studies in cognition and aging reiterate what has been seen in previous research. "Age-related deficits have been documented in tasks assessing episodic memory, semantic memory, as well as different forms of priming" (Bäckman *et al.* 2001: 349). What older persons need for learning are new and stimulating tasks: environmental demands that require adaptation and manipulation. Neurobiologist Marilyn Diamond, herself in her seventies, has been exploring the role of stimulation with older adults. She had previously found that after eighty days, there was a 6 per cent increase in the size of the cortex of rats who had been treated to an "enriched environment." Indeed, later experiments found cortical thickness changed in as few as four days. As she turns to human subjects, she stresses the need for newness (activities that are novel), challenges (activities that require mental effort) and adequate blood supply (spurred by good diet and ample exercise) (Diamond 2000; Schaie and Willis 2002).

Emotional refueling: new paths

Furthermore, it must be acknowledged that emotional development is on-going in adulthood. Research indicates that "the qualitative experiential core of elation, fear, anger, or shame ... do not change with age, although the feelings may become more cognitively complex and elaborated" (Magai 2001: 400). Emotions are found to be "prewired and functional within the opening months of life, and the emotion system is viewed as the primary organizer of human thought and behavior" (Magai 2001: 399–400). The path to adaptation in a life course review of development involves the on-going repetition of the need to be attached, to let go, and to return so as to grow and differentiate (the "refueling") (Kegan 1996). Each of us will experience loss, rebound and return to self-nurturing modes of behavior based on our life experiences. Chateaubriand wrote, in *Voyage en Italie*:

> Every man carries within himself a world made up of all that he has seen and loved, and it is to this world that he returns, incessantly, tho he may pass through, and seem to inhabit, a world quite foreign to it.
>
> (In Greenberg and Mitchell 1983: 9)

The role of reminiscence in learning for older adults has been the subject of considerable exploration (*Generations* 2003; Johnson 1995; Vaillant 2002; Webster and Haight 2002; Wolf 2002; and others). Reminding oneself of sorrows, achievements and pranks brings the older adult into a process not unlike Margaret Mahler's "refueling," where one touches base with a familiar environment, and the emotional connection can be sustenance for the elder. Here is a Jamaican elder now living in the Hartford, Connecticut, community recalling his travel to the United States some sixty-five years ago:

> At night we could not use any light on deck because if we were spotted we could be torpedoed. We had to go down in the "hole" to sleep and to smoke. The sailors were very strict about the rules. Sometimes down below deck it was extremely hot, especially near the engine room. Several of the men got seasick, especially those who were from the interior sections of the island. Many men traveled with a nutmeg in their mouths to help prevent seasickness, but I had no problem because I was born and grew up by the sea.
>
> (Johnson 1995: 33–4)

The ability to recall past strengths allows the elder to reconnect, "refuel." He integrates his current and past self. When feeling vulnerable, he is able to reestablish a sense of strength and power through the long-term memory. And, as he articulates this phenomenon to others (in the case of the Jamaican above, to a textbook author), he strengthens his backbone a bit more. The past self can nurture the present reality (Berger and Luckmann 1966; Vaillant 2002; Webster and Haight 2002). The image of sailing away is recurrent in stories of elders: explorations and experiences that can be related to coming generations. Attachment and loss are at the heart of emotional well-being, growth, differentiation, and human connection. George Vaillant (2002) found that those individuals who age most success-fully have the following characteristics: the ability to let others in, mature defense mechanisms, and the ability to identify compensations with age.

Older people are not trying to be young. They are trying to have what-ever adventure they can at their own place in the life cycle. Helen, my 92-year-old neighbor, had two hip replacements and was told not to even *think* about venturing out on the ice last winter. Further, she was *not* to drive on the lethally icy road. Nonetheless, I watched her car drive out one Sunday morning. Infuriated, I began pacing the floor, only to see her drive back in. I phoned right away: "Where did you go? Don't you know …?" I asked in my best middle-aged nagging voice. "Oh," she responded, "I just drove to the end of the driveway to get the Sunday paper. I hate to start my day without the comics." Helen's adaptive strategy might be labeled as "compensation with selective optimization." Where one facility (biological) fails, another (cognitive) prevails. The aging mind accommo-dates to the loss of physical strength: the "fluid-like *mechanics* with crystallized *pragmatics*" (Baltes 1993: 581). This is an automatic adapta-tion of the aging mind, "general adaptation, *selective optimization with compensation*" (p. 589).

Sister Millie waved me down one early morning after I had dropped a colleague off at the convent. "Oh, Mary Alice," she beamed, "lucky me. I found you! I need a ride to Saint Mary Home. I have a funeral to attend." Looking at Sister Millie, dressed in a suit with pearls, I had no difficulty assuming that she was late for a formal function and agreed to drive her to Saint Mary Home. We chatted amiably on the drive. Yet, after leaving her at the doorstep of Saint Mary Home, I did have a moment's concern. Aha! I used my cell phone to call the convent. "Hi," I said, "I just gave Sister Millie a ride." "Oh," came the disgruntled response. "OK. We'll go pick her up." Of course, Sister Millie had made an escape from the convent where she was confined with Alzheimer's disease and, because she had the wily ability to adapt to the environment, was successful in duping me. Even in times of dementia, elders have resources to compensate and adapt! "The Brain is wider than the Sky," observed Emily Dickinson of the elasticity of the human mind.

Transforming the last years

What, then, helps the facilitator of older adult education to best appreciate the potential for development in her population? The following suggestions touch on the life course perspective of human learning: The first is that the instructor examine and appreciate her own potential for development. She might explore how she negotiates each transformation, each new differentiation, and each challenge in her own life. There can't be a "them" and "me" approach to working with older adult learners. Each of us, too, will need to solve environmental crises on a daily basis well into our nineties (see Chiva 1996; Merriam 1998; Tennant 2000; Wolf 1999, 2002.) Nothing works as well as connecting with the needs of the learners. Giving time, listening, and allowing for narrative and reminiscence are the keys to a powerful interactive approach to the classroom experience. (See *Generations* 2003; Webster and Haight 2002; Berger and Luckmann 1966.)

Certain human development principles are essential in understanding the older adult learner. One is that personality is lifelong; each of us is born with an emotional makeup which will not change with age. Sensitivity to the continuity of self in older persons can be a key to connection (Beatty and Wolf 1996; Magai 2001; Neugarten 1964). I recently called my Aunt Gwen to let her know that I would be visiting Florida and would like to see her. "Hello, Aunt Gwen, how are you?" I began. "Oh, exhausted," she answered, "so much to do, so many people. They keep coming and going and I never get any rest!" "Well, guess what, Aunt Gwen?" I said. I didn't need a gold-plated invitation to know that I was welcome and I was not put off by Aunt Gwen's negative affect: Haven't I known her for over sixty years? I also know that she would be severely hurt if I *didn't* visit. Acceptance that each of us has our own personal quirks can be a powerful asset in creating comfortable holding environments.

Another caveat in adult development is that each of us sees the world from our own stance; we come from generations with differing values. An appreciation of this factor is essential in working with elders. Each group of elders comes with historical and social mandates for behavior and tastes for what is customary. These values are formed in our earliest years and often include gender roles. (See Beatty and Wolf 1996, Fisher and Wolf 1998: 73–84; Modell 1996.) Recently an 18-year-old student marveled that the elderly were so polite. We asked: Is it aging that makes them polite or is it typical of that cohort? Surely early training made for a lifelong mode in manners. Yet, there *are* role changes in aging: Gerontological research indicates that there is a gender shift that occurs. Men of the current aged cohort will become more affiliative, women more assertive. (See Neugarten 1964; Wolf in Wolf and Leahy 1998: 72–8.)

Cognitive changes also occur: Older adults are less linear, possess crystallized intelligence as opposed to fluid intelligence, and engage in meaning-making, integrative thinking modes (Baltes 1993; Fisher and Wolf 2000; Schaie and Willis 2002). Learning needs will be reflected in these areas. Further, older adults need multitasking, new tasks, things never tried before in order to remain alert and stimulated in the learning environment. (See Diamond 2000; Restak 2004/5; Schaie and Willis 2002.) It may be helpful to incorporate a physical exercise routine into the schedule of every older person. (Two good sources are videotapes *Exercise: It's Never Too Late,* produced by Films for the Humanities and Sciences, Box 2053, Princeton, NJ 08543–2053; and *Exercise: A Video from the National Institute on Aging*, Washington, DC.)

Finally, we must assume that elders need to find replacements for attachments now lost and enhance existing attachments. In the end, one is the sum of one's attachments. At the center of existence is connection. Elders often need to take stock of their own internal resources or core strengths. A useful resource is the work of Helen Kivnick who uses an "inventory of life strengths" to promote reflection and reevaluation of older adults' identity (see Kivnick and Murray 2001; Wolf and Whitman 1997). Elders can also reconnect with neighborhoods and villages that surround our learning centers. Instructors might explore roles that older people can play, outlets for wisdom to share unique gifts of experience and lore. "A human being," wrote Carl G. Jung, "would certainly not grow to be seventy or eighty years old if this longevity had no meaning for the species to which he belongs" (1933: 109). Frequently older people can be trained to teach computer skills, drawing, cooking, etc., in elementary and daycare settings.

The paradox: loss and new directions

There is no question that aging and learning are intimately related to relationship, environment, generativity, and links to coming cohorts. In learning to initiate, survive and adapt, older adults provide models for future development. Through biological, social and historical time we are bound together as a civilization. The life cycle is only one means of bringing full humanity to each. Patterning our world is a lifelong task; initiating separation and returning to attachments are our full-time endeavors. As Margaret Mahler observed, we must experience a loss before we move on – this is true at every age in life (Erikson 1968; Kegan 1996). Each person's existence depends on the biological, psychic and communal processes complementing (Erikson 1982).

We recognize the interweaving of emotional, physical, social, spiritual and cognitive dimensions in becoming fully developed human beings. The ability to learn is the mode of achieving our fullest potential as meaning-making creatures. In our memory are our identity and our means of touching our highest selves, or attaching to the full environment. We are granted the opportunity to achieve full integrality with the world anew. As Erikson

(1968) observed: Anything that grows has a found plan, and out of this ground plan the parts arise, each part having its time of special ascendancy, until all parts have arisen to form a functioning whole.

Notes

1 Theorists still talk about the mother as central to this dynamic, but new gender-neutral language could be on the horizon.
2 Although gerontological scholars in reminiscence have found that storytelling can be a form of reconnecting with the self (i.e. Kastenbaum 2003), the concept of refueling remains in the realm of early developmentalism.
3 Bernice Neugarten often talked about "body monitoring," "rehearsal heart attacks," and an obsession with hair by mid-life men.

References

AARPTheMagazine (November/December 2003) Cover.

Bäckman, L., Small, B. J. and Wahlin, Å. (2001) 'Aging and Memory, Cognitive and Biological Perspectives', in J. E. Birren and K. W. Schaie (eds) *Handbook of the Psychology of Aging* (fifth edition), New York: Academic Press, pp. 349–77.

Baltes, P. B. (1993) 'The Aging Mind, Potential and Limits', *The Gerontologist* 35 (5): 580–94.

Beatty, P. T. and Wolf, M. A. (1996) *Connecting with Older Adults: Educational Responses and Approaches*, Malabar, FL: Krieger Press.

Belenky, M. F., Clinchy, B. M., Goldberger, N. R. and Tarule, J. M. (1997) *Women's Ways of Knowing*, New York: Basic Books.

Berger, P. and Luckmann, T. (1966) *The Social Construction of Reality*, Garden City, NJ: Doubleday.

Cassidy, J. (1999) 'The Nature of the Child's Ties', in J. Cassidy and P. R. Shaver (eds) *Handbook of Attachment; Theory, Research, and Clinical Applications*, New York: Guilford, pp. 3–20.

Chiva, A. (1996) 'Managing Change in Mid and Later Life', in J. Walker (ed.) *Changing Concepts of Retirement*, Brookfield, VT: Ashgate, pp. 71–84.

Diamond, M. (2000) *Older Brains: New Connections, a Conversation with Marion Diamond at 73, Learning Guide*, San Luis Obispo, CA: Davidson Films. Available at http://www.davidsonfilms.com

Erikson, E. H. (1968) *Childhood and Society* (third edition), New York: W. W. Norton.

—— (1982) *The Life Cycle Completed*, New York: W. W. Norton.

Fisher, J. C. and Wolf, M. A. (eds) (1998) *Using Learning to Meet the Challenges of Older Adulthood, New Directions for Adult and Continuing Education No. 77*, San Francisco: Jossey-Bass.

—— (2000) 'Education for Older Adults', in A. L. Wilson and E. R. Hayes (eds) *Handbook of Adult and Continuing Education*, San Francisco: Jossey-Bass, pp. 87–100.

Generations (2003) *Listening to Older People's Stories* (special edition, 27 (3) Fall), San Francisco, CA: The American Society on Aging.

Greenberg, J. R. and Mitchell, S. A. (1983) *Object Relations in Psychoanalytic Theory*, Cambridge, MA: Harvard University Press.

Johnson, F. C. (1995) *Soldiers of the Soil*, New York: Vantage Press.

Jordan, J. V., Kaplan, A. G., Miller, J. B., Stiver, I. P. and Surrey, J. L. (1991) *Women's Growth in Connection, Writings from the Stone Center*, New York: Guilford.

Jung, C. G. (1933) *Modern Man in Search of a Soul* (trans. W. S. Dell and C. F. Baynes), New York: Harcourt Brace Jovanovich.

Kastenbaum, R. (2003) 'Where is the Self in Elder Self-narratives?' in *Generations, Listening to Older People's Stories* (special edition, 27 (3) Fall), San Francisco, CA: The American Society on Aging.

Kegan, R. (1994) *In Over Our Heads: The Mental Demands of Modern Life*, Cambridge, MA: Harvard University Press.

—— (1996) *The Evolving Self*, Cambridge, MA: Harvard University Press.

Kegan, R. and Lahey, L. L. (2001) *How the Way We Talk Can Change the Way We Work*, San Francisco: Jossey-Bass.

Kivnick, H. Q. and Murray, S. V. (2001) 'Life Strengths Interview Guide: Assessing Elder Clients' Strengths', *Journal of Gerontological Social Work* 34 (4): 7–32.

Magai, C. (2001) 'Emotions Over the Life Span', in J. E. Birren and K. W. Schaie (eds) *Handbook of the Psychology of Aging* (fifth edition), New York: Academic Press, pp. 399–426.

Mahler, M. S. (1968) *On Human Symbiosis and the Vicissitudes of Individuation: Vol. 1*, New York: International Universities Press.

Merriam, S. B. (1998) 'Adult Life Transitions: Opportunities for Learning and Development', in M. A. Wolf and M. A. Leahy (eds) *Adults in Transition*, Washington, DC: The American Association for Adult and Continuing Education, pp. 8–81.

Merriam, S. B. and Caffarella, R. S. (1999) *Learning in Adulthood* (second edition), San Francisco: Jossey-Bass.

Miller, J. B. (1986) *Toward a New Psychology of Women* (second edition), Boston: Beacon Press.

Miller, J. B. and Stiver, I. P. (1997) *The Healing Connection: How Women Form Relationships in Therapy and in Life*, Boston: Beacon Press.

Modell, A. H. (1996) *Other Times, Other Realities*, Cambridge, MA: Harvard University Press.

Neugarten, B. L. (ed.) (1964) *Personality in Middle and Late Life*, New York: Atherton Press.

Piaget, J. (1968) *Six Psychological Studies*, New York: Vintage Books.

Piaget, J. and Inhelder, B. (1969) *The Psychology of the Child* (trans. H. Weaver), New York: Basic Books.

Restak, R. (2004/5) 'All in Your Head', in H. Cox (ed.) *Aging* (sixteenth edition), Guilford, CT: McGraw-Hill/Dushkin, pp. 37–9.

Schaie, K. W. and Willis, S. L. (2002) *Adult Development and Aging* (fifth edition), Upper Saddle River, NJ: Prentice Hall.

Stern, D. N. (1985) *The Interpersonal World of the Infant*, New York: Basic Books.

Tennant, M. (2000) 'Adult Learning for Self-development and Change', in A. L. Wilson and E. R. Hayes (eds) *Handbook of Adult and Continuing Education*, San Francisco: Jossey-Bass, pp. 87–100.

Vaillant, G. E. (2002) *Aging Well*, Boston: Little, Brown.

Vaillant, G. E. and Koury, S. H. (1993) 'Late Midlife Development', in G. H. Pollock and S. Greenspan (eds) *The Course of Life: Late Adulthood* (vol. VI), Madison CT: International Universities Press, pp. 1–22.

Volz, J. (2004/5) 'Successful Aging: The Second 50', in H. Cox (ed.) *Aging* (sixteenth edition), Guilford, CT: McGraw-Hill/Dushkin, pp. 76–9.

Webster, J. D. and Haight, B. K. (eds) (2002) *Critical Advances in Reminiscence Work: From Theory to Application*, New York: Spring Publishing.

Winnicott, D. W. (1965) *The Maturational Processes and the Facilitating Environment*, New York: International Universities Press.

Wolf, M. A. (1999) 'Transformations within the Classroom Experience', paper presented at the 25th Annual Conference of the Association for Gerontology in Higher Education, Saint Louis, MI.

—— (2002) 'Differentiation and the Adult Learner', paper presented to the Annual Conference of the Association for Gerontology in Higher Education, Pittsburgh, PA.

Wolf, M. A. and Leahy, M. A. (eds) (1998) *Adults in Transition*, Washington, DC: The American Association for Adult and Continuing Education.

Wolf, M. A. and Whitman, C. (1997) *Gerontology for Companions, A Leader's Guide*, West Hartford, CT: Saint Joseph College.

Chapter 14

Learning trajectories

Reconsidering the barriers to participation

Stephen Gorard

Introduction

Greater attention than at present needs to be given to patterns of adult participation in learning opportunities. This is so for several reasons, most importantly because the determinants of participation are so widely misunderstood. Much research in this area considers only the views of current and recent participants, and so biases any policy recommendations. This approach tends to obscure the scale of lifelong non-participation in formal learning episodes, to ignore the often very valid reasons for non-participation, and to downplay the valuable self-directed learning evident among seeming 'non-learners' (Gorard and Rees 2002). In addition, there is often a confusion between changes over time for successive age cohorts and for individuals. Most policies are directed at improving measurements of learning such as participation among working-age adults that have no impact at all on the life of the adults themselves. For example, most of the growth towards UK targets for lifelong learning is explained by the annual addition of qualified 16-year-olds to the working-age population, and the subtraction of less qualified retirees. Growth towards the target is, thus, achieved without any increase at all in education or training for adults (Gorard *et al.* 2002). In fact, formal participation in later life is reducing over time *and* becoming more inequitable in terms of sex, social class and employment (Gorard *et al.* 1999a). The results of the new study outlined in this chapter begin to explain why the multiplication of learning opportunities and the removal of barriers to participation are not being effective, in isolation, in attracting those on a non-participation 'trajectory'.

Policies to widen participation in lifelong learning can be exhortative, involving the use of local target setting and monitoring. They also involve providing a wider range of opportunities and localities, such as drop-in centres, and publicising these widely. And they involve trying to overcome the barriers to participation faced by more disadvantaged individuals. The potential of information and communications technology (ICT) to 'free' adult education from the barriers that previously prevented people from participating has now been prioritised at the core of the current 'lifelong learning' ICT agenda in the UK and elsewhere. Existing barriers to learning, whether they are categorised as cultural, structural and personal (Maxted 1999) or situational, institutional and dispositional (Harrison 1993), are now seen as resolvable through the use of technology (Hawkey 2002).

The UK government has introduced a number of technology-based lifelong learning initiatives under the aegis of 'learndirect' and 'UK Online'. Learndirect most prominently takes the form of a telephone-based helpline for directing individuals to approved and kite-marked learning opportunities, as well as providing its own technology-mediated learning opportunities via a network of over 7,000 'UK Online' centres in community sites throughout the UK. The initiatives aim to widen participation, and also to reduce the current inequalities in participation among those groups traditionally under-represented in adult education, i.e. women, the elderly, some ethnic minorities, those on low incomes, ex-offenders and people with learning difficulties (Selwyn 2002). ICT can, apparently, solve many of the problems of the lifelong learning conundrum in one go:

> E-learning is a relatively new tool with the potential to *radically improve participation* and achievement rates in education. Benefits include the ability to customise learning to the needs of an individual and the flexibility to allow the individual to learn at their own pace, in their own time and from a physical location that suits them best. This could be in their local library, at their work or at home. Through e-learning we have the opportunity to provide *universal access* to high quality, relevant training and education.
>
> (DfES 2002: 4, emphasis added)

But is this really so? To answer this question, I present the results of 1,001 household interviews with adults aged 21+ in England and Wales in 2002, and sections of the transcripts of 110 follow-up interviews with a sub-sample of these. The first interview was concerned with what people had done in relation to formal learning, and the second with their reasons. Respondents gave a life history including demographic details, family, educational and employment histories, plus details of current and past ICT use (see www.cf.ac.uk/socsi/ict). I focus here on whether people continued with formal education or training within one year of reaching school-leaving age, and whether they then participated in any later education or training. 'Non-participants' are those who reported no episodes of education or training since leaving school at the earliest opportunity. 'Transitional' learners reported at least one episode of immediate post-compulsory education or training and nothing subsequently. 'Delayed' learners reported no episodes of immediate post-compulsory education or training but at least one subsequent episode as an adult. 'Lifelong' learners reported at least one

Table 14.1 Frequency of four patterns of participation

	Frequency	Percentage	Mean age (years)
Non-participants	371	37	58
Transitional	175	18	45
Delayed learners	246	25	52
Lifelong learners	209	21	44

immediate episode of post-compulsory education or training and at least one other episode.

The frequency of these four patterns or trajectories is shown in Table 14.1. The most common pattern is a report of no formal education or training since reaching compulsory school-leaving age. This is similar in scale to the figure reported by La Valle and Blake (2001). Also similar to their study, and many others, is the finding that participation is patterned by sex, age, ethnicity, disability, caring responsibilities, educational background, employment and local deprivation. These patterns are discussed in the next sections on personal background, family, initial schooling and adult life.

Background determinants of participation

Table 14.1 shows considerable disparity in patterns of participation by age. This is particularly powerful, since it shows clearly how older groups are less likely to have been involved in *any* learning, despite the longer time they have had to do so. Table 14.2 shows the changes over time in each age cohort. Non-participation has declined, and has largely been replaced by transitional learning, as the expectations of what was 'normal' have also changed over time. A story that appeared in various forms among the older cohort involved leaving school at the earliest opportunity, because that was normal and because there were jobs or family responsibilities to be taken on. In the second example below, this led to frustration and therefore, perhaps, to a later return to formal learning.

> I was only 14 [when I left school] ... it was just the primary school in the village, you didn't go on to higher education [then] unless you won the 11+ scholarship ... I [tried and] failed ... I was brought up on the farm and my father said, well there were three girls and one boy, and he said, 'Well, one of you will have to stay home and help your mother, so it may as well be you.'
>
> (non-participant, older female)

Table 14.2 Patterns of participation by age range

Trajectory	21–40	41–60	61+
Non-participant	26	27	54
Transitional learner	22	17	12
Delayed learner	23	29	25
Lifelong learner	28	27	22

Note
The cells contain the percentage within each learning 'trajectory'.

My dad was very Victorian or Edwardian or whatever, and his theory was that girls left school, got a job, and then got married and had children ... He was very reluctant to push us into higher education, which is what I should have done.

(delayed, mid-age female)

Jobs were easy to get, and there is an implication in these stories that staying on in education has no inherent merit. It fills in time while waiting for a job, or prepares for a job. Note that the next respondent also mentions a very common theme among older and mid-age respondents – that of learning-by-doing and common sense. As I have noted before (Gorard *et al.* 1999b), quite considerable changes in skilled tasks have been undertaken in the past without any formal training.

I didn't leave with nothing [qualifications]. I left school on the Friday, no, on the Thursday, because my birthday was on the Friday, and I started work on the Wednesday because it was Easter ... everybody went in to get an apprenticeship then, you know ... nobody stayed on after fifteen then, unless you was in grammar school ... there was plenty of vacancies in boot and shoe. And plenty of vacancies in engineering.

I went down for a driving job and the bloke said to me, 'Can you drive?' so I said, 'Yeah' ... 'Have you got a licence?' I said, 'Yeah.' 'Can you start Monday?' I said, 'Yeah.' And I got there on the Monday and the biggest thing I drove then was a [van], and I got there on Monday and there was this bloody great pantechnicon. He said, 'There you are, you're off to London.'

(delayed, older male)

Transitional learners are more common among the younger and mid-age respondents. This is partly due to the increase in opportunities and the expectations, both parental and societal, that go with them. This does not, in itself, lead to an increase in lifelong learning – perhaps the reverse, as explained by the following respondent.

> I hated every minute of it ... I thought it was the most boring waste of time ... I stayed in the sixth form because I was expected to ... nobody I knew left school at 16 ... well, I met my husband when I was 17.
>
> [On applying for jobs] They all wrote back and offered me jobs. Because at that time if you had two arms and two legs and could write your name you were in, you know.
>
> (transitional, mid-age female)

As expected, more women are delayed returners to education, and more men are lifelong learners by virtue of their different historical employment rates. There were several stories from female respondents about the clash between family commitments and the desire to take part in formal learning episodes. For example:

> Yes, she was pushing me to go back, but with the children – it's not easy at all you know. I've got Mum and Dad as well with me. My dad's got Alzheimer's disease ... maybe later, not now.
>
> After I had my daughter, I wanted to know all about the way I could play with her, the way I can teach her, the way I can enjoy things with her. And I absolutely loved it.
>
> (transitional, younger female)

> I couldn't wait to get out. I got out of there early, and I left when I was 14 ... I used to sign in and naff off ... I don't think I was put on this earth to be told what to do.
>
> I thought I'd put it on a back burner for a later date, then I had Cory and Charles and it's just the way it goes ... I would go back now if I could.
>
> Anything at all. I love to read. I read biographies and thrillers, anything ... yes always, I could read when I was 4, so I always like to.
>
> (non-participant, younger female)

What both of these extracts also exemplify is that lack of participation in formal episodes is often not the result of lifelong lack of motivation, or the lack of opportunities. Sometimes personal circumstances are a hindrance, but they are often also the start of another, less formal, way into learning by reading or child-care.

Table 14.3 contains one of a number of indicators that show how participation is strongly related to place and to geographic mobility. In general, participation increases with the distance between current area of residence and area of birth (also with minority first language, ethnicity and distance

Table 14.3 Patterns of participation by area of birth

Trajectory	Neighbourhood	District	Area	UK	Abroad
Non-participant	50	47	24	24	14
Transitional learner	17	12	19	21	24
Delayed learner	23	29	30	20	24
Lifelong learner	10	13	26	35	38

from parents). The most mobile are the least likely to be non-participants. In these explanatory extracts, the first example is of a non-participant living in the same rural area all of her life, and the second is of a lifelong learner showing that the link between education and mobility is a complex one.

> We lived in a sort of well out of the way place in the woods. So we had to walk a long way to school anyway. So if the weather was really bad and there was snow up to here, that was another good excuse to stay home ... I think moving out of that environment and going to school, there's so many people, it's so annoying, see.
>
> I [left school at 14 and] went to work in Woolworths ... They only just, you know, showed you what to do and you should have got on with it. People didn't have any special training as such.
>
> (non-participant, mid-age female)

> The problem was that my family ran – we did pubs – so we were moving constantly ... what we used to do was buy a pub ... redecorate it, revamp it, refurbish the whole thing ... then sell it on and go on to the next one ... the big issue was moving constantly, because you'd move from school to school ... so my education went up and down, so I didn't do as well in my O levels as I could have done, and I know that, and I think that's what probably spurred me on.
>
> (lifelong, young female)

Family influence on participation

Tables 14.4 to 14.6 show clear relationships between participation and the characteristics of parents. In general, the patterns are the same for father and mother, and only a selection of the results is shown here. These relationships are not new, and have been remarked before by a variety of commentators (Gorard *et al.* 1999c; San-Segundo and Valiente 2003). Post-compulsory ('continuous') participation for the respondent is also reflected in the elevated age of leaving education for the mothers and fathers of transitional and lifelong learners.

Table 14.4 Patterns of participation by parents' education

Trajectory	Age father left school	Age mother left school
Non-participant	14.2	14.3
Transitional learner	16.3	16.0
Delayed learner	14.5	14.6
Lifelong learner	16.4	16.1

Here is an example of the 'reproduction' of education patterns within families, and of the power of initial schooling, with family influence, to help create a lifelong attitude of confidence in face of objective learning opportunities.

> It was a fee-paying school, a private school. There wasn't anything different or special. It was just a normal school [in Australia]. My father attended this school, so it was pre-ordained that I would attend this school as well ... I enjoyed it very much. It was a good school ... It was kind of, sort of, ingrained that we would be conscientious and do the best we could. They were not the type of parents to push things. At the same time, I guess, they led by example. They were fairly well-learned themselves ... my father's an orthopaedic surgeon and did a lot of study to get that far. My mother ... she was a young children's teacher for a while ... I think it set the basis for confidence ... I'm not scared by anything.
>
> (lifelong, younger male)

Table 14.5 shows that respondents from families with non-manual and service class (professional/managerial) fathers are substantially more likely to continue to further education or training than those from families where fathers are not working or are part/unskilled. Family background, in general, is one of the most important predictors of participation.

> I come from a very rural area in West Cornwall. My father was a tin-miner ... we were a bit poverty-stricken.
>
> (delayed, older male)

Table 14.5 Patterns of participation by father's social class

Trajectory	Father service	Father non-manual	Father skilled	Father part-skilled	Father other
Non-participant	5	13	24	49	55
Transitional learner	40	27	20	12	18
Delayed learner	18	22	29	26	18
Lifelong learner	37	39	28	14	8

Table 14.6 Patterns of participation by mother's place of birth

Trajectory	Neighbourhood	District	Area	UK	Abroad
Non-participant	56	49	26	23	25
Transitional learner	12	13	22	21	23
Delayed learner	23	27	27	23	16
Lifelong learner	9	11	25	32	36

My father was very keen for me to succeed at school and put a lot of pressure on me ... I think my father was disappointed I left. I did not really think about a career, I just wanted a job ... I began in the lab testing steel quality. I was not trained – simply told to go and look at someone else and then get on and do it myself.

(delayed, mid-age male)

Table 14.6 links also to Table 14.3 in showing the association between mobility (both geographic and social) and learning. Participation for respondents increases with the distance between their current area of residence (the study site) and the area their mother was born.

Influence of initial schooling

Those who reported not attending school regularly were also less likely to report adult participation in learning of any sort (Table 14.7). Indeed, 60 per cent of them reported no adult education or training at all (and this despite their average age of 52). It is notable, however, that 22 per cent of them did report a return to some formal learning at a later date, and it is important therefore that this 'delayed' route back into learning remains feasible in future funding and qualification regimes.

As might be expected, many more respondents with a private or selective education have become lifelong learners (using the current definition) than those attending secondary modern or elementary schools (Table 14.8, see also above). These patterns are clearly determined historically, geographically and

Table 14.7 Patterns of participation by attendance at school

Trajectory	Regular school attender	Not regular attender
Non-participant	35	60
Transitional learner	18	10
Delayed learner	25	22
Lifelong learner	22	8

Table 14.8 Patterns of participation by school attended at age 16

Trajectory	Comprehensive	Grammar	Secondary modern	Private	Elementary
Non-participant	33	19	55	14	73
Transitional learner	20	25	8	32	6
Delayed learner	24	27	30	9	15
Lifelong learner	24	29	8	45	7

socio-economically as much as educationally. For example, attending a private school could be a proxy variable for many of those above (such as having a parent in a service-class occupation).

Nevertheless, Tables 14.7 and 14.8 together show that, despite the importance of early family background, initial schooling is also part of the pattern set for later life participation. Some respondents explain:

Hated it. I didn't like school at all ... I used to play up a lot ... It wasn't relevant to the job I got in the end. I was lucky really.

(delayed, young male)

[On passing the 11+] So, yes, my schooling played an important part in my future – I didn't know it then but I know now with the benefit of hindsight ... I didn't leave with any qualifications ... I walked into a job. See, that was a different thing then ... Half the class I was in had jobs before they left school ... Engineering. Most in that school went into engineering.

[On not being allowed to sit exams at 16] I was offended more than anything. I mean, I wasn't a brilliant student ... but then as an apprentice my employer sent me to day release and then I got qualifications.

(delayed, older male)

My sister went to grammar school and I went to a technical school ... I would have liked to [go to the grammar school] but I wasn't as clever as she was ... my father was a teacher and my mother didn't work at all. So it wasn't really a big deal that I didn't go to the school that she went to. No. Not really. It's just that I didn't like school. But I did more night school later on.

I just watched her. She would tell and show me. That's all really ... So I was then doing calf-rearing, milking, sheep ... Just by people showing you, the farmer showing you. I loved it. I didn't find it hard.

(delayed, older female)

The complete model

The respondents' current family setup can also be a key indicator of later learning patterns, especially in interaction with the respondents' sex (and occupational class). For men, living with a partner does not seem to be the barrier to participation that it can be for women; in fact, it is linked to enhanced participation. The same applies even more strongly to having children to look after. The relatively high proportion of delayed learners among those who have children suggests that some respondents' learning ambitions were initially frustrated by the need to care for the children (Table 14.9, and see above).

Putting all of the above factors together in a multivariate analysis, it is possible to 'predict' using logistic regression which of the four 'trajectories' is reported by each respondent with considerable accuracy using only what is known about their non-educational or initial education background (i.e. year of birth, sex, father's occupation, type of school attended and regular/irregular attendee at school). For example, it is possible to predict whether any individual reported extended initial education or training with 84 per cent accuracy (i.e. our prediction would place the individual on the correct trajectory 84 per cent of the time). In predicting their later episodes of participation, the overall accuracy is 77 per cent (Table 14.10). In both cases, therefore, the accuracy of predictions is improved by around 50 per cent compared to chance. More significantly, by creating the model in a hierarchical way, it is calculated in terms of explanatory variables entered in batches representing periods in the individual's life from birth to the present. In this way, each batch of variables can only improve the prediction based on the previous batch(es). This gives a clue as to which variables are the determinants of learning episodes and which, like qualifications, are largely proxy summaries of others.

Table 14.10 shows that the vast majority of variation in patterns of participation that can be explained is explained by variables that were known when each person was born. Other than that, a key issue in explaining continuous post-compulsory learning is the experience of initial schooling, whereas a key issue in explaining later-life learning is experience of work and family life as an adult.

Table 14.9 Patterns of participation by family setup

Trajectory	Single	Have partner	Have children	Have no children	Number of children
Non-participant	49	30	36	29	1.6
Transitional learner	17	18	15	24	1.2
Delayed learner	21	27	29	15	1.9
Lifelong learner	13	26	20	23	1.5

Table 14.10 Predictive power at each life stage

	Chance	Birth	Schooling	Adult	IT access
Continuous	62	79 (0.45)	84 (0.58)	84	84
Later life	54	71 (0.36)	71	77 (0.49)	77

Note
The use of information from adult lives cannot be said to 'predict' episodes of continuous initial education. The figures in brackets are the amount of variance explained by the variables at that life stage.

Is access to ICT a determinant of learning?

The model also included a final batch of variables relating to access to and use of computers and the internet. As Table 14.10 shows, these make *no* difference to the accuracy of our predictions. Once all of the preceding variables are taken into account, the model explains both continuous and later learning as accurately as is possible with the available variables. This section describes the implications of this finding for the strong simple relationship between access to computers and patterns of learning, and for attempts to widen participation via technology.

Probably the first and most obvious observation about patterns of formal learning and access to and use of ICT is that the two are strongly related. This has been observed before (e.g. Selwyn and Gorard 2002; Gorard 2003) and most commentators are agreed (e.g. Sargant and Aldridge 2002). The same relationship appears again in this new study (Table 14.11). All of the indicators of computer/internet access and use show the same pattern – those who undertake formal learning are also those individuals who are more likely to use ICT.

However, I do not immediately draw the same conclusion as others have done. It is not necessarily the case that use of ICT leads to greater participation. The causal model could be the reverse of that, or both phenomena could have a common cause. The majority of the variance in patterns of participation that *can* be explained in Table 14.10 is explained by what could have been known about the respondents when they were born (year of birth, sex, father's occupation, etc.). Our model improves through the addition of what could have been known about the respondents when they reached school-leaving age (type of school attended, for example). Our model for participation in later life also improves through the addition of information about the respondents as adults (occupation and number of children, for example). But adding all of the generic variables about experience of ICT, access to ICT and current use of ICT does not improve the model any further. While this model is not in any way a definitive test, it does suggest that ICT in itself is not a key determinant of adult participation in formal learning.

Table 14.11 ICT use by trajectory

Trajectory	Used computer	Not used computer	Computer last year	No computer last year	Internet last year	Not internet last year
Non-participant	19	67	16	61	12	55
Transitional learner	20	13	22	13	24	13
Delayed learner	30	16	29	20	26	23
Lifelong learner	31	4	34	6	38	8

Discussion

Non-participation in formal learning is partly a product of the fact that people do not see education and training as appropriate for them. These views are, in turn, structured by factors that occur relatively early in life. This suggests that policies that simply make it easier for people to participate in the kinds of learning opportunities that are already available, by removing barriers such as cost or travel, for example, will have only limited impact. Over a third of the adult population are not engaging in any learning at all and those individuals who are participating in adult education are heavily patterned by 'pre-adult' social factors such as socio-economic status, gender, year of birth and type of school attended. This confirms a long line of studies, from the 1950s onwards, which have provided compelling evidence that the determinants of participation (and non-participation) are long term and rooted in family, locality and history (e.g. Glass 1954).

An important conclusion from this analysis is that the 'e-learning' society is remarkably similar to its non-technological predecessor. Of particular interest from the most recent data is the 'failure' of ICT and technology-based adult education to make any noticeable difference to these deep-rooted patterns. There is no evidence of ICT having a positive effect in terms of *widening* participation in adult education. At best ICT is *increasing* levels of participation within the social groups which were learning anyway (a trend I have referred to previously as attracting the 'usual suspects'). More fundamental change to the patterns described in this chapter would have to come from improvements in the social and economic structure from which they emerge, from an increased recognition of the importance of self-directed learning, and from a radical reappraisal of the nature of the opportunities available. Rather than viewing non-participants merely as a group of potential clients to be tempted into the existing setup, we can use the lessons from research of the kind dealt with in the other chapters in this book to change that setup into something 'really useful'.

References

Department for Education and Skills (DfES) (2002) 'Thousands More "Get On" as Adult Learners' Week Kicks Off', DfES Press Notice 2002/0098, 14 May.

Glass, D. (1954) *Social Mobility in Britain*, London: Routledge.

Gorard, S. (2003) 'Lifelong Learning Trajectories in Wales: Results of the NIACE Adults Learners Survey', in F. Aldridge and N. Sargant (eds) *Adult Learning and Social Division: Volume 2*, Leicester: NIACE.

Gorard, S. and Rees, G. (2002) *Creating a Learning Society?* Bristol: Policy Press.

Gorard, S., Rees, G. and Fevre, R. (1999a) 'Two Dimensions of Time: The Changing Context of Lifelong Learning', *Studies in the Education of Adults* 31 (1): 35–48.

Gorard, S., Fevre, R. and Rees, G. (1999b) 'The Apparent Decline of Informal Learning', *Oxford Review of Education* 25 (4): 437–54.

Gorard, S., Rees, G. and Fevre, R. (1999c) 'Patterns of Participation in Lifelong Learning: Do Families Make a Difference?' *British Educational Research Journal* 25 (4): 517–32.

Gorard, S., Rees, G. and Selwyn, N. (2002) 'The "Conveyor Belt Effect": A Re-assessment of the Impact of National Targets for Lifelong Learning', *Oxford Review of Education* 28 (1): 75–89.

Harrison, R. (1993) 'Disaffection and Access', in J. Calder (ed.) *Disaffection and Diversity. Overcoming Barriers to Adult Learning*, London: Falmer, p. 2.

Hawkey, R. (2002) 'The Lifelong Learning Game: Season Ticket or Free Transfer?' *Computers and Education* 38: 5–20.

La Valle, I. and Blake, M. (2001) *National Adult Learning Survey 2001, Research Report 321*, Nottingham: DfES.

Maxted, P. (1999) 'Understanding Barriers to Learning', *t Magazine* July. Available at http://www.tmag.co.uk

San-Segundo, M. and Valiente, A. (2003) 'Family Background and Returns to Schooling in Spain', *Education Economics* 11 (1): 39–52.

Sargant, N. and Aldridge, F. (2002) *Adult Learning and Social Division: A Persistent Pattern, Volume 1*, Leicester: NIACE.

Selwyn, N. (2002) 'E-stablishing an Inclusive Society? Technology, Social Exclusion and UK Government Policy Making', *Journal of Social Policy* 31 (1): 1–20.

Selwyn, N. and Gorard, S. (2002) *The Information Age: Technology, Learning and Social Exclusion in Wales*, Cardiff: University of Wales Press.

Chapter 15

Human learning
The themes

Stella Parker

Introduction

This book is one of many that attempts to explore the nature of human learning, but it differs from most other publications in that it views the topic from a range of perspectives. Our view is that such a range is necessary and important because human learning is the focus of research in so many disparate disciplines that there is the possibility of researchers in one discipline working in isolation from the others. This is particularly likely to be the case where there are significant differences between the disciplines, such as between the sciences and the humanities. Why should this isolation be a problem? One answer, aimed at researchers, is that the fruits of research in one discipline can throw light on problems and issues in another. Another answer, aimed this time at practitioners, is that research questions are rooted in theoretical positions that can inform professional practice. We are not suggesting that practitioners need to be aware of all the research on human learning coming from all the disciplines, but we are suggesting that a knowledge of the major themes running through the various disciplines can provide a useful resource base on which to build models of practice. This final chapter brings together the various themes that have emerged previously in this book.

Nature via nurture

Learning (whatever its form) is a function of the human condition, and as such is it dependent on human nature or on human nurture? The answer to this question is woven into the structure of the book and into the themes running through each chapter. The answer here is that human learning is dependent on both nature and nurture or, more accurately, it is nature via nurture. The outcome of nature via nurture is the individual. The individual is a unique creation, whose biology more or less follows its predetermined course but which does so within the confines and opportunities of her or his physical and social environment. This book includes chapters that cover all three factors – nature, nurture and the individual. The first chapters concentrate on those aspects of learning which are dependent on nature, particularly the internal processes of learning. These are drawn from the sciences, such as evolutionary psychology, neuroscience and psychology. The chapters that follow concentrate on human nurture, meaning the various factors external to individuals that shape her or him and that affect the internal processes of learning. Nurture includes the affects of other individuals, of groups and of culture and of society. Yet other chapters cover learning from the learner's point of view. This book is thus attempting to span differing traditions or approaches to human learning. If we are to make sense of these differences, then we need common ground between them. At the risk of reductionism we suggest that there is one denominator common to the meaning of learning, from whichever discipline it is drawn. This common denominator is 'change'.

Learning, then, at its most basic level, implies changes on the part of the learner. Studies in the sciences tend to concentrate on the internal aspects of these changes, while the humanities/social sciences tend to focus on agents of change in the environment. The changes associated with learning may take place clandestinely within an individual and may be available only to her private self. Or changes can be expressed in such a public way that they are obvious to all. But whatever its origin, the change associated with learning is always a response to an external stimulus or agency.

If change is associated with the meaning of learning, then we need to note that the methods for studying it differ between the sciences and the humanities/social sciences; this implies that different questions are being asked too. For example, in a science-based study of learning, methods generally involve the setting up of controlled conditions and the manipulation of known (and relatively simple) variables such as the effect of (say) sleep deprivation on learning. Experiments can be repeated time and again, generalisations are made, giving the possibility of reasonably accurate predictions about the effect of the stimulus on others. In contrast, in the humanities/ social sciences, experiments cannot be set up in laboratories to study learning, because the focus of such studies is the complexity of human affairs. The methods used generally rely on post facto studies of phenomena and can only indicate the effect that various external factors could have had on samples of learners (see Gorard's chapter for a good example of the limits of this predictability). Such studies cannot predict accurately the effect of the environment on an individual's learning because there will always be exceptional individuals who buck general trends. And because human interactions are influenced by so many very different factors, the results of studies on learning in the humanities/social sciences can appear to be woolly and indeterminate when contrasted with the crisp results of scientific studies (say) on the effect of a controlled stimulus on learning ability. The apparent certainty with which science can provide answers to questions about the human condition is appealing in a world full of uncertainty. But it is inappropriate to assume that questions about human affairs can produce answers that are simple because these questions focus on many variables; in contrast, the questions posed by scientists focus on as few variables as possible. These differences in method contribute to the differences.

There is little agreement on how many learning theories there are, and so for the sake of argument the theories implicit in this book can be divided roughly into three schools of thought. One school studies the changes dependent on biological abilities; another studies how changes in social interactions affect learning; and the third school focuses on the individual's perceptions of learning.

The first of these three schools, in its most extreme form, implies that human brains are 'wired up' or preprogrammed, so that only a meagre amount of environmental stimulus is required to set off a train of predetermined, complex internal processing. The implication here is that the learning properties of the human brain are genetically inherited and passed on intact from one generation to the next. In its extreme form (not supported in this book) the 'wired up brain' theory of learning implies that fecklessness begets fecklessness, highly achieving parents will have highly achieving children and that talents (such as musical ability) run in families. In its less extreme form, which is supported in this book, the human brain is considered to have certain generic and inherent properties that are common to all. Despite the mass of evidence indicating that the extreme form does not have a tenable position, the idea that an individual's behaviour is predetermined by her/his biology is a powerful one in our society. Not only can it be used as an argument for maintaining the status quo, but it can also be used to explain (and sometimes justify) atrocious behaviour. Educational theories too emanate from such a theory of learning, so (for example) separate curricula for the sexes can be justified by reference to the biological differences between males and females, as can separate curricula for other groups perceived to be inherently different.

The second of the two schools is the environmentalist school, where learning is considered to be an outcome of environmental factors on the learner. In its most extreme form, this theory of learning implies that nothing in the human brain is programmed or predetermined before birth. In other words, rather than being pre-wired, the human brain is a *tabula rasa* at birth, waiting for the inscription of lifelong learning experiences. This view too is a powerful one in our society because it implies that nothing is fixed; it implies we can enable people to learn anything as long as we make sure their environment is right. This view is in part a reaction to the biological determinism (outlined above) which implies a monotonous predictability and little possibility of changing individuals or society by means of education. For these reasons in particular, theories based on the *tabula rasa* notion are appealing to the liberal minded, but they are flawed.

The flaws lie (first) in the Cartesian view that the human brain can be regarded as somehow distinct from the remainder of the human body, which certainly has been built according to a predetermined plan. Second, this assumed mind/body separation implies that the human brain has not been subject to the forces of evolution. If this were to be the case, the human brain is likely to be the only biological organ on earth in this situation! For these reasons, theories claiming that the external environment is the most important factor in understanding human learning are unlikely to be accurate. And yet they are at the root of certain educational theories about learning, such as behaviourism, including Skinner's theory, which assumes that learning is merely the sum of repeated environmental stimuli on an unstructured brain. It is little wonder that extreme forms of behaviourism have fallen into disrepute.

The two views outlined above – that of a pre-wired brain and that of a wire-less brain – can be regarded as two opposite ends of a spectrum. While extreme versions of each are no longer in vogue, the pre-wired version persists, but in a less extreme form. One example (attributed to Rousseau) is that a 'natural' human state is inherently temperate; another (attributed to Hobbes) is that the natural human state is inherently intemperate. Although opposite in their views of the human condition, both theories agree that it has inherited components. Educational practices based on these two theories differ according to whether the aim of learning is to develop potential or whether it is to develop submission through discipline.

Somewhere in between the internal biological processes and the external environment is the concept of the individual learner; this is the third school of thought. According to this school, the learner is neither a pre-wired automaton nor at the mercy of constant environmental stimuli. The learner is an individual with a life history of experience deriving from her or his upbringing, gender, class, culture, temperament, and so on. The learner mediates between environmental input and biological processes, and, through learning, constructs her or his own knowledge about the world.

It is not just academics who contemplate the meaning of learning; everyone has their own views about learning (whether explicit or not). We all use views of learning to enable us to go about our everyday business; if we did not, then we would be unable to carry out the normal activities of living. Theories of learning are gleaned from a variety of sources that include the experience of our interactions with others, our observations of the behaviour of others, and what we learn through discussions and from the media. Learning (and particularly formal learning) is regarded by most societies as so important that collective efforts are made to ensure that young people (and adults) become educated and that their learning is controlled. Whatever the details of everyday views about learning are, it seems as if they have enough in common to enable people to agree (albeit implicitly) on them as a basis for the learning that goes on in schools, colleges and universities.

Within these educational institutions, we find a variety of professional practices influenced by all three schools of thought – the *tabula rasa* (or behaviourist) theories of learning, wired-up (or cognitive) theories, and theories about the central importance of the learner (constructivist theories). All this suggests that these three theories are implicit in everyday thinking about learning.

The various themes

Innateness of human learning abilities

One of the distinguishing characteristics of humankind is its ability to learn. This ability is quite distinctive, and sets humans apart from other animals. The distinctiveness lies in our ability to use abstract thought, spoken and written language, symbolic representation, and so on; we are the only animals on this planet that have these abilities. Although our learning ability separates us from other animals, this does not mean that humans represent a discontinuity in evolutionary terms. There is sufficient fossil evidence to indicate that we are closely related to the other great apes and the evidence from genetics indicates that we share around 98 per cent of our DNA with chimpanzees.

The human brain is an organ which, like all other organs in the human body, is the product of millions of years of evolution by means of natural selection. This means that the human brain has been subjected to forces in the external environment (both physical and social), and as a result it has become altered over time and is a superb learning organ. The information about these evolutionary alterations is stored in the genes in all cells of the body; genes can be regarded as parts of an information system that collects data about the world in the past and incorporates it into the design of future generations.

In the same way that the human body is structured according to a common plan, so is the human brain. This means that all humans have the same overall plan, the same basic abilities and brains that can perform some tasks more easily than others. For example, all healthy humans learn to speak, but learning to write is not so easy. This previous sentence is written with a caveat, meaning that it does not apply to individuals whose brains malfunction. In the case of healthy human beings, any major differences between the achievement of groups or individuals are more likely to be due to differences in upbringing or culture than due to differences in brain structure; once again this general rule does not apply to those suffering from brain dysfunction.

Although there is a common pattern of brain structure, people do exhibit some individual differences. For example, for some people the brain's control of the eye muscles is not as strong as normal and gives rise to a condition known as 'wobbly eyes'. This can affect their reading ability, but the problem can be alleviated by treatments designed to steady the eyes. However, poor achievement in education in general cannot be explained in terms of defects in brain function.

The brain is structured in such a way as to respond to and be changed by certain external stimuli, and although it continues to respond throughout life, the rate of response diminishes after puberty. Stimulating the brain (by means of formal learning, for example) can cause permanent changes to its structure. The cells that make up the brain form complex neural networks that are intricately interconnected. When one part of the brain is stimulated (such as when noise stimulates the auditory centre) the stimulation travels across networks to other centres, meaning that the brain can respond to one set of stimuli on many different levels at the same time.

Particulate nature of human abilities/multiple intelligences

There is a certain amount of evidence to suggest that all humans find the achievement of some learning tasks very easy. These include learning to speak, to relate to others, to evaluate the behaviour and feelings of others, and so on. Because these abilities are common to all, then they are likely to be inherited, and their distinctiveness implies they are located discretely in the brain. This is the basis of Gardner's theory of multiple intelligences, a theory which could be regarded (at first glance) as being in the school of the wired-up-brain determinists. However, the developmental state of any one of the multiple intelligences depends on whether or not it is suitably stimulated by agents in the environment and/or whether or not an individual has the means and the will to develop it. Motivation is another word for stimulation, and individuals differ in terms of their motivation; this can account for individual differences in achievement.

Because some learning is easy, this suggests that the human brain is not an empty vessel waiting to be filled up with knowledge; rather, it is fully equipped with complex mental tools. These innate tools are responsible for our smartness, for the survival of our species, and their malleability means they can be pressed into service for ensuring human existence in many different circumstances and modes of living. Some learning is difficult because it requires the brain to perform tasks for which it is not designed, such as writing, adding up large numbers or learning the language of academic disciplines. This is the type of learning that takes place in formal education, and hard and anti-intuitive though it is, it can be more easily achieved if agents in their environment motivate learners.

The idea that uneducated human brains are empty and that educated ones are full is a crude caricature, but it does encapsulate an extreme version of the *tabula rasa* theory of learning. Such extreme versions are no longer tenable, but this does not mean that the environmental context has no effect on learning; on the contrary, the machinations and processing of cognitive tools in the brain are activated by context. Social context and social interactions are considered to have been pivotal to the development of human learning abilities, and interactions within a social context sustain learning abilities and enable the dissemination of the fruits of learning. In turn, the fruits of this learning (including culture) serve as a 'glue' that holds groups and communities together – groups and communities that learn together share a common identity.

Learning within the context of socio-political and economic forces

In the economically developed world and elsewhere, the socio-economic context in which an individual is born and bred has a significant impact on whether she or he achieves within a formal education system. Those from backgrounds where they are brought up to believe that education and training are not appropriate for them, learn to fail. The evidence underpinning this statement comes from numerous studies on the achievement of young people in school and the participation of adults from a range of socio-economic backgrounds. Learning to fail takes a long time, and if it is constantly reinforced by everyday experiences then it cannot be immediately reversed. No matter how many learning opportunities are made available to those who have learned to fail, they are unlikely to be taken up unless there is also some means of reversing learning-to-fail attitudes. Studies such as those delineated in Gorard's chapter show the importance of the external environment on shaping the learning about self, about society and about life in general.

Women's learning experiences, according to Stalker (Chapter 12) are different in comparison to men's. The differences exist because of the position of women in society, which (she argues) tends to be at a disadvantage in comparison to the position of men. Thus, there is a tendency for some knowledge bases to become associated with women and others with men. The knowledge bases of women become seen as trivial, as 'ladies' work' and thus outside of the rational and the 'normal', simply because men do not engage with them and/or because such knowledge bases do not draw upon research. In addition to 'ladies' work', women also have unique learning experiences which are biologically located (those in particular concerned with childbirth) and this again sets them apart from men. Although few would argue today that women's intellects are inferior to men's, the differences alluded to above can contribute to the impression that there is a dichotomy between the learning abilities of women and men. Rather than ignore these arguments, it is possible to use them as the starting point for analysing why they exist in the first place. This is the challenge that Stalker brings to our attention.

Jarvis's chapter on the relationship between one's socio-historical position and one's learning draws our attention to different forms of knowledge and how they can be hierarchically arranged across a spectrum, with 'primitive' forms at one end and more 'advanced' technological knowledge at the other. Different societies and cultures differ in terms of the make-up of their knowledge bases. For example, in highly economically developed societies, technological knowledge holds precedence over (say) the knowledge associated with myth and legend; in an economically underdeveloped society, the reverse may be the case. A society based on either of these two examples will have its particular view of the world, of 'how things should be' in the light of its predominant knowledge base(s). The political consequences arising from these differences in knowledge bases (or points of view) probably do not need to be spelled out here.

Learning and the individual; the effects of ageing, experience and feelings and gender

The idea that young people's learning abilities develop over time is not new, but the idea that adult learning abilities continue to develop is relatively new. There is evidence to indicate that London taxi drivers' brains have a larger than normal centre for orientation, implying that the biological development of the brain continues into adult life. There is evidence to indicate that learning a new skill or engaging in a new hobby can enhance the wellbeing of older people. Older people are now becoming recognised as a valuable group, partly because of their relative wealth and their increasing numbers, and partly because they expect to be more involved in society than did their predecessors. Old age is being redefined in developed countries by the 'baby boomer' generation that is now becoming 'the new old'. These factors, coupled with the ideas underpinning lifelong learning, are likely to change commonly held views about the old being incapable of learning.

An individual's life experience, together with her/his biological make-up, contributes to the making of a human learner. These contributory factors give rise to the notion of 'self', and emotions are central to the sense of self. When sensations and perceptions are disconnected from the emotions, this can lead to dissolution of self. 'Self' can be regarded as:

- continuity (a sense of time past and of future);
- unity (you experience yourself as one person);
- embodiment (your sense of being anchored to your body);
- agency (your sense of free will, of being in charge of your own destiny).

Emotions are thus central to the development of intrapersonal knowledge or learner identity. Emotions are central too to the development of morality, based on a sense of responsibility to and for others. This interpersonal sensitivity (arguably) is a distinguishing human characteristic. Learners with healthy interpersonal abilities assimilate the emotional data of others through comparison with their own experience. The wider general learning emanating from this assimilation enriches moral learning. Thus, moral learning presupposes emotional development, and emotions are crucial to learning.

The accumulation of experiences gives us a basis for operating in the world; if that basis is no longer reliable then we can become disoriented. We may try to learn the reasons for the mismatch between our experience and new realities, and then incorporate what we have learned into a new basis of experience. If we have the time and the inclination to do this, then we can continue to operate in everyday life. But in late-modern societies (characterised by rapid change, driven *inter alia* by technology), there is the possibility of being unable to do this effectively. This can give rise to disorientation and disaffection, and one of the challenges facing us is how to learn to operate in a rapidly changing context.

Theories (such as Gardner's) supporting the particulate nature of human learning include interpersonal and intrapersonal abilities. The potential to perceive the emotional state of one's self and of others is bound up with the ability to learn; for example, if one feels bad about oneself, the resultant poor self-esteem can hinder learning. Similarly, if one feels bad about a subject or a teacher, then learning can be hindered too. The idea that emotions have the power to inhibit or enhance learning is not new and is part of everyone's experience. The significance of the idea is that human learning is not simply the outcome of cognitive processes set in motion by external agencies. In other words, the emotions of an individual mediate between the external and internal aspects of learning and, indeed, may also be the primary organisers of thought and behaviour. Without the mediating effects of emotions, learning could be viewed as a simple model of stimulus/response.

This book starts with a chapter by Jarvis in which he makes the case that learning is an existential phenomenon, his case being built on many years of self-reflection as a learner and of reflecting on how others perceive their learning. Learning results from a combination of processes emanating from social situations. These processes affect an individual's body and mind, giving rise to experiences that are transformed cognitively, emotively or practically and integrated as experience into an individual's biography. They contribute to one's perception and thus affect future learning. This particular view puts the learner's perceptions of learning at the heart of understanding about learning. This particular view, emanating as it does from learners explaining how they understand their learning, gives us a subjective account of learning as a human activity. Learning is conceptualised in terms of both specific and individual characteristics. Conceptions of learning are derived from second-order analysis of first-order data, obtained from being self-aware of learning as a phenomenon which is 'in here' (inside the individual) because it is the individual's experience of learning.

In contrast to the above, there are environmental and cognitive perspectives on learning. They contrast with existentialist perspectives because they are objective, and regard the learner as someone to whom things get done, inside of whom things happen. Learning is conceptualised in terms of both universal and contextual characteristics. The conceptualisations derive from second-order analyses of first-order data obtained from observations on the learner. Learning is seen as a phenomenon that is 'out there' and not part of the experience of the investigator of learning. We suggest that the existential line of thinking about learning is a fruitful one. It gives us insights into learners' experiences of learning.

Future research

The topic of learning (in this book) has been examined from several perspectives. Some have chopped learning into bits, and examined it from specific points of view – for example, from that of brain biology, of cognitive functioning or from the effect of certain factors in the social environment. Others have examined learning in terms of a complex whole, with the learner as the centre of this whole. Neither approach can represent reality accurately, but we consider that we can continue to increase our understanding of learning by recognising and using the strengths of each type of approach. The complex-whole approach reminds us that the boundaries of understanding about learning extend beyond the results obtained from individual studies using the piecemeal approach. The piecemeal approach enables us to study in depth small areas of the big picture. Neither approach is in competition with the other.

We suggest that a fruitful way forward could involve researchers from two or three disciplines working together, in teams, on particular aspects of learning. Such aspects include the learning needed for living in complex technologically driven societies. People living in such societies, for their own survival and for the wellbeing of others, need to acquire cognitive tools that are more robust than our inherent, intuitive ways of thinking. Formal learning generally provides these tools, but the topics covered in educational institutions tend to lag behind developments in society. Furthermore, significant proportions of students are failed by education, giving rise to disaffection, economic deprivation and other social problems. These problems can be mitigated by worthwhile learning experiences, as explored in projects on the wider benefits of learning, which have only recently become the subject of research (see ESREA 2001 and relevant Institute of Education publications). The results demonstrate the non-economic benefits of learning, which include its beneficial effects on health, families, citizenship and its role in the prevention of crime, and off-setting the effects of ageing. These benefits arise from learning, and one way forward is to understand more about how we learn, and use this understanding in education, be it formal, non-formal or informal. We need also to understand what is necessary (but difficult) to learn, and how learning can be made more accessible.

Our potential to learn about our learning is only just opening up, and learning – with its ability to help us understand more about how we develop, how we can educate and control our emotions, how we can learn to live with others, how we can mediate our health throughout life and so much more – has many possibilities for enabling humanity to make the world a better place.

References

ESREA (2001) *Wider Benefits of Learning. Understanding and Monitoring the Consequences of Adult Learning*, Spain: Xativa.

Schuller, T., Bynner, J., Green, A., Blackwell, L., Hammond, C., Preston, J. and Gough, M. (2001) *Modelling and Measuring the Wider Benefits of Learning 1. A Synthesis*, London: Institute of Education (one of four in the Wider Benefits of Learning series).

Index

Ability 19, 91; cognitive 19; innate 20;
  perception of 59–60
Action 4, 5
Adams-Webber, J 104
Adaptation 184, 187
Ageing 187–8, 191
Agent 5, 109
Agreeableness 71
Albaili, M 67
Aldridge, F 205
Allport, G 149
Altzeimers, Disease 189
Appleyard, B 26
Argyris, C 95, 97, 143
Aristophanes 184
Aristotle 139
Art 173
Asher, C 162
Aspy, D 149
Associative stage 102
Attachment 185–6, 189, 190
Autonomous stage 102
Autonomy 109, 185–6
Awareness 10–11, 12

Backman, L 187
Bagshaw, M 144
Baltes, P 187, 189, 191
Bandura, A 146
Bar-On, R 142, 144
Barber, B 125
Barber, E 172, 173
Bauer, M 175
Baum, S 64
Beale, R 130
Beane, R 147
Beard, C 139
Beatty, P 184, 187, 190

Beck, U 99
Beder, H 53,
Behaviourism 5–6, 101,
Belenky, M 169–70, 186
Berger, P 10, 116, 117, 186, 189, 190
Bergson, H 10,
Bickham, P 70
Biddell, T 107
Biggs, J 66–7
Billett, S 111–13
Binet, A 51, 140
Biology 16–31, 169, 184, 216
Blake, M 197
Body 2, 4,
Booth, S 3
Borger, R 6
Botkin, J 117, 119
Bourdieu, P 171
Bowlby, J 186
Boyatzis, R 144
Braham, P 175, 176
Brain 19–21, 24, 32–49, 128–9, 130–4,
  187–8, 211, 212, 213–14;
  development of 33–6; left hemisphere
  40–2, 48; right hemisphere 40–2, 48
Bransford, J 59, 60,
Brookfield, S 21
Broughton, J 106
Brown, G 24, 27, 28, 147
Bruner, J 21, 97–98
Bulut, S 151
Bureaucracies 121–2, 124
Burke, G 177
Buzzi, S 176

Caffarella, R 17, 158, 184
Calhoun, A 177
Cano-Garcia, F 70

Career Personality Types 67, 70–1, 76–8, 79
Carkhuff, R 145
Cassidy, J 186
Cattell, R 71
Cerebral cortex 36, 48,
Chadwick, W 176
Chi, M 102, 105
Child, D 67
Chiva, A 186, 187, 180
Christal, R 71
Class, social 173
Cognition 20, 25, 32, 69, 90–3, 153, 218
Cognitive 184, 187; development 148, 190–1; stage 102; structuralism 101, 106–13
Cohen, J 132–3
Colin III, S 170
Collard, S 170
Communication 24, 92, 132
Community 177
Community of practice 110, 112
Computer-based systems 102–6
Connection 186, 190
Consciousness, Everyday 96
Constructivism 104, 107–8; internalisation model 108–9; participation 108–9, 110–13
Cooper, R 142,143–4, 153
Cosmides, L 18,
Costa, P 68, 71, 72
Costanzo, M 61–3
Cotord's syndrome 134, 136
Coustan, T 55, 57,
Covington, M 60,
Craft 173
Craik, F 66
Crane, D 175, 177
Creationism 29
Creativity 69
Culture 24, 26, 27, 171–2, 176, 178, 186, 209–13
Cusack, S 13

Dahlin, B 67
Dai, D 70
Damasio, A 92, 129, 130–1, 134, 137
Daniels, H 107–8, 109, 113
Darwin, C 23, 27, 28–9
Davis, D 157
Denton, E 161
Deoxyribonucleic acid (DNA) 17–18, 213

Department for Education and Skills (DfES) 196
Descartes, R 1, 2
Determinism 25, 29,
Diamond, M 187–8, 190
Digman, J 71
Disadvantage 195
Disciplines, academic xiii, 2, 5, 14, 20–1, 209
Disjuncture 10–11, 117-
Donnell, R 174
Drennon, C 54
Dualism 2–3, 5, 6, 7
Durée 10,
Dyslexia 42, 46

Education 122, 123, 129, 137–8; affective 147–8, 149; initial 202–3; moral 132; nursery 152; teacher 150
Elsey, B 175
Emmons, R 160
Emotional Competency 150; quotient (EQ) 142, 143
Emotions 12, 40, 41–2, 71, 90–3, 94–5, 128, 130–1, 134–5, 137, 185, 186, 188, 190, 191, 216–17; and maturity 149; educating 150–3
Empathy 137–8, 143, 147
Engestrom, Y 94, 97
English for Speakers of Other Languages (ESOL) 53–5, 59, 60, 61
English, L 157, 159
Engram 37
Entwistle, J 178
Entwistle, N 66, 67
Environment 90–3, 116
Erikson, E 184, 186, 191–2
Evans, C 168, 175
Evolution 23–4, 28–9
Exercise 187
Existentialism 3–6, 9–14
Experience 1, 2, 5, 7, 10, 11–14, 102, 103, 105, 116, 130, 139, 151, 157, 178; episodic 11–12, 117; lifelong 11, 117, 184, 216; emotional 135, 148–53; primary 12; prior 158; secondary 12; spiritual 158; transformation of 12–13; women's 170–1
Experientialism 6
Expert 102, 104–5, 106; domain 104
Extraversion 71
Eysenck, H 71, 72

Facilitator 149, 151, 178–9
Family 202–202
Fashion 173, 175–8
Feelings 152–3
Feldhusen, J 70
Femininity 175
Feminism 18, 185
Field, J 129
Fierros, E 64
Fingeret, A 54
Fisher, J 187, 191
Fiske, D 71
Flannery, D 170, 174
Flavell, J 93, 97
Ford, K 104
Free will 135–6
Freire, P 159
Freud, A 96
Freud, S 92, 96, 141, 173
Frieberg, H 149, 151
Functionality 91–2
Fundamentalism 125
Furer, M 183, 184
Furnham, A 76
Furth, H 92, 97
Fusco, C 177

Gardner, H 9–10, 13, 20, 51–64, 141,
    143, 160, 214, 217,
Gasgoigne, F 152
Generalisability 26
Genes 17–18, 25, 27, 32, 47
Genetics 32, 38, 46–7, 48
Gergen, K 89, 99
Giddens, A 99
Gill, L 178
Gilligan, C 133, 134–5, 137, 169
Glass, D 205
Glidden, R 70
Globalisation 87–8, 123, 124, 179
Goldberg, L 71
Goldsteni-Gidoni, I 175
Goleman, D 12, 139, 140, 141, 144, 149,
    150
Gorard, S 195, 198, 205, 210
Gordon, S 102, 103
Gould, S 51,
Gow, D 67
Greenberg, J 183, 184, 188
Greenfield, S 2, 132,
Greeno, J 110–111
Grigorenko, E 70, 102
Guglielmino, C 27,

Haight, B 184, 188, 189, 190
Hall, C 142, 148, 149–50, 152, 153
Hall, E 150
Hallinan, L 172
Hammond, C 13,
Harding, S 172
Harris, J 25
Harrison, R 196
Havinghurst, R 22
Hawley, R 196
Hayes, E 170, 174
Hedges, E 174, 176
Hippocampus 36
Hoffman, M 134–5
Holland, J 68, 70–1, 76
Hood, Y 174
Holzkamp, H 97
Hornby, G 141, 149
Howes, M 101,
Huang, J 72
Hughes, E 70
Human, becoming 2, 9; being 1,2, 9–10;
    learning 27–9; species 22–3
Human Genome Diversity Project 25
Humanistic psychology 147–8
Humanity xiii, 1, 17

Identity 174–5, 178, 187, 191; defence 96
Ideology 106
Illeris, K 5, 17, 87, 96, 98
Illiteracy 42, 53–4
Independence 183–4
Individual 90
Influence 144
Information and communications
    technology (ICT) 195–6, 205–6
Information processing 101
Inglis, S 176
Inhelder, B 184
Inner world 139, 146
Integration 92
Intellectual 142; multiple intelligences
    50–64, 214–15 (crystallized 190–1;
    eight 52; instruction 54–8; reflections
    54, 58–61; practical 101, 102, 105);
    quotient (IQ) 50, 51, 52, 140–1, 143,
    149, 153; spiritual 160–1
Intelligence 50–64, 105; definition of 51;
    emotional 139–54 (components of
    144, 150; defined 143–4); fluid 190,
    191
Interaction of learner and external
    world 89

Internal psychological processes 89
Intuition 21
Isaacs, J 174

Jackson, T 130
Jarvis, P 5, 7, 13, 14, 17, 99, 117, 216, 217–18
Jeffries, J 173
Jersild, A 140–1, 150
Johnson, F 184, 188
Jones, D 152
Jones, S 18,
Jordon, J 186
Joyce, B 151, 153
Jung, C 184, 191

Kallenbach, S 57–8, 61, 63
Kegan, R 186, 191
Kelly, G 147
Kember, D 67
Kerr, C 123
Kivnick, H 191
Knowledge, artificial 118, 120–1, 122, 123, 124; cultural 119, 121, 126; declarative 102; deep 103, 106; engineer 104, 105; experiential 103; expertise 103, 104, 105; ownership 179; practical 102, 111; procedural 102; production 179; rational-legal 121–2; shallow 106; society 123; tacit 102, 105; types of 118
Knowles, H 27
Knowles, M 27, 158
Kohlberg, L 133, 135, 137
Kolb, D 6, 7, 97, 152, 158
Kornhaber, M 52, 64,
Koury, S 187
Krechevsky, M 52
Krishnamurti, J 142

LaValle, I 197
Lacey, A 10
Lahey, L 185
Lakweink, K 173
Laland, K 24, 27, 28
Language 20, 41, 48, 67, 173
Lauer, J 175
Lauer, R 175
Laurillard, D 21,
Lave, J 89, 110
Lawrence, D 145
Lawrence, K 173
Leahy, M 184

LearnDirect 196
Learners 151–2, 178–9; adult 159, 196–207; delayed 196, 197–206; lifelong 196–206; transitional 197–206
Learning, accelerated 152; accommodative 94; active 37; adult 158–9; and achieving 66, 67; and drugs 38; approaches to 66–82; artificial 118; assimilative 94; barriers to 195–6; concept of 129–130; contracts 158; covenants 158; crafts 168–9; cumulative 93–4; cycle 6; deep 66, 67, 73, 80, 81; definition 6, 7, 88, 117; E- 196, 207; educative 130; episodes 195; experiential 105, 139–54, 159; generative 124; holistic 161; innovative 117, 122, 123, 124, 125, 126; lifelong 14, 88, 129–30, 195; maintenance 117, 122, 123, 124, 125, 126; model of 8; moral 133, 137–8; organisation 124; over socialised 112; perspectives on 17; philosophy 1–15; pre-conscious 12; self-directed 158, 159; situated 110; society 124; spiritual 163; styles 66, 67; surface 66, 67, 73, 80, 81; survival 124,130 ; trajectories 195–207; transfer 111; transformative 94–5, 159; types 93–5; women's 168–82, 215
Lefcourt, H 146
Leicester, M 132–3
Leiceister-Smith, W 121
Leithauser, T 96
Leontyev, A 97
Lewis, M 171
Life, cycle 183–92; history 196; mid 186
Lifeworld 116
Liminality 119–20, 121, 122
Lin, J 173–4
Lipka, J 147
Literacy 50, 52, 54–61,
Lockhart, R 66
Lodge, D 137
Long-term depression (LTD) 36, 48
Long-term potentiation (LTP) 36, 48
Lorenzer, A 98
Luckmann, T 10, 116, 117, 186, 189, 190

McCrae, R 68, 71, 72
MacDonald, D 71–2

MacGill, I 6, 151
Macmurray, J 4, 6, 14, 139, 142, 148, 150
Macquarrie, J 3,
McRobbie, A 175
McWorld 125, 126
Mahler, M 183, 184, 186, 188, 191
Magai, C 188, 190
Mager, R 95
Mahoney, M 139
Management 88
Marshall, I 144, 154
Marton, F 2–3, 67
Marx, K 92
Maslow, A 147
Matusov, E 108
Maxted, P 196
Mayer, J 139, 142, 143, 149
Maynard, M 175, 177–8
Meaning 91,187
Memory 36–7, 38, 135; episodic 36
Mental, self-government 68–70; forms
    68–9; functions 68; leanings 69; levels
    69; scopes 69
Merriam, S 17, 158, 184, 186, 190
Mezirow, J 12, 22, 94, 159
Mill, J, S 121
Miller, J 186
Mind 2, 4; brain 129
Mitchell, S 183, 184, 188
Mitroff, I 161
Modell, A 184, 190
Morality 128–138
Motivation 214
Mountford, V 176–7
Mruk, C 145
Muir, K 177
Multiple intelligence 21, 50–64
Murray, S 191
Murray-Harvey, R 66, 67
Murray-Thomas, R 137

Nature 209–13
Negt, O 98
Neugarten, B 190
Neural networks 130–2
Neurone 32, 33–5, 46; connectivity 35;
    magnocellular 46, 49
Neuroticism 71
Newman, M 171
Nicholson, H 173
Niles, F 67
Non-learning 95–7
Non-participation 195, 196, 197–200, 207

Norman, W 71
Nouwen, H 159
Novice 106
Nurture 209–13

O'Connell, A 146, 147
O'Connell, V 146, 147
O'Neil, M 67
O'Sullivan, E 12–13, 159
Objectivity 27
Olson, S 22, 25,
Oppression 176, 178
Orr, J 162

Parenting 143, 145–6
Parker, R 177
Parkinson's disease 42
Participation 195, 200–3; barriers to 195;
    continuous 203–4; family influence
    on 200–3; initial education and
    202–4; later life 203–4
Passeron, J-C 171
Pavlov, I 6,
Paxton, D 61,
Perry, P 144
Perry, W 169
Personal 6, 13–14
Personality 190; traits 67, 68, 71–2,
    76,79; types 70–1
Peters, R 129
Piaget, J 92, 93, 95, 97, 106, 107, 184
Pinker, S 20
Pogson, P 102
Postiglione, G 69
Prerau, D 103, 104, 106
Preston, J 13
Primates 22
Protest 176–8
Psychology, developmental 97
Purcell-Gates, V 54

Ramachandran, V 128, 134–5, 136
Ramsden, P 66
Ratner, C 109
Raynor, S 66
Reading 42–6; auditory skill 44–6; visual
    analysis 43–6, 49
Reason 128
Rees, G 195
Relationship 154
Reminiscence 188–9, 190
Renfrew, C 22
Resistance 176–8; mental 96

Restak, R 187, 190
Richards, M 177
Riding, R 66, 76
Ridley, M 25, 27
Rocka, L 56
Roebuck, F 149
Rolley, K 175
Rogers, C 10, 21, 94, 147, 149, 150
Rose, R 67
Rowley, S 176
Ryle, G 2, 4

Sadler-Smith, E 66
Salovey, P 139
San-Segundo, M 200
Sargant, N 205
Sawaf, A 142,143–4, 153
Schaie, K 186, 187, 188, 191
Scheler, M 118
Sheared, V 170
Schon, D 95, 97
Schutz, A 10, 116, 117
Schutz, W 147
Scientism 10, 116, 117, 186
Seaborne, R 6
Self 4, 136–7, 151, 216; concept 144–6;
    defined 136; esteem 144–6; moral
    136; understanding 160
Selwyn, N 196, 205
Senge, P 124
Sewing 174–5; circles 175,177
Shapiro, S 177
Significant other 116
Simon, R 171
Simon, T 51, 140
Siren, A 142
Skill 105
Skinner, W 6, 212,
Smith, F 161
Socialisation 117
Society 117; Late modern 123–5;
    Modern 120–2; Open 123; Primitive
    119–20, 125 ; types of 118
Socio-biology 27
Spiritual 157–66, 191; audit 161–2;
    direction 163; intelligence 160–1;
    journey 162
Spirituality 159–60, 163
Staff development 67
Stagnation 186
Stalker, J 170,171,172, 176, 215
Stanford-Binet IQ Test 51
Steele, V 177

Stehr, N 123
Steiner, C 144
Stern, D 183, 186
Stern, W 51,
Sternberg, R 68, 69, 70, 73, 76, 102
Stevens, J 148
Stiver, I 186
Stroke 38
Stubenrauch, H 98
Study Progress Questionnaire 66–7
Survival 186
Sykes, B 25,
Synapses 34, 35–7
Synaptic modulation 36

Tang, C 67
Taylor, A 71–2
Teaching 21, 67
Terman, L 51
Tennant, M 22, 102, 190
Thinking styles 67, 68–70, 73–6, 79,
    80–1; inventory 69, 73; Type, I 69, 73,
    79–80, 82; Type, II 69, 73, 79–80
Thompson, W 13
Thornton, M 168, 175
Time 10,
Tisdell, E 170
Tooby, J 18,
Torrens, K 178
Tough, A 158
Turner, J 186
Turner, V 119

Unlearning 169, 171–5

Vaillant, G 184, 187, 188, 189
Valiente, A 200
Van, Gennep, A 119
Viens, J 57–8, 61, 63
Volz, J 186
Vygotsky, L 92, 95, 97, 108

Wagner, R 69
Watkins, D 67
Weber, M 121–2
Webster, J 184, 188, 189, 190
Weil, S 6, 151
Wendt, I 174, 176
Wenger, E 89, 99, 110
White, C 172
Whitman, C 191
Wicket, R 158
Wigley, S 76

Willis, S 186, 187, 188, 191
Wilson, A 67
Wilson, E 27
Wilson, J 139
Winch, C 3,
Winnicott, D 186

Wisdom 120
Wolf, M 184, 187, 188, 190, 191

Zhang, L 67, 69, 70–1, 72, 73, 76, 79, 80
Ziehe, T 98
Zohar, D 144, 154